Re-Viewing Classics of Joyce Criticism

Re-Viewing Classics of Joyce Criticism

EDITED BY

Janet Egleson Dunleavy

UNIVERSITY OF ILLINOIS PRESS
Urbana and Chicago

© 1991 by the Board of Trustees of the University of Illinois
Manufactured in the United States of America
1   2   3   4   5   C   P   5   4   3   2   1

This book is printed on acid-free paper.

Library of Congress Cataloging-in-Publication Data

Re-viewing classics of Joyce criticism / Janet Egleson Dunleavy,
   editor.
      p. cm.
   Includes bibliographical references and index.
   ISBN 0-252-01774-9 (cloth: alk. paper). — ISBN 0-252-06166-7 (paper:
alk. paper)
   1. Joyce, James, 1882–1941—Criticism and interpretation.
I. Dunleavy, Janet Egleson.
PR6019.09Z78438 1991
823'.912—dc20   90-19589
                                                        CIP

For Richard Morgan Kain,
whose contributions to Joyce studies include
not just his own works
but the works of so many others
who have benefited from
his example, assistance, and encouragement

Contents

Janet Egleson Dunleavy

Introduction

One remarkable fact of Joyce criticism is the continually increasing number of new studies that are introduced every year. Another is that—despite radical changes in critical theory and method since 1960—a significant number of studies published thirty and more years ago are still quoted in contemporary texts, listed in current bibliographies, referred to in lectures, and cited in reviews. What is it about these early works that preserves their relevance? What links, if any, are there between contemporary critical writing and the classics of Joyce criticism that shaped Joyce readership and scholarship in the years between 1929 and 1959?

In this volume, fifteen contemporary scholars tackle such questions, reassessing the best-known pioneer texts in the light of today's critical standards. For established Joyceans, their essays offer new perspectives on the development of Joyce criticism—and the opportunity to experience vicariously the excitement of discovery that characterized the years 1929 to 1959, when Joyce scholarship was a literary frontier. For new Joyceans, they provide an introduction to the history of Joyce studies as well as to the foundations of much of modern criticism. For everyone, they recapture a time when the variety of ideas to be examined was limited only by curiosity, imagination, and a reader's willingness to find new puzzlement, insights, and delights on every page.

Bernard Benstock explains how Richard Morgan Kain's *Fabulous Voyager* (first published in 1947 and revised in 1959) "marks the boundary between the generalized and the specialized, the tentative and the assertive" in Joyce criticism and demonstrates the reciprocal relationship between the earlier *Dubliners, Exiles,* and *Portrait,* on the one hand, and

Ulysses and the *Wake*, on the other. Although Benstock acknowledges that Kain's analysis of Leopold Bloom and the background characters of Joyce's 1904 Dublin respond to critical concerns of the fifties, he points out that its progressive reading of the development of Joyce's perspective in both major and minor texts anticipates the scholarship of the eighties. Further evidence of the continuing relevance of *Fabulous Voyager*, declares Benstock, is the debt that a number of full-length studies published since 1959 owe to the appendixes of the 1959 edition.

Patrick McCarthy cites the continuing demand for Stuart Gilbert's *James Joyce's "Ulysses"* as the most persuasive evidence of its continuing influence on, and importance to, contemporary critics. First published in Great Britain in 1930, republished in the United States in 1931, revised in 1952, and issued in paperback in 1955, it has been regularly reprinted since. McCarthy attributes the popularity of Gilbert's *Ulysses* to a number of factors: its demonstration of the logic, coherence, and readability of the novel, encouraging to new Joyceans; the evidence that much of its contents may be traced back to Joyce himself; its historic role in the court decision that allowed the publication of *Ulysses* in the United States; its inventory of motifs to which even its detractors return again and again; and its significance as an early model of literary exegesis.

Michael Begnal declares that, like Gilbert's *Ulysses*, Campbell and Robinson's *Skeleton Key to Finnegans Wake* is still the first study of the text for which many new readers of Joyce reach, often before they have progressed through more than ten pages of the *Wake*. This fact establishes the significance of the *Skeleton Key*, even though it never has received the approval of most scholars. But as Begnal notes, Campbell and Robinson wrote their text for general readers, not specialists; their task was to introduce the reader to expanding guidelines of what constitutes literary art. They alert readers to the narrative trails, cultural landmarks, and submerged themes embedded in the *Wake*, then encourage them to progress on their own; for this, Begnal forgives the bombastic style and novelistic descriptions of characters and events that have troubled so many of his professional colleagues.

Bonnie Kime Scott maintains that no single reference work offers both general readers and specialists as much useful information interestingly presented as Adeline Glasheen's *Census of Finnegans Wake*, first published in 1956 and expanded in 1959 and 1977. The book is a basic scholar's tool, written in a lively and personal prose style into which both experienced and inexperienced Joyceans may dip with profit and pleasure. She recommends it, in any edition, to anyone bound for a desert island with a copy of the *Wake*. From first to third edition, the format has remained essentially the same: in addition to the census proper, it consists of a preface, a synopsis of the *Wake,* and a table indicating "Who's Who When Everybody Is Somebody Else." Scott's only criticisms of Glasheen are that (1) users are directed to elemental part rather than whole and to a novelistic rather than a conceptual approach and (2) while generally accurate, the text is not error-free and sometimes requires checking. Scott regards these, however, as mild defects, not serious detractions.

Suzette Henke acknowledges that probably the most curious example of *Wake* scholarship is *Our Exagmination round His Factification for Incamination of Work in Progress,* a collection of essays by twelve different authors published in 1929. A review of a work that would not be completed for ten years—that in fact existed in print at the time of the review's publication only in random fragments published in an avant-garde periodical—it was, as Henke notes, often parodied by Joyce himself between 1929 and 1939 and was then incorporated in part into the metafiction that it purportedly reviewed. Samuel Beckett wrote the opening essay; other contributors were Marcel Brion, Frank Budgen, Stuart Gilbert, Eugene Jolas, Victor Llona, Robert McAlmon, Thomas McGreevy, Elliot Paul, John Rodker, Robert Sage, and William Carlos Williams. Each, as described by Henke, had his separate role in the cleverly orchestrated whole.

Fritz Senn explains why James Stephen Atherton's *Books at the Wake* (1959) is often regarded, together with Glasheen's *Census* and Clive Hart's *Concordance to Finnegans Wake* (1963), as one of three essential items in every Wakean's library. A technical high school teacher in a coal-mining town in the north of England, Atherton developed on his own the author-centered thesis that prompted him to seek the sources of Joyce's art in the books that Joyce had studied and read. What Atherton discovered, Senn points out, was much more, including answers to frequently asked questions of fact, insights into Joyce's working habits, and clues to Joyce's working methods, all of which make *The Books at the Wake* an indispensable and reliable aid to the study of *Finnegans Wake* and an important source of information on Joyce's other works as well.

Morton P. Levitt notes that Harry Levin's review of *Finnegans Wake* in 1939 changed Levin's life, for after it was printed, Joyce himself suggested to New Directions Press that the young scholar (of Elizabethan drama!) be asked to write the volume on Joyce's work for its new series, The Makers of Modern Literature. Mystified by his good fortune but willing to accept it, Levin worked on his New Directions book, *James Joyce* (1941)—the first full critical study to examine the whole of Joyce's career—between editions of Ben Jonson and the Earl of Rochester. Levin thus became, serendipitously, a renowned Joycean, the first to explore, with implications for the direction of Joyce criticism, the idea that Joyce's use of myth and symbol might be but the scaffolding of the artist.

Richard F. Peterson describes the development of William York Tindall's opposite conviction, developed in *James Joyce: His Way of Interpreting the Modern World* (1950), that myth and symbol were in fact central to Joyce's art. It was with this thesis before him, writes Peterson, that Tindall mapped the myth-inspired, labyrinthine landscape into which Joyce transformed the streets of Dublin, creating a setting that dramatized the complexities of human nature and converting Daedalean flight into the theme of exile and the aesthetic strategy of detachment. For Tindall, it was a landscape replete with domestic, nationalistic, and religious features, as well as geographical markers, in which Leopold and Molly Bloom represent the human condition and affirm the human spirit. Tindall's contemporaries responded cautiously but favorably to his thesis, Peterson reports, warning against overemphasis on analogy but applauding his ability to lead readers through a forest of symbols to confront the question of Joyce's central meaning.

Clive Hart notes that as an artist himself, a self-taught painter who worked in the impressionist mode in the era of dadaism and surrealism, Frank Budgen, author of *James Joyce and the Making of "Ulysses"* (1934), brought credentials very different from those of either Harry Levin or William York Tindall to his study of Joyce and his work. Budgen was convinced, writes Hart, of the essential humanity of Joyce as a literary artist. He in turn appealed to Joyce in part because he shared Joyce's belief in the artistic value of hard work and the rational application of technique, in part because he played Leopold Bloom to Joyce's Stephen Dedalus. A Bloomian study, *James Joyce and the Making of "Ulysses"* is in fact a reading of the novel based on what it says, not what it suggests. As such, Hart declares, its particular value to biographers and literary historians is that, like Gilbert's *Ulysses*, it is a book to which Joyce himself contributed, through "sheet after sheet of suggestions" that he sent to the author.

Melvin J. Friedman points out that readers eager for information about the life of the controversial author of *Ulysses* had little more than Frank Budgen to rely on until Herbert Gorman (also aided by Joyce, sometimes to their mutual dismay) published his *James Joyce* in 1939. For the definitive biography, a model of biographical-critical scholarship not just for initiates but for all readers of modern literature, they had to wait for Richard Ellmann's *James Joyce*, first published in 1959 and revised in 1982. Reviewers of the 1959 edition called Ellmann's work "a model for future scholarly biographies" of which "nobody interested in . . . the novel or the literature of the twentieth century" should remain ignorant; "a critical experience in depth" and "a work of art" "written with . . . skill and warmth," "wise in its completeness." Reviewers of the 1982 edition pointed to the extent to which the book had inspired new insights into Joycean interpretation in its twenty-three years. Friedman emphasizes the current critical value of Ellmann's work, as it continues to serve both casual and serious readers as well as teachers and scholars.

Michael Patrick Gillespie acknowledges that to some extent *Dublin's Joyce* (1955) by Hugh Kenner overlaps the ground covered by both Budgen and Ellmann. He asserts, however, that it is more memorable for its differences. Digression, Gillespie observes, is the hallmark of Kenner's style; provocation—comfortably executed by Kenner because he knows where lies the bog and where the firmer ground—is his preferred rhetorical technique. Gillespie regards Kenner as a kind of scholarly Oscar Wilde who "delights in making prose . . . and in assaulting the complacency of his listeners/readers through paradox." Always questioning, never accepting conclusions that he himself has not tested, admitting no prescriptions, regarding nothing as irrelevant, Kenner is less concerned with being either right or wrong than with maintaining an open and curious mind and encouraging others to do the same.

Thomas F. Staley reexamines responses to issues raised by William T. Noon in *Joyce and Aquinas* (1957), such as the impact of Catholicism on the characters of Joyce's fiction and the extent of Thomistic influence on Joyce's aesthetic theories. The significant facts established by Noon, Staley explains, are that there are indeed Thomistic strains in the works of James Joyce but that these are not derived from direct or accurate use of the writings of St. Thomas Aquinas. He notes that Noon questions even Joyce's much quoted employment of such Aquinian terms as *integras, consonantia,* and *claritas* to refer to "qualities of things . . . the mind comes to know." Acknowledging that many critics disagree with Noon, Staley declares that nevertheless they must take into account both his argument and his evidence, for more than thirty years after publication, *Joyce and Aquinas* is still a "cornerstone work" that has not yet been superseded.

Mary Reynolds observes that since the earliest days of Joyce criticism, Joyce's allusions to Shakespeare have been noted frequently and incorporated peripherally into various critical studies. But it was not until publication of William Schutte's *Joyce and Shakespeare* (1957) that the subject received the full attention it merits. Reynolds traces Schutte's investigation through the ninth chapter of *Ulysses*, "Scylla and Charybdis," in which Stephen finally develops the "Shakespeare theory" tantalizingly promised, chiefly by Buck Mulligan, as early as "Telemachus." It is from this starting point, Reynolds says, that Schutte explores the Shakespearean allusions that recur in the mind of Stephen Dedalus throughout *Ulysses* and *A Portrait*. The result is a careful documentation of how Shakespeare is woven into the fabric of Stephen's character and experience — and how the Shakespearean allusions that occur in the thoughts of Leopold Bloom differ from those that permeate Stephen's consciousness.

Shari Benstock examines the ways in which David Hayman's *Joyce et Mallarmé* was both of and ahead of its time. Published in Paris in 1956, it is, she notes, in many ways characteristic of other influence studies of this period. Yet it also reveals ambiguities and dualities more appropriate to critical concerns of the 1980s. In part, these postmodernist qualities may be attributed to its unusual origin: Hayman did not set out, Benstock explains, to trace the evidence of Mallarméan influence in *Ulysses* and *Finnegans Wake* but to investigate why, abandoning *Stephen Hero* for *Portrait*, Joyce had turned away from the direct statements of realism. Analyzing the replicating juxtaposition of words and the association of ideas that Joyce substituted, Hayman perceived them as the stylistics of suggestion. It was his discovery of a similar methodology in *Un Coup de dés* that was the impetus for his two-volume study of Joyce's and Mallarmé's texts. Benstock points to the continuing significance of *Joyce et Mallarmé* to contemporary readers interested in Joyce's multidimensional verbality; she places it in the critical canon as a work that is simultaneously about Joyce and, self-referentially, about a Joycean critic.

Ruth Bauerle tackles a concept more complex for most literary scholars: music in the writings of Joyce. She observes that from 1930 to 1956 the significance of the subject was often referred to by such critics as Stuart Gilbert, Frank Budgen, Harry Levin, L. A. G. Strong, Richard M. Kain, and Hugh Kenner. In 1956, in *James Joyce: The Man, the Work, the Reputation*, Marvin Magalaner and Richard M. Kain had declared that, throughout Joyce's works, "no reader can fail to detect the important role music plays, in fact and in spirit." Meanwhile, Hodgart and Worthington had decided to collaborate, bringing together material that, slowly and painstakingly, each had been accumulating separately. Their encyclopedic *Song in the Works of James Joyce* finally appeared in 1959. Since then, this study has proved invaluable. Bauerle notes the ways in which, with Hodgart and Worthington in hand, scholars have been able to investigate how time, place, milieu, popular culture, language, characterization, rhythm, mood, tone, emotion, and more are evoked, augmented, parodied, romanticized, dramatized, and undercut by Joyce through the use of techniques and devices derived from music.

These essays are followed by a list of other landmarks of Joyce criticism— articles, reviews, editions, concordances, and even judicial opinions—

compiled by the late Alan M. Cohn. Purposely open-ended, Cohn's useful compilation is an invitation to all Joyceans to add their own nominations to the list of pre-1960 studies that remain relevant in the 1990s.

Bernard Benstock

The Fabulous Voyaging of Richard M. Kain

Looking back at the year 1947 from the vantage point of 1987 is hardly a matter of gazing into the dawn of protohistory, even the proto-history of James Joyce criticism—the "official" beginning of which took place in 1929 with the *Exagmination*. Richard M. Kain's *Fabulous Voyager: A Study of James Joyce's "Ulysses"* is neither the first study of *Ulysses*, the first study of *Ulysses* by an American, the first book on Joyce since his death, nor the first by a critic who did not know him personally. Yet its place in the history of Joyce criticism remains unique: it marks the boundary between the generalized and the specialized, the tentative and the assertive, between awe and complacency. Although the years preced-ing publication of Kain's *Fabulous Voyager* provided the author with few and somewhat imperfect materials on which to build (and of these he was highly selective), the four decades since its initial publication have pro-duced an avalanche of Joyce criticism (and especially *Ulysses* criticism) without impairing its enduring usefulness.

There is every indication that Richard Kain would have preferred a totally empty field in which to maneuver, that the very existence of a handful of works on the Joyce text was somewhat unwelcome, although he reveals no displeasure at not finding himself the first in a series. For Kain, only two early books on Joyce proved particularly useful, and those both by Americans: Harry Levin's *James Joyce* and Edmund Wilson's *Axel's Castle* (it is significant that these two critics were singled out by Joyce for their reviews of *Finnegans Wake*). Yet Kain's treatment of the Levin and Wilson approaches to *Ulysses* never grants these predecessors any decisive victories. Allowing that Levin's book is "an excellent guide to the entire career of Joyce" and "a masterpiece of judicial and perceptive criticism," he nonetheless refers to it as a "brief handbook," "limited in scope." Although Wilson's essay remains for him "an unsurpassable introduction," the view that some excesses in the writing of *Ulysses* may not be defensible occasions Kain's assertion that "time will undoubtedly place these devices in their proper perspective."[1] It is soon apparent that his "use" of Levin, Wilson, and, to a greater extent, even Stuart Gilbert's *James Joyce's "Ulysses"* becomes a process of correcting their overemphases on aesthetics and symbolism: "It will be necessary," Kain notes, "in this study to evaluate Gilbert's findings and to assess their aesthetic significance" (5). And with a nod to the "important pioneer work" of Valery Larbaud, T. S. Eliot, and S. Foster Damon, Kain embarks on a fresh approach to James Joyce's *Ulysses.*

Between 1947 and 1959, the year in which *Fabulous Voyager* was reprinted in paperback, the literary world was awash with numerous books and articles on Joyce, as Kain's preface to the revised edition, titled "Joyce Studies 1947–1958," attests; it attempted to contain the flood in a scant five pages. Other books that appeared during the same year as the Kain reprint and therefore were unavailable for his preface include Ellmann's biography, Tindall's *Reader's Guide,* Hodgart and Worthington's *Song in the Works of James Joyce,* Atherton's *The Books at the Wake,* Morse's *Sympathetic Alien,* and Magalaner's *Time of Apprenticeship.* The flood-gates had opened. By comparison, 1947 was indeed at the dawn of protohistory.

Kain's 1959 preface takes into account the wealth of new material and new considerations of the Joyce canon and surveys the years between 1947 and 1958 for contributions to the opening up of various kinds of interests, including stage productions and library acquisitions. His own work receives the same scrutiny: he corrects a few mistakes made in *Fabulous Voyager* and adds to its appendices. These appendices are themselves eloquent testimony to the ground breaking undertaken by Kain in 1947: each has since been expanded by various hands into full-length studies. Appendix A ("The Temperament, Personality and Opinions of Leopold Bloom") is the genesis of John Henry Raleigh's *Chronicle* of the Blooms; appendix B ("A Biographical Dictionary of *Ulysses*") provides the basis for the Benstock and Benstock *Directory;* appendix C ("A Directory of Shops, Offices, Public Buildings and Civic Personages") evolves into the Hart and Knuth *Topographical Guide;* and appendix D ("An Index of Verbal Motifs") underlies William Schutte's *Index.* In both first edition and revision, Kain's *Fabulous Voyager* has not only encouraged but directed subsequent scholarship.

Yet there appears to be an underlying sense of relief in the 1959 preface, as if the author were aware of how well his text had stood the test of time. When he notes that "the watershed remains where Harry Levin located it years ago, at the boundary of naturalism and symbolism, the meeting place of map and myth" (x), Kain must be aware of the extent to which his *Fabulous Voyager* contributed to fixing that boundary, to overlaying the map of Dublin and of human existence on the grid of mankind's mythologies. Carefully plotting his coordinates, he avoided the chapter-by-chapter analysis of *Ulysses* that has tended to be the common approach, dealing instead with the text as an entity and finding conceptualized approaches to the complex maze. Kain's fifteen chapters are designated by subtitles that indicate the range and depth of his analytic directions: "James Joyce in the Modern World"; "The Tonal Pattern"; "The Epic Structure"; "Integrating Themes"; "The Isolation of the Individual"; "The Intellectual in Modern Society"; "The Minor Characters"; "The Geography of Dublin"; "Psychological Associationism"; "The World of Sound"; "The 'Sirens' Scene"; "Social Institutions"; "Bloom's Humanitarianism"; "The Rhythms of Life"; "The Cosmic Overview." By casting a net with so precise a weave, Richard Kain had no problem in accumulating so much good material.

Vieus Von DVbLIn

Prior critical approaches either had capitalized on first-hand knowledge from Joyce himself or had maintained lofty New Critical perspectives, emphasizing the Homeric correspondences, stylistic variations, modernist techniques, or symbolic structures in *Ulysses* (none of which Kain ignores). Despite the overwhelming evidence that Dublin as a city was at the center of Joyce's Ulyssean scheme, it was not until the American scholar looked at maps and Dublin newspapers for 16 June 1904 that a detailed study of the Dublin scene and its significance, the verities of Joyce's cartographic mythography, were applied to the text. There is little evidence from *Fabulous Voyager* that Richard Kain walked the streets of Dublin to scout out the terrain (as he and many others have since done) and not much likelihood that there were opportunities to do so in the days immediately after the Second World War when his book was in composition. But Kain established contact with the assistant librarian of Trinity College, Dublin, and acquired microfilms of the pertinent issues of the *Freeman's Journal* and the *Evening Telegraph*. *Ulysses* criticism has never been quite the same since.

The strategy of establishing the broadest critical base possible works in various ways in *Fabulous Voyager* and includes investigation of that now indispensable guide to *Ulysses*, Thom's *Dublin Directory* (that Bloom once worked for Thom's should send the reader to that particular source). Kain discovered in it that on 16 June 1904 the premises of 7 Eccles Street were vacant and could therefore be tenanted by Joyce's fictional Blooms. (To return a degree of historical reality to the fiction, Joyce has one of the rooms of the house advertised for rental.) In addition to such external documents as newspapers, maps, and city directories, Kain also avails himself of the 1937 Miles Hanley *Word List* and the 1944 publication of *Stephen Hero*, as well as references to other Joyce texts, not only *A Portrait* and *Dubliners* but most particularly *Finnegans Wake*. That *previous* texts would shed light on *Ulysses* should have been a critical commonplace; that the later *Wake*, difficult and obscure as it may be, could also illuminate its predecessor proves to be a masterstroke. What Kain achieves is a progressive reading of the development of Joyce's perspectives, and although he never openly takes issue with it, his overview contrasts sharply with that of David Daiches, who in *The Novel and the Modern World* (1939) allows that *Dubliners* is the work of an "observer," *A Portrait* that of a "liberal," and *Ulysses* that of a "cynic." Kain insists that "Joyce's early works were pervaded either by astringent bitterness or by sentimental sympathy. Looking back upon his country now [i.e., in *Ulysses*], his perspective mellowed by reminiscence, he creates an Irish background that is amusing and tender as well as sordid" (99). Against the charge of cynicism Kain remains firm: "to accuse the novel of being uncompromisingly nihilistic is to fail to sense the presence of the buried hopes of humanity that lie concealed in its buried pages" (210).

To read *Ulysses* through *Finnegans Wake* has become standard practice in the 1980s, but it must have appeared novel, if not idiosyncratic, in 1947, with little more than the *Skeleton Key* available to the *Wake* exegete. Yet Kain took the challenge in stride: "Hence it should be possible to understand *Ulysses* more clearly now that the themes of *Finnegans Wake* have been probed" (35). And the thematic approach is very much at the heart of his analyses in *Fabulous Voyager*, despite the eclecticism of perspectives and the constant interweaving of the many threads indicated by the chapter subtitles. Kain therefore insists that "*Ulysses* can be understood much more clearly in relation to the work, for in *Finnegans Wake* appear the two basic themes of *Ulysses* —social criticism and philosophical relativity—the first somewhat submerged, the second considerably magnified" (4). The ease with which he makes such claims attests to his own confidence and inspires a concomitant confidence in his reader. Only by the mid-1940s could a commentator begin to assess the Joycean canon as an entity, as a constantly developing work in progress, and so state with assurance that the "cosmic perspective is to be found in each of his major works, and in each with an increasing emphasis, until in *Finnegans Wake* cosmic background and realistic foreground are but two aspects of the same material" (227). Kain is always aware of the dualistic facets of Joyce's maneuvering, tunneling from two directions toward a center, but most important for Kain's reading of the text(s) is the evaluation that "like Rabelais, who saw with amusement the crumbling of medieval ideals, Joyce portrays the decline of bourgeois values with the abandon of reckless laughter. *Finnegans Wake* goes even further in this direction" (34).

Themes have thimes / The age demanded

Fabulous Voyager is very much a document of a certain time and a certain place: it reflects basic American attitudes during the closing days of World War II, when a victorious campaign against political fascism gave rise to a heady optimism tempered by the retrospective analysis of the horrors endured. Kain balances that euphoria with a cold eye on *Realpolitik*, and although his enthusiasms pervade the book, they never descend into the world of pollyanna. At his most exuberant, he credits Joyce with an "understanding of the plight of modern society" and a "pity for humanity" that overshadows the overpraised "technical virtuosity, great as that may be" (47). The balance, however, is quickly restored and that virtuosity returned to the realm of major attributes: "one must be impressed by the amazing technical skill of the writing, as well as the deep human feeling that pervades it" (34). On an even larger scale, Kain acknowledges the various dualities that sustain *Ulysses*, the Joycean focus that proves itself many faceted, as he renders an expanded verdict: "Joyce was both naturalist and symbolist, social realist and mystic visionary. His keen observations of the contemporary scene are permeated by a feeling for the panorama of history and a vision of the mysteries beyond" (213). But the "contemporary scene" had altered considerably since the almost halcyon days of 1904 or even those of 1922, and Kain quickly shifts from Joyce's mastery of the specifics of a time and place to a comprehensiveness of their universalities. "Unlike the social reformer," he adds, "whose attention is directed exclusively to the immediate scene, he is constantly attracted to the ultimate problems of existence itself" (213).

Despite Kain's protestations, vestiges of nihilism still adhere to Joyce's reputation, and Kain refuses to dodge the issue; he instead reexamines the nature of the Joycean vision to arrive at a realization of the satiric thrust. He invokes the spirit not only of Rabelais but also of Jonathan Swift and of Henrik Ibsen in shaping the contours of Joyce's antecedence: "As Swift mercilessly demolished the eighteenth century idols of the tribe and Ibsen those of the nineteenth century, so Joyce has done for our day" (3). To emphasize the point, he adds "Joyce is a satirist" and later indicates specifically what is being satirized when he judges the work to be "as final a satire on bourgeois values as anything in modern literature" (191–92). Characteristic of the literary critic of his time, Richard Kain seeks the intellectual precedence that underpins Joyce's outlook and creates a four-cornered structure, supplementing Swift, Ibsen, and Rabelais with Sterne and Flaubert: "Joyce's tone is difficult to analyze: at one time it seems to partake of the carefree gusto of Rabelais or the comic *esprit* of Sterne, again of the savage indignation of Swift. . . . But frequently it has the mood of the aging Flaubert, devoting his energy to the excoriation of human falsity and stupidity" (193).

In addition to setting Joyce within the context of his predecessors, Kain also sets him within the context of his contemporaries, relying heavily on the two modernist giants with whom Joyce was constantly compared at midcentury, Proust and Mann. "Thomas Mann had examined with diligence the decline of bourgeois standards of value," he avers, adding that "a similar task was undertaken on a colossal scale by Marcel Proust in France; and during these years Joyce wrote his panoramic *Ulysses*, depicting the disintegration of moral and philosophic values" (8–9). Although Kain is careful to avoid comparative judgments, Joyce's supremacy as the major writer of the age is signaled quite clearly at various instances in the critique, and the critic's partisan allegiance is explicit. "Joyce is prophetic, as all great writers have been prophetic," Kain contends, establishing a classification for the creative artist in a time of triumph, change, and uncertainty, and underscoring the assumption that the artist is a barometer of the age and a beacon into the future. "His is the clearest and most incisive voice of our age," Kain concludes, "and we should do well to heed him" (2).

It is the multifaceted aspects of *Ulysses*, its varieties of human experience and all-inclusiveness, that are stressed in Kain's evaluation. Although a great deal of emphasis has been placed on the psychological impact of Joyce's novel, on the efficacy of Joyce's use of stream of consciousness as a psychological technique, Kain views that facet as part of a larger pattern: "The stream of life is rendered as it flows. In contrast to Marcel Proust, engaged on much the same quest, Joyce does not linger over the discoveries he makes regarding the action of the mind, weaving a tapestry of rumination about his theme and its implications; all is direct, immediate" (131). The directness and immediacy are contained for Kain in the political and the philosophic, literary attributes pertinent to the postwar period (he cites the events in the Cyclops, Eumaeus, and Ithaca chapters to offset the naysayers). Yet, as he sums up the qualities of

Joyce's masterpiece, he nonetheless negates the propagandistic possibilities of the prophet: "Social institutions, be they religious, economic, political, or aesthetic, are subject to the most searching mockery. The mood may vary from the facetious to the sardonic; the intent is, nevertheless, the same. Joyce has no panacea to recommend; his task is diagnosis rather than therapy. But his diagnosis is brilliant and often prophetic" (167).

The cautiousness, even hesitancy or perhaps contradiction, that one finds in such summings-up reflects the difference of the assessments of the 1940s from those of the 1930s, a decade in which Joyce was never credited with political prophecy or commitment. The era after the war introduced a corrective to the overpoliticized demand of the previous decade, a new skepticism that would soon become dominant in the early days of the Cold War. On the cusp between those extremes, Kain is judicious in his optimism and also politically astute in gauging the nature of Joyce's position, aware that Joyce remained disdainful of the political liberalism that turned a blind eye in Britain toward the legitimacy of Irish national aspirations and contributed inadvertently through political naiveté to the rise of fascism. His early allegiance to and continued interest in socialism have been the subject of renewed interest in the 1970s and 80s but were almost unknown at the time Kain wrote *Fabulous Voyager*. Nonetheless, Kain was capable of an estimation of Joyce's outlook that still has a precise relevance for current discussion: "One must not go so far as to interpret Joyce as a humanitarian liberal. He is too clear-eyed for that. It was as though he were setting himself the task of showing what a small part Christian idealism plays in the modern world and raising the question why it has proved so ineffectual, not to say ridiculous" (210).

Little Man, What Now?

At the heart of Richard M. Kain's *Ulysses* is the figure of Leopold Bloom. Not that there is any strong indication of the Stephen-hating that would be introduced almost a decade later, but Kain determines a qualified distinction between what each of the two principal male characters represents in the novel. In deciding that "what is wrong with the world is not that it fails to live up to the ideal of good will but that it is impossible, under modern conditions, to do so," Kain notes that "Bloom almost gets the point—indeed, comes closer than Stephen to seeing the point—and again proves that common sense may be a more reliable guide than sterile intellectuality" (198). Kain's estimation of Bloom marks a midpoint between the early overintellectualized attitude (*pace* Ezra Pound) that Bloom is too ordinary to merit much attention and the recent interest in the enigma of Leopold Bloom, a reading of the gaps and empty places in the complex characterization. Kain establishes the concept that held sway for decades, that "the little man of Eccles Street is undoubtedly the most completely characterized figure in the history of fiction, if not in all literature" (243).

It is not the psychological portrait of the cuckolded Poldy that takes the center stage for Kain: although there are several nods toward Sigmund Freud in *Fabulous Voyager* (of Circe he comments [45] that "the Freudian id, or subconscious, would be a more fitting bodily emblem than the locomotor apparatus"), much of the psychosexual versions and perversion in *Ulysses* receives little note. Masturbatory Bloom is played down, Gerty's exhibitionism acknowledged without comment, and even in an era when the list of Molly's twenty-five extramarital affairs was accepted as verified, Kain offers neither explanation nor analysis (much less censure). His approach is crystallized in the casual comment that Bloom's "sensuality, which has been unduly emphasized as an aspect of *Ulysses*, is largely a matter of sex frustration and, even so, is not so apparent as other qualities" (243).

"The story of Leopold Bloom," as read by Richard Kain, "is a dramatic exemplification of the corruption of innate decency by an alien environment" (87). There is little doubt that Kain wholeheartedly accepts Joyce's own casual assessment of his hero as a "good man," and he views him as the somewhat naive protagonist of a satiric novel, innocently navigating the dangers of a corrupt society and learning more than just how to survive. The Cyclops chapter proves to be the "eye-opener," and Kain suggests that it "might be entitled 'Bloom's Political Education,' for he is brought face to face with the appalling revelation that his doctrines of good will are inadequate as solutions for the chaos of modern industrialism and imperialism." (203). But revelation hardly brings him to the brink of political action, since Bloom is very much a part of the chaos, a contributing factor in the society that persecutes him as it sustains him. Kain determines that Bloom's religion is the modern secular religion of money and that his interest in science, for example, corroborates that religion, for which science serves as a "twin god" (185). Of particular interest are those expansively bourgeois dreams in Ithaca, those Bloomian get-rich-quick schemes and delusions of economic glory that Kain views as the most potent satiric elements in *Ulysses*. By contrast, Kain points to Bloom's economic failures, his series of insignificant jobs and period of unemployment, as well as the resultant paltriness of his present finances. "Yet the bank balance is only eighteen pounds, the bonds nine hundred pounds," Kain cites (193), as evidence of Bloom's financial insecurity (although later commentators have considered those bonds and the "endowment assurance policy of £500" as evidence of the financial stability of the cautious and prudent Bloom).

Nonetheless, the contradiction (other critics might term it the irony) of Bloom's position is that he is immersed in the bourgeois values that conflict with his altruism, more so because he never realizes the contradiction. "Nowhere is Joyce's social criticism more searing than in his portrayal of Bloom's humanitarian philosophy," Kain contends; "Essentially a man of good will, Bloom finds himself corrupted by a world given to crassly monetary values. This absurd little man has no difficulty in reconciling schemes for private profit with vague general visions of human betterment. He reproduces on a primitive, prethought level the inconsistencies of the political and economic liberal" (197). What Kain senses throughout is the multiplicity of the characterization of Leopold Bloom, the stages of his existence collapsed into a single day at age thirty-eight from which the various Leopold Blooms need to be retrieved. His skill in reading *Ulysses* as a composite produces the capsule of Bloom's political shades with exactness: "Joyce mocks the emptiness of political allegiance in a divided Ireland when he tells us that Bloom had been an adherent of the radical socialist program of Davitt but had also supported the constitutional agitation of Parnell and, to top all that, had advocated the reforms of Gladstone, who played a cat-and-mouse policy with the Irish throughout" (175). Kain concludes that this inconsistent Bloom is very much a gauge of his society, for "unaware of the course of history, Dublin carries on business as usual" (175–76). Stepping back from the vast panorama of Dublin in *Ulysses*, he notes that "here is the sensateness of modern materialistic civilization, the world of Leopold Bloom, quite different from the abstract meditations of the medieval-minded Stephen" (171).

Throughout his commentary, Richard Kain refers to Leopold Bloom as the "little man," "the little advertiser," and even the "absurd little man," hardly a reference to his height (5' 9½"), for which the statistics in *Ulysses* belie such a designation. Instead, the allusion is a timely one: the emphasis in the early part of the twentieth century on the notion of the era of the little man, brought to its heights in the 1940s in America by Henry Wallace's slogan, the "century of the common man" (with fanfares by Aaron Copland).

Kain's "little man" is also a "man of good will"; he shares both aspects with the democratic ideal of the era, an era in which such titles as *Kleine Mann, was nun?* and *L'Homme de bon volonté* were well known and characteristic. "What is the fate of a man of good will in the modern world?" Kain asks (198), aware that the answer is a relatively benign one in *Ulysses* compared to the fate of such men between 1941 and 1945. Yet optimism and pessimism, belief and skepticism, color Kain's perspective as he reads the events of 1904 as transmitted through the 1915–1921 period of the book's composition. At one end, he can insist that "it is impossible not to conclude that Bloom is superior to his environment" or that "in conclusion, there can be noted the deep melancholy that colors his political and religious opinions and pervades his philosophy" (243). On the other end, Kain can state defiantly that "to those who would accuse Joyce of utter nihilism the first answer would be, 'Ecce homo, Behold Bloom'" (199). The contradiction displayed by Richard Kain is his equilibrium, a characteristic he purposely shares with the little man of *Ulysses* and with Joyce's text as well.

What's This Here, Guv'nor?

The complex morass that we now recognize as the Ulyssean mine-field had been (and on occasion still is) the subject of grand overviewing, with Stuart Gilbert's study assumed to have placed all the necessary signposts for the basic directions. With *Fabulous Voyager*, Kain under-took to survey that terrain for himself, providing one of the first detailed investigations of the intricate minutia. Wherever possible, Kain labels the specific details as he find them, solving dilemmas that no one as yet knew existed. He has no difficulty in noticing that Bloom *rents* rather than buys *Sweets of Sin* (an error that perpetuated itself for quite a while before repeatedly corrected); that the Burton existed under that name and was not actually the Bailey (as that latter eating emporium later claimed in its self-glorifying advertising); and that Sceptre and Throwaway actu-ally ran in the Gold Cup on 16 June 1904 and were not merely phallic and onanic symbols for Boylan and Bloom. But Joyce had set many traps for the unwary in *Ulysses* and even for the most wary of navigators, and Kain falls occasionally into some of them, as his 1959 preface admits. He sets the time of the Molly-Blazes assignation at 4:30, following Boylan's delayed arrival and accepting Bloom's stopped watch as diagnostic. The complexity of recorded voices within an interior monologue proves to be overly opaque, and he assumes that Stephen had paid the rent for the tower and that Mulligan was therefore a "roomer" there. The similar prejudices of Haines and Deasy cause them to be confused with each other, and the appearance of *two* parental figures in Bloom's hallucina-tions (father Rudolph and grandfather Lipoti) causes a similar confusion.

Matching up the evidence gleaned from Thom's *Dublin Directory* and the *Evening Telegraph* with the clues with which *Ulysses* is impregnated clears away a great deal of confusion, but being physically present in Dublin also has its advantages to the investigator, who would have seen that access from the Blooms' areaway would have been through the kitchen door rather than through a window. And problems of interpreting information separated by hundreds of pages are difficult for any reader of *Ulysses*. Fortunately, Kain's conceptualized method brings diverse facets of the text under tighter scrutiny than is usually available to commentators who track the chapters sequentially, although there are instances where the threads are few, even when brought together from distant places. When Kain views the relationship between Bloom and his daughter ("One might expect that the presence of his daughter Milly would alleviate Bloom's brooding loneliness. But Milly is too closely associated in his mind with his unfaithful wife, and he feels the distance between father and daughter acutely" [75]), he opens up an area of interest that has had only the most casual scrutiny in the forty years since *Fabulous Voyager*, despite recent psychoanalytic probings. Nor has the relationship between Bloom and Stephen, where massive speculations have taken place, yielded to critical pressure: Kain in particular emphasizes the continued lack of rapport that runs through Eumaeus and into Ithaca as a "cruel distance between them" that, due to the "reluctance of Stephen to respond to any of [Bloom's] overtures," (85), allows for no change in Stephen's attitude at the end of Eumaeus. Kain's stress on "Bloom Alone" is particularly severe, as he reads *Ulysses* as embodying "the difficulty of establishing vital personal contact in the maelstrom of metropolitan life" (26).

An unusual area of controversy in *Fabulous Voyager* centers on the schema reproduced from Stuart Gilbert's 1930 study of *Ulysses*, with which Kain seems particularly uncomfortable. His inclusion of the "Plan of *Ulysses*" may well have been intended to allow him the opportunity to contest certain specifics of it (for Eumaeus he asserts that "to choose the sailors as symbol is less convincing than the deserted streets of the city, so relevant to the spirit of isolation evoked" [45]), and his various suggestions are often quite apt. What becomes apparent, however, is that Kain had no way of knowing that the schema is the brainchild of the author of *Ulysses* and therefore carries a certain imprimatur: finding it in *James Joyce's "Ulysses,"* Kain assumes that it was put together by Stuart Gilbert ("Gilbert finds here flesh as the organ" [45]). Few commentators on *Ulysses* who have been aware of the provenance of the "Plan of *Ulysses*" (and therefore have treated it as sacrosanct) have had the audacity to challenge its component elements, although indeed they ought to be challenged. Kain's handling of the schema as a suspicious document to be judiciously scrutinized is especially welcome, and had he also possessed the Carlo Linati schema for comparative purposes at the time, his method of close analysis might well have tumbled these flawed and somewhat arbitrary touchstones. The placement of the Gilbert schema, however, has a somewhat disruptive effect as well. Kain's meticulous effort to fix time in *Ulysses* concludes: "The bells of St. George's toll 1:30 or 1:45 as they retire; the final peal of 2:00 A.M. interrupts Molly's soliloquy" (50). Yet, only a few pages before, the "Plan of *Ulysses*" reads: " 'Ithaca.' 2:00 A.M." and " 'Penelope.' 2:45 A.M." (38). The unspoken indicator is that Kain is uietly "correcting" Gilbert.

The Charictures in the Drame

Despite his professed emphasis on the political and philosophical aspects of *Ulysses* and his disassociation from the psychoanalytical, Kain's major strength is in evaluating characterization in *Ulysses*, his reading of the people in the action of the novel. For someone who as yet has no reason to discount the list of Molly's twenty-five "lovers," he is obviously without prejudice and succinctly accurate when he states that "Molly's heart is, after all, in the right place. And her greatest virtue is honesty." (102). His treatment of Stephen is certainly determined by lack of evidence that the young man has as yet understood what the heart is and what it feels, but Kain never indulges in calling Stephen a prig and acknowledges that when others ridicule Bloom, Stephen does not (not having noticed him). The overwhelming sympathy and even affection that Kain has for the maligned Bloom (few have stressed the pathos of Bloom's isolated and despised position in Dublin as keenly as does Richard Kain) is clearly the central issue in *Fabulous Voyager*. But the three major characters of *Ulysses* are accommodated by the vast amount of evidence about them in the text (thus Bloom is "the most completely characterized figure in the history of fiction"), while minor characters offer little evidence for accurate treatment. Nonetheless, Kain undertakes to discuss several of these in his "All Too Irish" chapter on "The Minor Characters." His views on Father Conmee are unusually cogent, considering how flummoxed most commentators are in accepting a saccharine evaluation of the priest, primarily because Joyce himself had later had a kind word to say about the real priest he had known. Kain compares him to Martin Cunningham, insisting that a "comic counterpart to the generous spirit of Cunningham is the unctuous Father Conmee" and citing the "perfect depiction of the contrast between genuine and professional Christianity" (111).

The case against Conmee could include snobbism, elitism, secular and even sensual interest, as well as condescension (an extended portrait is available in the Wandering Rocks chapter), but Kain's attitudes toward most of the characters in *Ulysses* are relatively benign (his reign, too, is mild). Where there is very little evidence for really minor characters, he often allows them the benefit of the doubt. Even the collector of bad and doubtful debts—himself often viewed as a bad and doubtful debt—is credited (again quite aptly) with a "stratum of horse sense in this vulgar mind" (112): he should surely be credited also as the only person in Dublin who has guessed about Boylan and Molly Bloom. Perhaps calling Larry O'Rourke "goodnatured" (122) is too generous. After all, when Bloom greets him in the morning, he does so by name and calls him "sir," yet the pubkeeper answers without either concomitant politeness or graciousness. That Bloom may have sensed something of a snub there might be the reason for his caution when he confronts Hornblower; instead of actually greeting him, he has an imaginary conversation in which he is granted the honorific ("How do you do, Mr Hornblower? How do you do, sir?"). Kain mistakes the intention for the deed in their encounter and assumes that "Bloom passes the time of day with the porter of Trinity College" (124). The Sirens' allure also may have been convincing, since Kain has them "playfully scolding the boots" (159), where other readers may see them as genuinely annoyed. The two major stumbling blocks for determined readers of Joyce's *Ulysses* invariably have been following the vagaries of the method of internalized speech and accounting for the rationale that governs the phantasmagoria in Circe (133). Kain's attempt to deal with the latter (137) is to assume that Bloom as well as Stephen is intoxicated (so much for ginger cordial!).

Nostos: He Travelled

There can be no doubt that for Richard M. Kain in the mid-1940s James Joyce's *Ulysses* was a literary work that still needed study, and particularly a fresh approach. Without necessarily indicting predecessors who misread the text, Kain determined his own paths of investigation and had no compunctions about indicating areas left unexplored. The Homeric structure so vital to Gilbert's study disturbs him, so he insists that "even to the reader who is unfamiliar with this framework, *Ulysses* has a narrative pattern of its own. It is created by a skilful modulation of the fictional tone, with styles appropriate not only to the time of day described but to the characters involved and to the implied philosophical outlook. Strangely enough, this feature of the work has never been fully interpreted" (21). Kain carves out for himself a territory very much his own. There is ample reason to infer from it a very early stage of scholarly exploration, Cortez supplanting and subsuming Balboa, almost at the dawn of protohistory. Again he obliquely chides his predecessors: "The tonal pattern, the emotional and stylistic rendition of the time-scheme, has, strangely enough, never before been pointed out. Nor has the geographical coverage of the city of Dublin" (37). Eventually, he even replaces the Homeric with his preferred urtext, *Hamlet*, claiming that "certainly, as important as the much-heralded resemblances to the *Odyssey* is the identification of these two isolated individuals with the dilemma of the noble Dane" (94). For Kain, the lonely, sensitive, introspective, inactive Bloom is as much a Hamlet as the intellectual Stephen Dedalus.

Fabulous Voyager is a "cough mixture with a punch in it," a critical study not without its thesis, a thesis that insists that *Ulysses* has a punch in it, too: "With microscopic exactitude Joyce revealed the inherent contradictions and shortcomings of modern civilization" (10). Whatever else the work contains, and Kain can be quite all-inclusive in his descriptiveness, that Joycean revelation looms as paramount. Kain enumerates "the unquestioned values of the novel—the vigor and rhythm of its style, the amazing vividness of its setting, its rich humor and pathos, its understanding of human character, its analysis of the dilemmas of modern civilization"—invariably returning to the "punch" (47). Yet Kain constantly expands his focus on the novel, constantly catalogues the ingredients of the mixture in his conceptualized approach, so that his summing-up reads like a sectional breakdown of the elements contained in his *Fabulous Voyager: "Ulysses* is a mosaic of psychological recalls, topics of the day, Dublin landmarks, social, political, and cultural themes, mystic correspondences and philosophical concepts. Its tone changes with kaleidoscopic rapidity—from irony to pathos to ridicule to poetry. In its cubistic arrangements of contrasting planes and perspectives it is a perfect art form for the modern era" (240).

There is every indication that Kain is of two minds regarding the tonal pattern and world outlook incorporated into the polymorphous and polytropic mass that is *Ulysses*, unable to shake off the horrors of his age as he embraces its hopes. He quickly notices that his basic introduction to the satiric tone of the novel ignores the comic tone: "Nor is *Ulysses* as grim as this introduction might seem to make it," he adds, in order to right any implied imbalance. "Joyce's humor is infectious, his gusto irrepressible. He has much of the 'joyicity' of the grasshopper of *Finnegans Wake*" (3). But the grimness is there nonetheless, and Kain militates against any implied charge that it is there for its own sake, exuding an aura of nihilism: "throughout Joyce's career," he contends, drawing the Wakean joyicity into the Ulyssean context, "a heartbreaking pity throbs behind the facade of impersonality" (239). A parallel accusation to that of negativism might well be that of a godlike aloofness and indifference, a "facade of impersonality" often considered characteristic of the modernist period, so that the specified targets of Joyce's satiric jabs need to be identified. "By the very scope of its indictment and the bleakness of its atmosphere, the novel constitutes a most powerful challenge to commercialism, vulgarity, ignorance, prejudice, and inertia," Kain concludes, positing a *Ulysses* that is very much a text of its time, an epic looking back in anguish and forward in joyicity (241).

NOTE

1. Richard M. Kain, *Fabulous Voyager: A Study of James Joyce's "Ulysses"* (New York: Viking, 1947), 4, 47. All further references to this work are made parenthetically in the text.

Patrick A. McCarthy

Stuart Gilbert's Guide
to the Perplexed

It would be difficult to imagine a Joyce critic and scholar who played a greater variety of significant roles, at crucial times, than Stuart Gilbert. A retired member of the British civil service who first read *Ulysses* while serving as a judge in Burma, Gilbert met Sylvia Beach in 1927 and, at her suggestion, wrote to Joyce to point out errors in Auguste Morel's translation of a selection from *Ulysses*. This introduction led to the first of Gilbert's major Joycean efforts, a collaboration with Morel and Valery Larbaud on the first full-scale French translation of *Ulysses*.[1] Later, Gilbert contributed to Joyce scholarship by proofreading the 1932 Odyssey Press edition of *Ulysses* and, more importantly, by editing the first volume of Joyce's letters. In addition, Gilbert might well have earned some recognition as a Joyce critic solely on the basis of a succession of articles, among them one of the better essays in the 1929 collection *Our Exagmination round His Factification for Incamination of Work in Progress*.

More important than all his other contributions, however, was Gilbert's seminal volume, *James Joyce's "Ulysses": A Study*, which first appeared in England in 1930 (with an American edition early in 1931) and was revised for a new hardbound edition in 1952 (a paperback edition appeared in 1955).[2] Written under Joyce's supervision, and apparently carrying his endorsement, the book was the first extended study of *Ulysses* to leave a permanent mark on Joyce scholarship. In 1932, Charles Duff described the Gilbert volume as "a detailed exposition of *Ulysses* . . . the best substitute for the original,"[3] and Gilbert continues to find admirers among more recent Joyce critics. Sidney Feshbach and William Herman, for example, call Gilbert's study "indispensable for understanding the possibilities of each chapter of the novel," and Paul van Caspel, whose own book consists largely of a recitation of errors in previous readings of *Ulysses*, has little but praise for Gilbert, describing his analysis as "an excellent introduction to *Ulysses*," a book by "a reliable mentor," and even "an epoch-making study."[4] The pervasiveness of Gilbert's influence may also be seen in the way some of his working assumptions, and even specific observations, have come to be regarded as common property and are often repeated without attribution to their original source.[5]

The importance of a Joyce critic may be measured in another way as well: by the regularity and eagerness with which later critics seek to challenge their predecessor's judgments. Here again, Gilbert has attracted considerable attention. The most frequent objection to Gilbert's influence is the feeling that, as Marvin Magalaner and Richard Kain put it, Gilbert gave "undue emphasis" to the Homeric parallels in *Ulysses*.[6] In 1951, the year before Gilbert published the revised version of his book, Marshall McLuhan dismissed the original study as one "of incidental use," a book whose "effect . . . has been to promote the acrostic and naturalistic fallacies about *Ulysses*."[7] Critics as different in other respects as S. L. Goldberg and Hugh Kenner have essentially agreed with McLuhan's assessment, Goldberg concluding that Gilbert's mythic interpretation of *Ulysses* "is generally felt to be wrong" and Kenner calling Gilbert's study "a solemn deadly lead-footed schematization, from which the world learned that Mr Bloom was Ulysses thanks to an algebra of correspondences that turned the Cyclops' fiery club for instance into Bloom's 'knockmedown cigar.'"[8] It is no wonder, then, that in 1976, Michael Seidel, whose Bérardian analysis of *Ulysses* had its genesis in Gilbert's commentary, found it necessary to defend "the much maligned Stuart Gilbert"[9] in the process of advancing his own thesis.

That Gilbert's presentation is often pedantic, that it involves the analysis of symbolic esoterica, that it lays out an overly schematized structure for the novel—all these common complaints must be admitted. These faults were far from inadvertent, however, for Gilbert cultivated the scholarly air as a means of lending weight and dignity to his study at a time when Joyce was still widely regarded as a controversial experimentalist rather than as one of the major figures in the modernist literary canon. In the preface to the revised edition of his book, Gilbert cites three reasons for not attempting "to alleviate the rather pedantic tone of much of the writing in this Study":

> For one thing, Joyce approved of it; and, for another, we who admired *Ulysses* for its structural, enduring qualities and not for the occasional presence in it of words and descriptive passages which shocked our elders,

were on the defensive, and the pedant's cloak is often a convenient protec-
tion against the cold blasts of propriety. Moreover, in those early days
most readers and many eminent critics regarded *Ulysses* as a violently
romantic work, an uncontrolled outpouring of the subconscious mind,
powerful but formless. Thus it was necessary to emphasize the "classical"
and formal elements, the carefully planned lay-out of the book, and the
minute attention given by its author to detail, each phrase, indeed each
word, being assigned its place with *pointilliste* precision. (1955:ix)

Gilbert's analysis, then, was not meant merely (or even primarily) as
an objective assessment and explication of *Ulysses*: it was also intended
to be an essay in critical propaganda, with an elaborate exegetical apparatus whose main purpose was to demonstrate the rationality, and therefore
the respectability, of *Ulysses*. The emphasis on rationality was all the
more important since at the same time, Joyce was issuing fragments of
Finnegans Wake under the title "Work in Progress," and the apparent
randomness and irrationality of his new work lent weight to the argument that the same elements lay at the heart of *Ulysses*. The increasing
acceptance of *Ulysses* during the 1930s may be traced in part to the work
of Gilbert and of Frank Budgen, whose *James Joyce and the Making of
"Ulysses"* (1934) complemented Gilbert's depiction of Joyce as a scholarly novelist by portraying a humane (and relatively accessible) Joyce,
one more concerned with human values than with technical experimentation. Breon Mitchell has commented at length on the impact of Gilbert's
book on German-language criticism of *Ulysses* during the 1930s, observing,
for example, that in 1932 most German articles on Joyce "mentioned
Gilbert's work specifically," while Carl Jung's reading of Gilbert led him
to rewrite his essay on Joyce "in a mellower tone."[10] It also seems likely
that Gilbert had an impact on the 1933 court decision allowing *Ulysses*
to be published in the United States, for Morris L. Ernst, the attorney for
Random House, quoted Gilbert, along with other critics, in his brief,[11]
and Judge Woolsey surely meant to include the Gilbert volume among
the "satellites" that he believed "it is advisable to read" (and implied that
he *had* read) in order to understand and evaluate *Ulysses*.[12] By pointing
to a coherent pattern of meaning in *Ulysses*, Gilbert helped to make the
novel accessible to a generation of readers. To T. S. Eliot's rather grand
declaration that Joyce's "mythical method" was "a step toward making
the modern world possible for art"[13] we might add that Gilbert's detailed
analysis of that method was a step toward making *Ulysses* possible for
much of its audience.

James Joyce's "Ulysses": A Study is divided into two parts of
unequal size, each aimed at a rather different audience. In the original

version, part I, comprising at most a quarter of the whole book, consists of four chapters of general analysis of themes, techniques, and background material; the revised edition adds a fifth chapter, "The Climate of *Ulysses*," which reviews some of the literary influences that exerted pressure on Joyce during the late nineteenth and early twentieth centuries. The chapters in this part take a broad view of *Ulysses* and set forth Gilbert's assumptions about the novel as a whole. The remainder of the book, part II, is less useful for scholars but more likely to be scanned by general readers whose main reason for consulting a critical study is to help them follow the narrative line of a somewhat imposing novel. In this section, Gilbert summarizes and discusses, in sequence, each chapter of *Ulysses*. Being (in 1930) in the odd position of writing an analysis of a novel that most of his audience had not yet read, and often could not read unless they had found a means of circumventing the American and British bans on *Ulysses*, Gilbert produced, in effect, a substitute *Ulysses*, a critical volume with such extensive passages from the original that, if necessary, it could be read without reference to *Ulysses* itself.

Earlier studies of *Ulysses* —Herbert Gorman's *James Joyce: His First Forty Years* (1924), Paul Jordan Smith's *A Key to the "Ulysses" of James Joyce* (1927), and numerous articles—had laid down some of the general lines of interpretation of Joyce's novel, but Gilbert's study was the first thorough explication of such crucial motifs as the return, the omphalos, and paternity, as well as of the book's roots in Irish history and Greek myth; it was also the first detailed examination of the individualizing styles, narrative strategies, and images of particular chapters. The best-known aspect of the book, however, and the one most closely associated with the belief that Joyce had absolute control over his materials, is the schema for *Ulysses* that Joyce gave to Gilbert and allowed him to reproduce in his study. (Gilbert actually reproduces it twice: first, the whole schema appears in part I [28/30], and then each chapter of part II begins with the details from the schema that are relevant to the episode under discussion.) Gilbert's is an abbreviated version of a plan for *Ulysses* that Joyce had shown first to Carlo Linati,[14] and in one form or another the schema had circulated among Joyce's confidantes during the 1920s: Valery Larbaud used it in his preparations for a public lecture on *Ulysses*, and around 1927 Herbert Gorman received a version intended to help him in preparing a corrected version of his 1924 study.[15] Working only from the final published text of *Ulysses*, and citing a schema that gives the impression of predating the novel's composition, Gilbert not only implies that Joyce had the finished product in mind all along but emphasizes the reader's need to discover, and keep in mind, the relationship of even the most minute elements to the book's larger structures and themes.

For Gilbert, the book's true significance lies in its rhetorical principles and its formal design:

> The meaning of *Ulysses* ... is not to be sought in any analysis of the acts of the protagonist or the mental make-up of the characters; it is, rather, implicit in the technique of the various episodes, in nuances of language, in the thousand and one correspondences and allusions with which the book is studded. Thus *Ulysses* is neither pessimist nor optimist in outlook, neither moral nor immoral in the ordinary sense of these words; its affinity is, rather, with an Einstein formula, a Greek temple, an art that lives the more intensely for its repose. (8/8–9)

Gilbert's analogies, it will be noted, are chosen carefully and imply the dual aspects of experimentation and conservatism that pervade literary modernism: like an Einstein formula, *Ulysses* is radically new and dynamic, while the comparison with the Greek temple suggests its classical heritage and its formal perfection. Nonetheless, when forced to choose between these two poles, Gilbert almost invariably stresses the conservative, orderly qualities of the book—its completeness, accuracy, and static beauty—over its more avant-garde aspects. Indeed, much of his analysis is an attempt to demonstrate that the apparently disparate elements of which *Ulysses* is composed actually form a coherent whole. Adopting from *A Portrait of the Artist* Joyce's use of the term "rhythm," which Stephen defines as "the first formal esthetic relation of part to part in any esthetic whole or of an esthetic whole to its part or parts or of any part to the esthetic whole of which it is a part" (*P* 206), Gilbert argues that "*Ulysses* is a complex of such relations" (23/24) and that its meaning may be found in the reader's discovery of the book's underlying rhythm of relationships.

The emphasis on order and control was a response to critics who regarded *Ulysses* mainly as a formless, chaotic outpouring of experience. In 1921 Richard Aldington, who found himself unable to wait for the full book publication of *Ulysses* to pronounce judgment on Joyce's novel, called Joyce "a modern Naturaliste" and complained that "from the manner of Mr. Joyce to Dadaisme is but a step, and from Dadaisme to imbecility is hardly that."[16] T. S. Eliot answered Aldington in his 1923 essay "*Ulysses*, Order and Myth," where the focus on the "continuous parallel between contemporaneity and antiquity" as "a way of controlling, of ordering, of giving a shape and a significance to the immense panorama of futility and anarchy which is contemporary history"[17] sketches out part of the argument that Gilbert was to elaborate in his book. Even so, the charge of formlessness recurred throughout the 1920s: Shane Leslie, for instance, discovered in *Ulysses* "an abandonment of form and a mad Shelleyan effort to extend the known confines of the English language," while Edmund Gosse wrote to Louis Gillet in 1924 that *Ulysses* "is an anarchical production, infamous in taste, in style, in everything."[18]

Nor did Aldington's alignment of Joyce with the naturalists readily disappear. The most intelligent, and most sustained, attack on the "naturalism" of *Ulysses* came from Wyndham Lewis, whose *Time and Western Man* (1927) contained a chapter entitled "An Analysis of the Mind of James Joyce."[19] Lewis believed there was an essential split between Joyce's modern and "progressive" craft and his retrogressive, cliché-ridden materials, which Lewis regarded as enmired in the morass of naturalism (109). From Lewis's viewpoint, Joyce succeeded only as a technician, and that success was insufficient to redeem his moribund subject matter, which was adopted from nineteenth-century Darwinian naturalism as modified by the discoveries of Freud, Einstein, and Bergson. "At the end of a long reading of *Ulysses*," Lewis declared, "you feel that it is the very nightmare of the naturalistic method that you have been experiencing" (108). Lewis attacked Joyce's method of "telling from the inside," which consists of "confining the reader in a circumscribed psychological space into which several encyclopaedias have been emptied" (107). The order of *Ulysses*, then, is merely superficial, whereas the core of the book is "unorganized brute material . . . a suffocating, moeotic [*sic*] expanse of objects, all of them lifeless, the sewage of a Past twenty years old, all neatly arranged in a meticulous sequence" (108). It is this apparent emphasis on process, on the undifferentiated flux of experience, that Lewis found most objectionable in *Ulysses*: "This torrent of matter is the einsteinian flux. Or (equally well) it is the duration-flux of Bergson—that is its philosophic character, at all events. . . . The method of doctrinaire naturalism, interpreted in that way, results in such a flux as you have in *Ulysses*, fatally. And into that flux it is you, the reader, that are plunged, or magnetically drawn by the attraction of so much matter as is represented by its thousand pages. That is also the strategy implied by its scale" (119–120). The result of Joyce's method in *Ulysses*, Lewis argues, is "a softness, flabbiness and vagueness everywhere in its bergsonian fluidity" (120).

Lewis's essential charge—that Joyce had used his talents as a craftsman to give the appearance of order to his materials, which nonetheless remain mechanical and chaotic—was more damaging, because more intelligently conceived, than most other hostile responses to *Ulysses* in the 1920s; it was typical, however, in its insistence that the inner world the book attempts to portray is both lifeless and disorganized. In response to these charges, Gilbert asserted that *Ulysses*, far from being "the manifesto of those forces of disorder which riot in the background of the mind," is "a work essentially classical in spirit, composed and executed according to rules of design and discipline of almost scientific precision" (1931:vi). Moreover, "the superficial disorder of Mr Bloom's and Stephen's meditations, the frequent welling up of subconscious memories and the linking together of ideas by assonance or verbal analogy, all in reality form part of an elaborate scheme" (11/11).

Gilbert's faith that everything in *Ulysses* could be explained, if only we could see the book's underlying plan or logic, grew out of the many hours he spent on the French translation, which entailed frequent consultation with Joyce as to the precise meaning and function of a word or phrase. To his painstaking work on the translation can be traced some of the strengths and weaknesses of his study. "In making a translation," Gilbert says, "the first essential is thoroughly to understand what one is translating: any vagueness or uncertainty in this respect must lead to failure. . . . One begins with close analysis, and only when the implications of the original are fully unravelled does one start looking for approximations in the other language" (1955:vi). This fundamentally inductive pattern of interpreting *Ulysses* —beginning with specific details and moving outward to larger structures—is ideally the method of all readers, although the experience of many readers of *Ulysses*, including most who have had recourse to Gilbert's study as a guidebook, suggests that it is difficult to interpret the details without some prior conception of the book's genre, techniques, and major themes. In any event, Gilbert's careful attention both to the smallest elements in the text and to the book's overarching patterns sets the style for much of *Ulysses* criticism, which—as critics have at times noted—frequently resembles Biblical exegesis in its emphasis on explication of details in relation to larger patterns of meaning as well as in the rather humorless reverence with which the book is often approached.[20] Regarding the critic's task as a combination of the translator's and the exegete's, Gilbert assumes in *Ulysses* a fundamental consistency of design that enables readers to anchor their interpretations of particular passages within the larger contexts of what he regarded as the novel's relatively stable and consistent themes and narrative strategies.

If the strength of Gilbert's analysis lies in its thorough and lucid demonstration of the logic of *Ulysses*, its most obvious weakness is its solemn insistence on that logic. Although earlier critics had called attention to Joyce's use of the Homeric motif, Gilbert was the first to follow that theme systematically through the novel, actually demonstrating rather than merely asserting its pervasiveness and importance. Gilbert was well trained for the task of interpreting Joyce's Homeric allusions—he had taken an Honours degree in Classics at Oxford—and he was an intelligent, conscientious, and perceptive reader. Unfortunately, his pedantic tone, whether or not it was largely assumed, made him an easy target for critics who regarded with suspicion Gilbert's willingness to accept at face value whatever lead Joyce offered him. William Schutte undoubtedly spoke for many others when he contended that "Stuart Gilbert's pedantry must have made him [Joyce's] inevitable victim" and suggested that Joyce's "hints," for example, his suggestion that Victor Bérard's *Phéniciens et l'Odyssée* was an important source for *Ulysses*, were often elaborate practical jokes.[21] The characterization is undoubtedly unfair to Gilbert, but its persistence in Joyce criticism points to a widespread feeling that Gilbert was too willing to introduce arcane lore in support of his reading of *Ulysses*. Similarly, few readers today would deny that the schema for *Ulysses* has some value, but in his willingness to fit his interpretations within the framework suggested by the schema, Gilbert demonstrated that his desire for order and continuity outweighed his sense of the ironic and incongruous.

One of the difficulties with Gilbert's emphasis on the *Ulysses* schema is the implication that the plan predated the novel; the result, as Kenner has observed, is that *Ulysses* appears to be "a great feat of planning, full of cunning esoterica"[22] rather than an artistic production whose levels of meaning emerged from the lively interplay of the artist's creative intelligence with his materials. The impression is somewhat misleading, for as A. Walton Litz has demonstrated, the elaboration of Homeric correspondences to specific episodes and passages of *Ulysses* was generally the result of Joyce's revisions, which Joyce carried out, in part, "to impose this elaborate pattern of correspondences upon [the episodes], to transform the entire novel into an 'epic' work."[23] To his analysis of Aeolus, which depends heavily on the analogy between the rhetorical windiness of the daily press and the bag of winds Ulysses received from Aeolus, Gilbert appends an extensive list of rhetorical figures employed in the chapter; but Litz and Michael Groden have observed that many of these figures, including "startling, unique phrases that make Gilbert's list seem like a dominant part of the episode," were added at a late stage in the chapter's composition.[24] The impression that the Homeric correspondences were incorporated into the text fairly early is one that Joyce wanted to encourage, however, for it made the parallels seem an integral part of the book's texture rather than an extraneous overlay of symbolism.

That the Homeric parallels are not central to the text had been the contention of both Ezra Pound, who found them merely "a scaffolding taken from Homer," and Wyndham Lewis, who dismissed them as "only an entertaining structural device or conceit."[25] Gilbert's analysis, as thorough and precise as it was, seemed to Harry Levin to point to a problem in *Ulysses* itself: while regarding the parallel with the *Odyssey* as "a useful contrivance for the reader" and granting that it could help the reader "to control an overwhelming flux of impressions," Levin argued that the parallel "seems more important to Joyce than it could possibly be to any reader." Like Pound and Lewis, Levin preferred to regard the Homeric framework as a device that "served as a scaffolding, while Joyce constructed his work."[26]

A more satisfactory view was set forth in the 1950s by Hugh Kenner, who argued in *Dublin's Joyce* that although the Homeric parallels were indeed important, they were not always important in the same way (Joyce was less schematic than Gilbert makes him appear), and that the most important parallels are between situations rather than between specific incidents (the parallels are less mechanically conceived than Gilbert's presentation would suggest). Moreover, whereas Gilbert had generally accepted the parallels in straightforward fashion, Kenner tended to regard them ironically: "it is unnecessary to heap up detailed parallels for the reader who can extract them from the text or from Mr. Gilbert's commentary; our object is to indicate their multivalent modes of functioning."[27] Kenner's use of Homer as a guide to Joyce's narrative strategies has been picked up and extended by Fritz Senn, who terms *Ulysses* a "Homerically polytropical" book, and by Brook Thomas, who focuses on the relationship between the Homeric themes of transformation and return and the many narrative and linguistic (re)turns of *Ulysses*.[28] Nor are the Kennerian and Gilbertian approaches the only ones open to scholars working on the relationship of *Ulysses* to the *Odyssey*: Hermione de Almeida, for example, analyzes *Ulysses* from the viewpoint of a cultural historian, emphasizing the attitudes toward art and society implicit in Joyce's links with Homer and with other interpreters of the Odyssean myth, rather than the sort of specific parallels between Homeric and Joycean incidents that had attracted Gilbert's attention.[29]

On the other hand, two recent critics owe a more direct debt to Gilbert for opening up the question of Homeric parallels. Richard Ellmann, in *Ulysses on the Liffey* (1972), builds on the Gilbert commentary to argue for an even more intricately patterned *Ulysses*, one in which the triadic principle of thesis, antithesis, and synthesis is the central organizing principle. More impressionistic than rigorous in its argument, Ellmann's book is nonetheless important for its emphasis on what Ellmann terms the Linati schema, an expanded version of the chart of Homeric parallels that Joyce sent to Carlo Linati in 1920. The chart had been published previously, but Ellmann's emphasis on this more intricate schema makes it difficult to argue that the elaborate interpretations contained in Gilbert's study were not intended by Joyce himself. The influence of both the Ellmann study and Gilbert's book may also be seen in another volume of the 1970s, Michael Seidel's *Epic Geography: James Joyce's "Ulysses."* Ellmann had observed that "for many promptings, as Gilbert makes clear, Joyce depended on Victor Bérard's attempt to locate the supposedly mythical topography of the *Odyssey* in actual places,"[30] and Seidel extrapolated from this—and from a careful reading of Bérard's *Phéniciens et l'Odyssée*—an analysis of *Ulysses* based on parallels between the narrative structure of Joyce's novel and Bérard's exposition of the geographical structure of the *Odyssey*. Seidel's interpretations of particular directions in *Ulysses* are sometimes open to objections, but he does seem to have demonstrated that Gilbert, far from overstressing the Bérardian influence on *Ulysses*, may at times have been guilty of underplaying his hand.

The principle of return, so crucial to Gilbert's reading of *Ulysses*, is also a major factor in Joyce criticism, where once-popular modes of interpretation fall out of favor and then return, like Odysseus, in disguise. Thus, it is unsurprising that the Homeric correspondences that received so much attention in the 1930s and were then disparaged by many subsequent critics of *Ulysses* came to be scrutinized from a variety of angles in the 1970s and early 1980s. Making an attempt at interpreting for Molly Bloom the strange word "metempsychosis," her husband, stalling for time while he thinks of a synonym, says "It's Greek: from the Greek" (*U* 4.341), thereby defining the provenance not only of the key word but also of the book in which the dialogue appears, a book whose Greek origins Joyce was at pains to demonstrate. That those origins remain important to any thorough understanding of *Ulysses* remains as clear to today's critics as it was to Stuart Gilbert six decades ago. If Gilbert's analysis appears somewhat pedantic and rigid; if its status as an authorized interpretation seems less important to a generation that has come to be suspicious about authors' statements regarding their intentions; if recent analyses of the styles of *Ulysses* have superseded Gilbert's theories about the representational quality of Joyce's style—even if all this is granted, it remains true that few books have done as much as Stuart Gilbert's to direct their readers' attention to the beauty and integrity of Joyce's masterful novel.

NOTES

1. Richard Ellmann, *James Joyce*, rev. ed. (New York: Oxford University Press, 1982), 600–601. For Gilbert's letter offering to point out "discrepancies" in the French translation, see *Letters of James Joyce*, 3 vols., vol. 3 ed. Richard Ellmann (New York: Viking Press, 1966), 3:158–59.

2. References to *James Joyce's "Ulysses": A Study* are cited parenthetically in the text of this essay. The first of a pair of page numbers (e.g., 161/177) refers to the original American edition (New York: Alfred A. Knopf, 1931); the second, to the revised paperback edition (New York: Vintage Books, 1955), whose pagination differs from that of the revised hardbound edition of 1952. A single page number preceded by 1931 or 1955 cites a passage found only in the indicated edition.

3. Charles Duff, *James Joyce and the Plain Reader* (London: Desmond Harmsworth, 1932), 75.

4. Sidney Feshbach and William Herman, "The History of Joyce Criticism and Scholarship," in *A Companion to Joyce Studies*, ed. Zack Bowen and James F. Carens (Westport, Conn.: Greenwood Press, 1984), 755; Paul van Caspel, *Bloomers on the Liffey: Eisegetical Readings of Joyce's "Ulysses"* (Baltimore: Johns Hopkins University Press, 1986), 2, 9, 23.

5. A perhaps extreme example may be found in Don Gifford and Robert J. Seidman, *Notes for Joyce: An Annotation of James Joyce's "Ulysses"* (New York: E. P. Dutton, 1974), 519–25, where well over half of the entries on rhetorical figures in Aeolus appear to be derived, without attribution, from Gilbert (176–79/194–98).

6. Marvin Magalaner and Richard M. Kain, *Joyce: The Man, the Work, the Reputation* (New York: Collier Books, 1962), 164.

7. Herbert Marshall McLuhan, "A Survey of Joyce Criticism," *Renascence* 4 (Autumn 1951): 14.

8. S. L. Goldberg, *The Classical Temper: A Study of James Joyce's "Ulysses"* (London: Chatto and Windus, 1961), 212; Hugh Kenner, "Who's He When He's At Home?" in *Light Rays: James Joyce and Modernism*, ed. Heyward Ehrlich (New York: New Horizon Press, 1984), 59.

9. Michael Seidel, *Epic Geography: James Joyce's "Ulysses"* (Princeton: Princeton University Press, 1976), 3.

10. Breon Mitchell, *James Joyce and the German Novel 1922–1933* (Athens: Ohio University Press, 1976), 80–81; see also 49–50, 79–80, 86, 101, 162–63.

11. Ellmann, *James Joyce*, 666.

12. Judge Woolsey's decision, prefaced to *Ulysses* (New York: Modern Library, 1961), viii. In his *Dictionary of National Biography* article on Joyce, Gilbert noted that "a growing understanding of the true nature of *Ulysses* (in no sense a pornographic work) gradually paved the way for a removal of the ban [on publication]"; he modestly omitted mentioning his own book's role in this process. See "Joyce, James Augustine (1882–1941)," in the *Dictionary of National Biography 1941–1950*, ed. L. G. Wickham Legg and E. T. Williams (London: Oxford University Press, 1959), 441.

13. T. S. Eliot, "*Ulysses*, Order and Myth," in *Selected Prose of T. S. Eliot*, ed. Frank Kermode (New York: Harcourt Brace Jovanovich/Farrar, Straus and Giroux, 1975), 178.

14. The schemata are reproduced and compared by Richard Ellmann in *Ulysses on the Liffey* (New York: Oxford University Press, 1972), appendix. See also Claude Jacquet, "Les Plans de Joyce pour *Ulysse,*" in "*Ulysses*": *Cinquante ans après*, ed. Louis Bonnerot (Paris: Didier, 1974), 45–82.

15. See the letter from Gorman to Joyce in H. K. Croessmann, "Joyce, Gorman, and the Schema of *Ulysses:* An Exchange of Letters—Paul L. Leon, Herbert Gorman, Bennett Cerf," in *A James Joyce Miscellany, Second Series*, ed. Marvin Magalaner (Carbondale: Southern Illinois University Press, 1959), 11–12.

16. Richard Aldington, "The Influence of Mr. James Joyce," excerpted in *James Joyce: The Critical Heritage*, 2 vols., ed. Robert H. Deming (New York: Barnes and Noble, 1970), 2:186–87.

17. Eliot, "*Ulysses,*" 177.

18. Shane Leslie, review of *Ulysses*, reprinted in Deming, *James Joyce*, 1:211; Louis Gillet, *Claybook for James Joyce*, trans. Georges Markow-Totevy (London: Abelard-Schuman, 1958), 31.

19. Wyndham Lewis, *Time and Western Man* (London: Chatto and Windus, 1927), 91–130.

20. "Because of the problems Joyce has presented to readers, the principal mode of discussion has been what scholars call exegesis—a term which implies that the Scriptures are being interpreted. The pattern was set by Stuart Gilbert's authorized commentary." Harry Levin, *James Joyce: A Critical Introduction*, rev. ed. (New York: New Directions, 1960), 237. Cf. Patrick Parrinder, *James Joyce* (Cambridge: Cambridge University Press, 1984), 122.

21. William M. Schutte, *Joyce and Shakespeare: A Study in the Meaning of "Ulysses"* (New Haven: Yale University Press, 1957), 3.

22. Hugh Kenner, *Ulysses* (London: George Allen & Unwin, 1980), 170.

23. A. Walton Litz, *The Art of James Joyce: Method and Design in "Ulysses" and "Finnegans Wake"* (London: Oxford University Press, 1961), 34; cf. 29.

24. Michael Groden, "*Ulysses*" *in Progress* (Princeton: Princeton University Press, 1977), 105; cf. Groden, 93, and Litz, *Art of James Joyce*, 49–50.

25. Ezra Pound, "James Joyce et Pécuchet" (1922), in *Pound/Joyce: The Letters of Ezra Pound to James Joyce*, ed. Forrest Read (New York: New Directions, 1967), 206; Lewis, *Time*, 121.

26. Levin, *James Joyce*, 75–76.

27. Hugh Kenner, *Dublin's Joyce* (Bloomington: Indiana University Press, 1956), 186.

28. Fritz Senn, "Book of Many Turns," *James Joyce Quarterly* 10 (Fall 1972): 41, reprinted in *Joyce's Dislocutions: Essays on Reading as Translation*, ed. John Paul Riquelme (Baltimore: Johns Hopkins University Press, 1984), 133; Brook Thomas, *James Joyce's "Ulysses": A Book of Many Happy Returns* (Baton Rouge: Louisiana State University Press, 1982).

29. Hermione de Almeida, *Byron and Joyce through Homer: "Don Juan" and "Ulysses"* (New York: Columbia University Press, 1981).

30. Ellmann, *Ulysses on the Liffey*, 34.

Michael H. Begnal

A Skeleton Key to Campbell and Robinson

When *A Skeleton Key to "Finnegans Wake"* was published in 1944, it was the first attempt at a full-length treatment of the narrative of *Finnegans Wake*, which had appeared in its final form only five years earlier. As might have been expected, the interpretation put together by Joseph Campbell and Henry Morton Robinson met with more catcalls than cheers, ranging from Harry Levin's opinion that "the collaborators 'render him no service' in making 'assertions which cannot withstand scrutiny'" to Edmund Wilson's conclusion that the study "'strips away most of the master's poetry.'"[1] More recently, the critics may have changed, but in general their reactions of irritation and dismissal remain the same. Assessing his experience of *Finnegans Wake* as interpreted through the *Key*, Roland McHugh says that "Campbell and Robinson paint over everything they don't understand and they are followed in this by their weaker imitators."[2] John Bishop fumes: "An example of coherent nonsense is what one will find elaborated in some of the commentary on *Finnegans Wake*, which explains, without irony, that the book is about a Nordic hunchback saddled with the improbable name of Humphrey Chimpden Earwicker, who is married to someone even more improbably named Anna Livia Plurabelle, and who has committed an indistinct crime involving two temptresses, three soldiers, and unclear quantities of urine in Dublin's Phoenix Park."[3] Yet *A Skeleton Key*, still in paperback, continues to be the first book of criticism read by the newcomer to *Finnegans Wake*. It is a fixture on every critical bibliography. Just how can this be?

What Campbell and Robinson set out to discover is a traceable narrative line in the *Wake*, the hint of a plot that may help to codify the chaos.

As they say: "Then the enormous map of *Finnegans Wake* begins slowly to unfold, characters and motifs emerge, themes become recognizable, and Joyce's vocabulary falls more and more familiarly on the accustomed ear."[4] Their work was never intended as a trot, a paraphrase, or a substitute for Joyce's novel, but rather as a supplement and an encouragement to an understandably baffled neophyte reader of the *Wake*. The authors repeatedly declare that this or that observation is only a guess, that this or that reading may be palpably incorrect, but they constantly exhort the reader to forge ahead, much as do Joyce's own narrative voices. Most importantly, they are convinced that the *Wake* does make sense and that it is the reader's burden to catch up with the artist's expansion of the guidelines for what might constitute a contemporary work of art. Certainly, they are proselytizers, and certainly they occasionally demonstrate excessive zeal in their pronouncements, but they are sincerely confident that the novel is not a hoax and that, through dedication and effort, it will be revealed as a monumental reaffirmation of human existence.

Consequently, the authors of *A Skeleton Key* begin in their "Introduction to a Strange Subject" to unveil the basic, underlying propositions that give a thematic form to the novel. They link Joyce's title to the Irish music-hall ballad, "Finnegan's Wake," and they introduce the concept of the Fall as essential to the evolution of all human history. In a single paragraph, they outline Giambattista Vico's theory of the four-part cycle of universal history (though they miss the fact that it is really a three-part cycle followed by a *ricorso*, or waiting period), and they indicate some parallels with Goethe, Spengler, and the Hindu Round of the Four Yugas. Their method is eclectic, inclusive, and quite Jungian in its emphasis, but it establishes their contention that Joyce's novel is a vast collection of histories and mythologies, allusions and references, which provide a vision of archetypal man and woman.

It is in the introduction to *A Skeleton Key* that the foundation for a novelistic approach to the text is most directly laid. The body of this section is devoted to descriptions of the narrative's principal characters and to the trials and tribulations of the Earwicker family in their residence at Chapelizod, just outside Dublin. Humphrey Chimpden Earwicker is a newcomer to Ireland, the successor to Tim Finnegan of a previous epoch, one of a series of the many earlier invaders of the Emerald Isle. His precursors are legion, ranging from, among a multitude of others, Thor, Manannan MacLir, Saint Patrick, and Oliver Cromwell. Yet Campbell and Robinson are insistent about one critical aspect of HCE: "He emerges as a well-defined and sympathetic character, the sorely harrowed victim of a relentless fate, which is stronger than, yet identical with, himself" (6).

Though it is not quite clear exactly what the last clause of their descriptive sentence means, the authors view Earwicker as a traditional character in an apprehensible plot. Though he can be seen as a representative of all humankind, his individual characteristics and foibles allow us to follow him through a series of narrational happenings in something much like a conventional manner of reading. HCE is no Leopold Bloom, but he is also not so elusive or *sigla*-like that we cannot get a reasonable understanding of what he does in his dream.

Thus the *Key* fills in the background to Earwicker's guilty dilemma, his Sin in Phoenix Park, which causes him to dream the nightmare of the *Wake* and which the authors do indeed take as having been a literal transgression. "Briefly, he was caught peeping at or exhibiting himself to a couple of girls in Phoenix Park. The indiscretion was witnessed by three drunken soldiers, who could never be quite certain of what they had seen; from them it went out to the world" (7). Continuing to transcribe an unfolding narrative whose basis is essentially cause and effect, Campbell and Robinson relate that the secret comes to be public knowledge when HCE is accosted in Phoenix Park a day later by a certain Cad with a pipe, who not so innocently asks for the time. Caught off guard (though why should he be on guard?), Earwicker blurts out a long defense of his actions, which the Cad takes home to his wife, and soon the rumors are spread across Dublin and result in the satiric and insulting "Ballad of Persse O'Reilly."

In the course of their account of the gossip's transmutations, the authors touch on some of the peripheral characters, such as the Twelve, drinkers at the pub owned by HCE, and the Four, whom they identify as senile judges who preside over the ill doings of the present. They are historians, the Four Masters of the Irish Annals as well as the Four Evangelists, and they drift in and out of these pages seemingly at will. Armed with this knowledge of what has been involved in Earwicker's past, the reader is now prepared to deal with the effects and consequences of the Sin. "In the last analysis, the universal judgement against HCE is but a reflection of his own obsessive guilt; and conversely, the sin which others condemn in him is but a conspicuous public example of the general, universally human, original sin, privately effective within themselves" (9). The plot, then, revolves around the central figure of the Father.

Continuing with their naturalistic catalog of the players in the drama, Campbell and Robinson reinforce one of the most controversial aspects of their critical hypothesis. They invariably make what are, in essence, moral judgments about the characters. Anna Livia Plurabelle, for example, in her various guises, is Eve, Isis, and Iseult, along with being a personification of the River Liffey, but she is also, in her primary manifestation as the wife of Earwicker, "the psyche of the book—bewitching, ever-changing, animating, all-pervading. . . . She is the eternally fructive and love-bearing principle in the world" (10). In many ways, she is a much more complicated character than HCE, splitting into two to become a younger Anna who points up her husband's sexual inadequacies and an older Anna who binds up his wounds and begins again. She is both the daughter, Issy, who is passed over very quickly in this account, and the older housekeeper, Kate the Slops. Although they are clearly aware of the archetypal nature of these characters (for example, HCE as mountain to ALP's river), Campbell and Robinson wish to eliminate as much distance as possible between the characters and the reader. They say that Anna Livia is both the writer and the receiver of the mysterious Letter, or "Mamafesta," uncovered in a dungheap by a scavenging hen (what happened to Shem's role in all this?), and in essence she moves through Joyce's pages as the Great Mother, a representative of all that has been lost through the Fall. Further, she herself is the hen, the lifegiver, and the keeper of the mysteries. She seems completely free of the psychic problems that incapacitate her husband. As Campbell and Robinson say, with something of a grandiloquent flourish: "Anna is the principle of vivid movement, ever setting in motion the river-flow of time" (11).

The list of *dramatis personae* is rounded out with thumbnail sketches of the twins, Shem and Shaun, and once again, characters are defined according to what their positions seem to be on the moral yardstick of virtue and vice. "If it is the typical lot of Shem to be whipped and despoiled, Shaun is typically the whipper and despoiler" (12). The two brothers together constitute a basic polarity and antagonism that exists in society between the artist and the bourgeois, between the exile and Bohemian and the man of the world. Strangely enough, we are told that the twins exist as Shem and Shaun on a symbolic level and as Jerry and Kevin on a domestic one, though none of the other characters is discussed as functioning on these separate levels. Equally debatable is the contention that, since Shem and Shaun embody opposing traits that are encapsulated and incorporated in their father, they are much simpler characters than Humphrey Chimpden Earwicker. Such statements could use a great deal more justification. "Compared with the rich plasticity of HCE, the boys are but shadow-thin grotesques" (13). Be that as it may, for Campbell and Robinson, the characters Shem and Shaun are still boys, whose struggles can be quickly smoothed over by the intervention of a parent. "Antipodal as the brothers may be, they are both easily embraced by the all-inclusive love of their wonderful mother ALP" (13).

The portraits of the players now complete, *A Skeleton Key* moves on to the overwhelming question: "What, finally, is *Finnegans Wake* all about?" And here is the answer: "Stripping away its accidental features, the book may be said to be all compact of *mutually supplementary antagonisms:* male-and-female, age-and-youth, life-and-death, love-and-hate; these, by their attraction, conflicts, and repulsions, supply polar energies that spin the universe" (14). Leaving out what might be meant by "accidental features," such a definition is not half bad as a starting point for the *Wake*. Additionally, it is interesting that this statement seems, momentarily at least, to transcend a novelistic approach, since it defines the narrative in terms of tension and opposition rather than in terms of the internal dissensions of a specific family in a specific place and time. What seems to be equally important are not the actual maneuverings of HCE and ALP but rather the timeless concepts they come to represent. "James Joyce presents, develops, amplifies and recondenses nothing more nor less than the eternal dynamic implicit in birth, conflict, death, and resurrection" (14). Campbell and Robinson expect that the reader will realize that, by comprehending and moving through individual scenes with halfway realistic features, he or she is witnessing any story and all stories. Though they assert earlier that "the chief contribution of the present volume is its thin line-tracing of the skeletal structure of *Finnegans Wake*" (x), it becomes clear that their ultimate purpose is not quite so simple. They hope to explicate what might be termed the archetypal story behind the literal one.

Before proceeding any further, it must be said that the most irritating aspect of *A Skeleton Key* is its euphoric, even gushy, rhetoric. In their admittedly admirable enthusiasm for Joyce's work, the authors are too often unable to restrain themselves from waxing rhapsodic about what they and we are learning from any given page. As Marvin Magalaner and Richard M. Kain state: "The flaw of the *Key* lies not in the inadequacy of the paraphrase—the authors are the first to admit that the *Key* is not the *Wake* —but in the unlimited hyperbole of the editorial comments."[5] We hear of Joyce that "his youth had been nurtured on such sacramental fare that he was nauseated by the sweetish, sawdust loaf offered to the populace as true bread" (362–63). The writing of the *Wake* seems beyond the limited powers of mortal man. "One acknowledges at last that James Joyce's overwhelming macro-microcosm could not have been fired to life in any sorceror furnace less black, less heavy, less murky than this, his incredible book. He had to smelt the modern dictionary back to protean plasma and re-enact the 'genesis and mutation of language' in order to deliver his message" (4). Phew! And when we confront the first sentence of *Finnegans Wake:* "Here the Joycean volcano in full eruption vomits forth raw lumps of energy-containing lava, a mythogenetic river still aflame as it floods across the page" (24). Such flights of excess are a tribute to the commentators' zeal, but too often, enough is enough. Perhaps the reader should take to heart the advice of one of Joyce's own narrative voices: "Now, patience; and remember patience is the great thing, and above all things else we must avoid anything like being or becoming out of patience" (FW 108.08).

Having provided an overview of the novel, Campbell and Robinson put theory into practice in a section entitled "Synopsis and Demonstration." In their synopsis, they attempt to give form to the four books of the Wake by designating them, in order, the Book of the Parents, the Book of the Sons, the Book of the People, and Recorso. These titles, they say, "are intended to serve as a handrail for the reader groping his way along unfamiliar galleries" (15), and again the stress is on the human. Their appellations can certainly be contested (what is the Shem chapter doing in the Book of the Parents, for example?), but it seems that their intention is to anthropomorphize the text to make it more readily apprehensible. Thus, they briefly trace in Book One a steady progression from Finnegan's wake to Earwicker's rise, his background, his trial and incarceration, and ultimately his fall and his resurrection. The last four chapters of this first book encompass Anna Livia's Mamafesta, twelve questions that introduce the main characters, Shaun's indictment of Shem, and the washerwomen's discussion of the history of Anna Livia Plurabelle. It goes without saying that things here are much too neat, but A Skeleton Key posits a simple frame within which the reader can begin working.

The Book of the Sons provides the same kind of apparent critical confidence and actual textual problem. The children play games before supper in one chapter, and they do their homework in the next. So far, so good, but the third chapter, "Tavernry in Feast," breaks away from the sons and continues a literal story with Earwicker serving drinks in his pub while the children are asleep. The complexity of the narrative forces Campbell and Robinson to switch gears and to return to HCE as the center of events, dominating the action in his roles as the Norwegian Captain and the Russian General. The concluding chapter, which they call "Bride-Ship and Gulls," poses the same difficulty, since the focus is on HCE as King Mark, cuckolded by Tristram with Iseult, while Shem and Shaun do not seem to make any literal appearance. It might be argued as well that Book Three should better be designated "the Book of Shaun," since the first three chapters reveal him in his various transformations, and the last leaps to a scenario that involves the parents in bed, but why quibble? This synopsis by Campbell and Robinson moves the reader along to the conclusion, Book Four, to the breaking of day and to the emergence, in their view, of the human spirit of renewal. We begin the final section on a symbolic level, with Saint Kevin, Saint Patrick, and the Archdruid, before returning to the realistic with Anna Livia and the River Liffey. "The moment of the triumph of wakefulness over deep mythological dream is represented as the arrival of St. Patrick (*ca.* A.D. 432) and his refutation of mystical Druidism. All thereafter moves toward enlightenment" (23).

With their overview in place, the authors substitute microcosm for macrocosm in a detailed examination of the novel's first four paragraphs. It should be noted that the first volume of Joyce's letters, edited by Stuart Gilbert, with its many hints and explications that Joyce sent to his correspondents, most notably to Harriet Shaw Weaver, was not published until 1957, so Campbell and Robinson are often groping in the dark. As always, they do not profess to reveal all the resonances or pun possibilities in a given word or sentence but rather set out an example of how to read the text. They are concerned with its method, and in this endeavor they are quite successful. Thus, along with exploring the connotative ripples of a Joycean word, they point out the peripheries of the technique, such as the initials HCE looming behind "Howth Castle and Environs" and the interplay of love and war that runs throughout the passage. Some of their precepts may sound a bit obvious to the accomplished reader of the *Wake*, but they are probably manna from heaven to the beginner. "Always seek in a Joycean expression an antimony or contradiction. He delights in saying two opposite things in the same words" (34). The ease with which the commentators move through these initial sentences almost makes it possible to accept without reservation their later claim that "amidst a sea of uncertainties, of one thing we can be sure: *there are no nonsense syllables in Joyce*" (360). If only we all could be so sure.

Shying away from any pretense of final authority, as usual, Campbell and Robinson, while apologizing that "these few lines of commentary are an admittedly inadequate gloss" (36), emphasize the fact that the fun and the fascination of untangling an individual word must always be tied to the application of more general themes. If nothing else, their explication of the first four paragraphs has revealed the presence of three central moments: the Fall, the Wake, and the Rise. They assert that the interpretative emphasis for the first page, as well as throughout *Finnegans Wake*, must be placed on the living, on the brawling and quarrelling of the Wake scene itself, which is only another version of the rises and falls that make up human existence. And at this point, too, they state what is one of the most important features of their work—what the reader must accomplish *after* he or she has read *A Skeleton Key*. "The present interpretation can only hint at some of the secrets of Joyce's language and indicate the great outlines of his method: the *experiencing* of the work must be left to the sensibilities of the apt reader" (36). In many ways, they see themselves as partners with the reader in a joint enterprise, and rarely is their tone limiting or dictatorial. This position is one of their great strengths, since, as pioneers in virtually unexplored territory, they wish to recruit fresh volunteers for their undertaking instead of staking out narrowly defined claims. For all their intermittent bombast, Campbell and Robinson are a jovial pair who approach their task with appreciation and devotion. Their stress on the necessarily collaborative nature of *Wake* reading underscores a concept that has become an integral part of the critical investigation, and it is evidenced by the longstanding importance of *A Wake Newslitter*, edited by Clive Hart and Fritz Senn from 1962 to 1984.

The bulk of *A Skeleton Key* is taken up with the explication of the text. "Henceforth a thin line-tracing of the basic story of *Finnegans Wake* will suffice to guide the reader. It is not our purpose to elucidate fully any page or group of images, but to weld together the fundamental links of the narrative itself" (38). It would be too easy to fire off potshots at various shaky moments of the plot elucidation; it is much more fair to take the authors at their word. They make no claim to omniscience. Ideally, the explication should be used as an introductory tool, something not necessarily read straight through, since a reader should probably investigate each section of Campbell and Robinson either before or after he or she has experienced a given *Wake* chapter. The reader is not to remain passive, allowing the *Key* to have the final word. Over and over again, the authors, often sounding like one of Joyce's kindly but stern professorial personae, implore the reader to get busy. Before they present their view of Earwicker's meeting with the Cad, for example, Campbell and Robinson intone: "These pages demand strict attention and very slow reading" (69). Again, mired in the middle of the chapter concerning Shem and Shaun at their lessons, they call the reader to attention: "We do not promise that we have correctly related the passages in the body of the text to the principles named in the margin; every reader will have to do this job himself! The present rendering is put forward only as a suggestion" (172). This is not false modesty; it is an indication to the reader that he or she must participate actively in a plausible approximation of the Wakean narrative.

True to their initial premises, Campbell and Robinson are convinced that *Finnegans Wake* tells a story about a middle-aged man who has seen better days and his wife who seeks to regenerate him. For all their citings of archetypal and mythological parallels, they always return to a pubkeeper in Chapelizod, beset by guilt and a quarrelling family, who strives only to get along in this world. They are highly sympathetic to the downtrodden man, and they heap high praise on the woman who will stand by him. About the sons, they are not quite so sure. While Shem may be admirable as the dedicated artist who must tell the truth about the hypocrisy he sees all around him, his nihilism and his gall make him somewhat suspect in their eyes. Though he is identified at one point as James Joyce himself, Shem is described as incomplete without the reconciliation with his brother that can never come to pass. "Shem, acutely aware of his need for assistance from the other half, has begged for help, but Shaun, unable to admit his need for the other, yet compelled to protest very elaborately his independence, has refused to collaborate and has insisted on his own unique power and right to occupy the seat of dictation" (132). Shaun is a necessary evil, the standard bearer of society's conventional vision of order and morality, but he, too, is doomed to fail. "He represents the last stage of a vast historical development; his is the period of the fully expanded and exhausted blossom. For all his world-filling bulk, he lacks durability. Whereas HCE was always up again and around, Shaun will quickly fade" (289). Affirmation will remain the province of the father and the mother.

In conclusion, then, the authors restate their claim that *Finnegans Wake* is a novel that takes language leagues beyond where anyone could have thought it might go. They are adamant that a reader's diligence will be repaid many times over with insight into the complexities of the human psyche, and they codify a "simple" method for piercing the book's shroud of mystery. "The task of opening the way into any passage thus divides itself into three stages: (1) *discovering* the key word or words, (2) *defining* one or more of them, so that the drift of Joyce's thought becomes evident, (3) *brooding* awhile over the paragraph, to let the associations running out from the key centers gradually animate the rest of the passage" (359–60). One of Joyce's greatest triumphs is that he has managed to utilize myth on a universal scale, going beyond the boundaries of Western literature to incorporate all times and all peoples in his work. He has, as well, plumbed the depths of dream to reveal man, along with the artist himself, in all his brilliance and in all his horror. As Campbell and Robinson say, with more than a touch of a foreboding, mystic warning about the book: "The baffling obscurity of *Finnegans Wake* may be due to the author's determination to muddy the track of his narrative with a thousand collateral imprints, lest we trace him to the scene of his own life-secret, which he yet describes in compulsive half-revelation" (361). Whatever this last sentence may mean, they defend Joyce against charges of decadence, and they end on the same upbeat that resounds from Molly Bloom's "Yes." "Emphatically, *Finnegans Wake* is not a book of sweetness and light, yet the underlying note is one of positive affirmation" (364).

To return finally to the initial question of why *A Skeleton Key to "Finnegans Wake"* continues to be cited by virtually every critic who deals with Joyce's masterwork, despite its obvious shortcomings and oversimplifications, it might be said that its weakness is its strength. As Sidney Feshbach and William Herman have commented: "Until its publication, nobody had done as much by way of taking on the *Wake* as a whole, suggesting its structural divisions, explicating some passages, and entertaining many correct ideas of the work's mythic dimensions. Nearly forty years later, we can see that, whatever its defects as an initial and ambitious work, it was indeed a key to opening the *Wake* to generations of readers."[6] The novelistic approach Campbell and Robinson champion still seems to be a requisite stage in the development of every Wakean critic. Before it is possible for a reader to move on elsewhere, if he or she so desires, it is necessary that the idea of a plot involving the Earwicker family be absorbed. Basic norms and ground rules must be set out for examination, and this is exactly what Campbell and Robinson provide. Though they had no access to Joyce's drafts and manuscripts, or to a census or a gazetteer or a lexicon, they had implicit faith that *Finnegans Wake* could make sense, that James Joyce was no hoaxer (though he may occasionally have been a trickster), and that their readers could benefit from the narrative that they saw peeping out from the pages of the *Wake*. Indeed, there are still those who conclude that Campbell and Robinson did not really go so far astray in tying the novel to its origins in story in the development of Western fiction. They hoped that the reader would go beyond them, no doubt expected as much. They would certainly approve what their successors have done.

NOTES

1. Quoted in Marvin Magalaner and Richard M. Kain, *Joyce: The Man, the Work, the Reputation* (New York: New York University Press, 1956), 249–50.

2. Roland McHugh, *The "Finnegans Wake" Experience* (Berkeley: University of California Press, 1981), 50.

3. John Bishop, *Joyce's Book of the Dark* (Madison: University of Wisconsin Press, 1986), 395.

4. Joseph Campbell and Henry Morton Robinson, *A Skeleton Key to "Finnegans Wake"* (New York: Harcourt, Brace and Co., 1944), 4. Further references will be drawn from this edition and included parenthetically in the text.

5. Magalaner and Kain, *Joyce: The Man, the Work, the Reputation*, 249.

6. Sidney Feshbach and William Herman, "The History of Joyce Criticism and Scholarship," in *A Companion to Joyce Studies*, ed. Zack Bowen and James F. Carens (Westport, Conn.: Greenwood Press, 1984), 762–63.

Bonnie Kime Scott

A Consensus on Glasheen's *Census*

"Indispensable" is the single word used most frequently to describe Adaline Glasheen's *Census of "Finnegans Wake"* by scholars who have employed it as a reference work in their own studies of Joyce's baffling final book. Some highly productive *Wake* scholars who have succeeded Glasheen cite James Atherton's *Books at the Wake* (1959) or Clive Hart's *Concordance to "Finnegans Wake"* (1963) as their basic tool. (Glasheen herself reports reaching for the latter "like a pair of reading glasses."[1]) But Glasheen's *Census* is consistently at or near the top of the list of essential works.[2] Many of the terms she introduced have become standard vocabulary for discussing the *Wake* and thus must be acquired by serious students of it. If a student bound for a desert island with a copy of *Finnegans Wake* were to ask me what single reference book he or she should also take, I would without hesitation recommend the latest version of the *Census.* I say this as much for Glasheen's attitudes toward the text as for her book's encyclopedic information; perhaps most important, I know that the *Census* will encourage the student to go on working on the *Wake* with a hopeful, inventive, joyful spirit and a sense of community, even in isolation.

I cheat slightly on the terms of this collection, namely, the "classics" of Joyce criticism, when I refer to the "latest version" of Glasheen's *Census.* Expanded three times since its first appearance in 1956,[3] Glasheen's work is most likely to come to students and scholars today in the 1977 *Third Census of "Finnegans Wake."* My own university library apparently never owned the first *Census,* and fewer than fifty libraries in the United States had copies available for interlibrary loan. Although later editions of some other works covered in this volume have been produced, Glasheen's additions and changes have been by far the most extensive; she has more than doubled the 146-page length of the original *Census*.[4] And though her basic format has remained consistent, her tone has become increasingly spirited, and occasionally outrageous, but such liveliness was there from the start.

Frank Glasheen, husband of Adaline, provides the following account of the beginnings of her *Census:*

> When Adaline started to work on *Finnegans Wake*, she had only two things in mind. One was to find something worth doing and that could be done in the brief, scattered intervals between tending her baby; the other, to find out all she could about a book that she already knew to be brilliant, complex, and hitherto not fully explored. She wanted an intellectual chore that would sustain her between cries and diapers.
>
> The first step to understanding *Finnegans Wake* was to find out what was in it. It was filled with people, known and obscure, so she started listing the names. The idea of compiling a census came as the list of names grew.

The village library in Farmington, Connecticut, proved inadequate for Glasheen's identification process, but such old friends as Charles Bennett and Warren Hunting Smith filled the gap by bringing requested books from a university library.[5] Glasheen mimeographed her growing, alphabetical list and sent it out for reactions to people she knew were interested in *Finnegans Wake*.

Those who provided encouragement, further identifications, and useful suggestions for revision included Thornton Wilder, James Atherton, and Matthew Hodgart; thus, the collaboration already involved a creative writer and scholars from the other side of the Atlantic. Glasheen was pleased by Wilder's description of her as "a lady who sits and thinks."[6] Far-flung contributors to later editions included Fritz Senn from Switzerland and Clive Hart from Australia. Two Americans who helped on the first *Census* were perhaps the most famous Joyceans of all, "Mr Hugh Kenner" and "Mr Richard Ellmann." Ellmann interested Northwestern University Press in publishing the first *Census*. His "Foreword" to that edition still bears rereading for its justification of Joyce's name-hiding "to stretch our daytime imaginations" and for his placement of Glasheen's work in the context of a growing Joycean critical apparatus.[7] Kenner took the *Third Census* to the University of California Press. Glasheen observes that her collaborators had not known her previously and that "they had nothing in common save an interest in Joyce and a desire that *Finnegans Wake* should become more available to the common reader" (*C* xviii). Glasheen considered even her *Third Census* an "interim report," and its reviewers had come to rely on new editions as regular events. Regrettably, given the present state of Glasheen's health, the third is probably the final issue of the *Census*.

In people's reminiscences of Adaline Glasheen, she emerges as a letter-writer to rival the hen of *Finnegans Wake*. "She began a correspondence which continued for thirty years. No one was safe. The U.S., England, France, Italy, India."[8] Her letters usually dealt with specifics, sharing her discoveries in areas where her correspondents were working but also asking questions about identities, behaviors, and patterns that puzzled her.[9] She makes her own appearance in scholars' acknowledgments for her tireless contributions to their work on the *Wake*.[10] When Joyceans first began to gather on an international scale, Glasheen was a part of the forming circle that has become the Joyce Foundation.

Even in her acknowledgments sections, Adaline Glasheen comes across as an individual. Up through the *Third Census*, she continued to use "Mr," "Mrs," and "Miss" as titles, never the informality of a name alone or the remote, hierarchical academic appelations of "Professor" or "Dr." She has called herself a "harmless drudge" (*C* xvi). But though her labor has the persistence and patience that mark devotion, her attitude is anything but dull and submissive. Her judgments of Joyce himself are neither reverential nor harmless. The maze of *Finnegans Wake* is described as a "vainglorious imitation of God and Masterbuilder Daedalus" (*3d C* vii). In the *Third Census*, there is an entry, its format like all the others, for "Joyce, James Augustine Aloysius (q.q.v.) (1882–1941)—Irish poet . . ." (*3d C* 148).[11] Glasheen is outspoken about Joyce as a father: "It seems to me that Joyce observed his daughter's madness with care and interest and wrote about it with great power and bad taste" (*3d C* 149). Glasheen is willing to draw on her experience of the world, including her female point of view, and on this basis to register the authenticity or the tragedy of Joyce's fictions. ALP is "a horrid warning to martyred mothers" (*3d C* viii), and Issy, a "triumph of feminine imbecility" (*C* 61; *3d C* 138); Lewis Carroll is, for Joyce, "the man and artist who responds to the feminine with sentimental, self-serving lust and sexual stinginess," and in this he is comparable to Swift and Wyndham Lewis (*3d C* 51). Elsewhere, I have credited Glasheen with displaying an "alerted feminist conscience," and this is truly remarkable for its early manifestations in 1956.[12] She also uses personal experience in discussing the four annalists: "As far as I know, Joyce was the first artist to set senility down at length. Listening to an educated man, dying of hardening of the arteries, I realized that he spoke in the manner and matter and very rhythm of the Four. Joyce does not prettify his senescent Four—they are boring, repulsive, sinister—but he does leaven them. A crazy beauty hangs about the honeymoon section, and at the inquest their maunderings are disciplined by numerical significance and structure" (*3d C* 97–98).[13] She can be very funny with familiar materials, as in her identification of Ajax as "a brawny not brainy Greek" (*3d C* 5). She can be hard on her academic colleagues: "It is high time that someone who knows FW should read books *by* Bruno, not just books *about* Bruno" (*3d C* 18). She turns even harsh judgments into useful materials, and lures us to them. Of Kitty O'Shea's book on Parnell, she remarks, "She wrote a book about him that cannot—by its naive vapidity—fail to fascinate" (*3d C* 218). She ventures some frank generalizations that students will not encounter in their usual scholarly sources: "Such Hermetic matter as I have read or read about is on an intellectual level with Kahlil Gibran—simple-minded mystical platitudes with a strong hate of sex and physical fertility" (*3d C* 126). She occasionally talks to herself, as in this struggle to limit the number of citations of Finn MacCool: "Also I think, what is unthinkable, that every fin-fan-fen-fon-fun-phin (see also Chin) names Finn MacCool—and of course every C–l, M-C-l, elegantly subjected to the ablaut. The foregoing statement is not lightly set down. Surely, Madam, you use 'every' loosely or in a purely Pickwickian sense? No" (*3d C* 92).

Glasheen's use of asterisks to admit that she doesn't know who somebody is and the question marks that register uncertain citations are refreshing in their honesty and mature appreciation of the provisional nature of knowledge that they demonstrate. Sometimes the gap would seem embarrassing, if the entry were not still full of information about conditions of occurrence, as when she admits, "I don't understand the use of Prince Hamlet in FW" (*3d C* 116). She sets for future scholars a model of the open-ended design, diligence, and patience needed to detect patterns that will unravel only with time and cooperation. She remarks on Daedalus, for example, that " 'Daedalus' is hidden cunningly all over FW, and will be but slowly unraveled" (*3d C* 67).[14] At times she disappoints with her flippancy. She writes for Wynn's Hotel that it "was (is?) near the Abbey (q.v.) theatre." It remained in the summer of 1987, and Glasheen very readily could have had this information from a Dublin telephone directory.

In describing her project, Adaline Glasheen employs several metaphors. The title uses "census"; the subtitle proclaims further that the work is an "index of the characters and their roles." "Census" suggests a real place, a world or a country, awaiting a resourceful official to find out what numbers and sorts of people it contains. Having left Dublin, Joyce recreated it in *Ulysses*; in *Finnegans Wake*, we have Dublin and the world, now and through history. The process of stock taking implied by a census is as limited as the tools of collection, and Glasheen is the first to admit the incompleteness of the gathering efforts. "Index" relates more to literary texts. As the most typical entries in book indexes are listings of persons, it seems appropriate that Glasheen felt her alphabetical listing could substitute for an index to the *Wake*. Glasheen also found meaning in the theatrical metaphor of the "role." Like a Dublin stock company, Joyce worked with a limited number of actors, all too familiar to the audience and forced to appear opposite each other in a bewildering variety of parts (*C* ix–x; *3d C* ix–x). In one entry, she tells us that "Alice is a principal role of Issy's (q.v.): girl-child rejected as a sexual object, used sentimentally by a father figure" (*3d C* 5). We also learn that Adonis is "a good role" for Shaun (*3d C* 3).

It took three metaphors to get at what Glasheen felt she was doing with her book. But it also took several sections: a preface, a synopsis, a chart, and finally, the extensive alphabetical listing of the census. In the census itself, as evolved in the third edition, typical entries offer the following: variant forms of the name, cross-references to other names listed in the census, and suggestions that one should see others (e.g., Mme. Blavatsky's theosophical associates); a historical or literary identification, complete with dates for historical figures. The identification emphasizes aspects of the person that Joyce centers on in his text (e.g., the gluttony of the great Irish tenor, John McCormack, would not be featured in typical write-ups of him but suits *FW* III.1–2). Where appropriate, Glasheen quotes from earlier works in the Joyce canon, as well as the Buffalo notebooks and the letters. There is often a paragraph of general remarks about the contexts, themes, words, syllables, or even just letters typically associated with the person in the *Wake* and about special difficulties in locating the entity. Next come locations where the entity may be found in the *Wake* text. She gives page number, followed by a period, followed by the line number, a convention that she may have originated. (It would be wonderful to have marginal line numbers provided in a future edition of *Finnegans Wake!*) Citations of individual appearances are followed by composites, made from the listed name plus one or more additional persons. For composites, citations are preceded by a plus sign and followed by "—with" and the name(s) of the additional person(s), with cross-listings signaled. The admission of composites to the listing reflects an important polymorphic structure of the *Wake*. Sometimes, Glasheen will remark on the special difficulties of detaching personalities from one another. She says of Molly Bloom: "I have tried to disentangle Marion Bloom from the Marys and Annes of FW, and I cannot do it, and concluded Joyce didn't want it done" (*3d C* 33). Some listings, like "Anna" and "Parnell," are usefully broken down into subaspects: "I Anna Livia Plurabelle," "II Anna Livia," "III Anne, Annie, Anna, etc.," "IV Livia, Liffey, etc.," "V Plurabelle," "VI ALP, LAP, PAL, PLA,

APL, LPA (see also One Hundred and Eleven)" (*3d C* 10–12).[15] "Hosty," "Cad" and "Man Servant" are very *Wake*-specific listings but also have interesting, miniature subaspects in their definitions. The listings in the *Census* give first general identifications, then *Wake*-specific ones. In its less-crowded pages, it was possible for the first *Census* to present a column of page numbers and the *Wake* spellings—a format that is in some ways easier to work with than the run-on lists of the *Third Census*, which provides only page numbers and often Glasheen's standard English rendition of *Wake* language. As knowledge of the *Wake* accumulates over the years, the problem of collecting it in a single volume becomes increasingly difficult. Roland McHugh's *Annotations to "Finnegans Wake,"* which spaces identifications on blank pages that correspond in number and line to the Joyce text, was of cumbersome dimensions in its first edition. I worry about the awkwardness of using a promised second edition. Glasheen's *Census* remains manageable, even in its last rendition.

The census is not really limited to "characters and their roles." Glasheen conveniently provides a set of lyrics to the song "Finnegan's Wake" in all editions of the *Census*. *The Third Census* lists quite a few numbers (three, four, seven, eleven), some solitary letters (A, E), "signs" (a selection of the *sigla* that have been extensively considered by Roland McHugh), and some nouns that are not proper ones but closer to themes (bull, fox, salmon, ear, atom).[16] Surprisingly, or perhaps sensibly (given their numbers), she rarely lists rivers. She does list Aeolus, even though she gives no specific citation, because he seems to lurk in the many references to the wind; I think perhaps she wants someone to pin him down. Glasheen is willing to talk about and work around her basic listing principles—discussions that often tell us a great deal about patterns of the *Wake*. Under Finnuala, she writes: "Some of the following indicate rather than name—e.g., 'silent,' 'moyle,' 'lonely' (q.v.) indicate the swan-girl. I don't know if a census can or should deal with indications (madness lies), but Joyce's glosses to paragraph #2 of FW (see *Letters*, 1:247–48) show plainly that he makes no distinctions between persons named and persons indicated" (*3d C* 94–95). We learn in the unusual first entry (A, An, Aleph, Alpha) of Joyce's use of acrostics. Characters that usually appear in pairs (usually couples) are listed that way (Abraham and Sarah; Adam and Eve). The most extensive entries may run to four half-page columns and qualify as small essays. Anyone interested in Lewis Carroll (or his Alice), Wyndham Lewis, Charles Stewart Parnell, Saint Patrick, King Lear, and (surprisingly to me) Betsy Ross must be sure to consult Glasheen's mini-essays. As a contrast, in their index of characters in earlier Joyce works, *Who's He When He's at Home*, Shari and Berni Benstock deliberately offer only a bare directory. In revising,

Glasheen has dropped some useful general material from the essays, perhaps because it no longer fit in the more specific subaspects that emerged. Take, for example, the second paragraph of her original Anna Livia Plurabelle identification:

> Joyce was romantic about women. Gretta, Bertha, Molly, Anna Livia are the eternal feminine that counters man's restless flux with a sweet permanence. Of all Joyce's heroines, Anna Livia Plurabelle is the most romantic, most poetic, most conventionally endearing. The parts of FW that are devoted to her will always be the most popular, and are becoming standard anthology pieces. There is nothing about Anna Livia that outrages expectation. She is a woman and a river, and women have been identified with water before this. The Greeks did it, Freud did it, a good many English poets did it, and Joyce did it because he needed a well-worn conceit. In the elaborate, shifting, sometimes fussy, complexities of FW, something must stand firm and comprehensible. Anna Livia, little, quick, red-haired, is always "the same anew." (*C* 5).

There are narrative summaries in Glasheen's census, too, elucidating the fables of the Mookse and the Gripes, the Ondt and the Gracehoper, and the Dublin stories of the *Wake*, like "Kersse the Tailor," as it relates to one of John Joyce's stories, the Norwegian Captain (*3d C* 154).

The primary approach to *Finnegans Wake* encouraged by Glasheen's census is a structural reading, calling attention to scattered positioning and recurrence of allusion, as opposed to a chronological reading. It contains encyclopedic knowledge, reenforcing for students this important aspect of Joyce. The two briefer sections of her books that precede the census encourage other paradigms for Joyce and the *Wake*. The first section is a "Synopsis," the defects of which she is quick to point out: "The synopsis omits Joyce's fine nonsense and infinite variety; it renders abrupt and broken the 'savage economy' of Joyce's language; it misses or mangles the elegant and ingenious flow of Joyce's variations on metamorphic experience" (*3d C* xxiii). Campbell and Robinson had provided the first synopsis in their *Skeleton Key*, which is now frequently found to be misleading. In 1956, Ellmann pronounced Glasheen's synopsis "an advance in fathoming the book's structure and plot" compared to the *Key* (*C* iv–v). Synopses continue to appear—as in Patrick McCarthy's useful contribution to the recent *Joyce Companion*, the specialized Shakespearean synopsis of Vincent Cheng, and the rather quirky book-length summary of John Gordon's *"Finnegans Wake": A Plot Summary*. The 48-page synopsis that appears in the *Third Census* grew from a bare 4½ pages in the first and is supplemented by the narratives of legends and fables in the census proper. Although the *Census* version still presents a fine, compact view of the *Wake*, the expanded version has special strengths, including a stronger mythical dimension than most. Perhaps the most debatable aspect is the identity of the speaker at given points in the "narrative." But however simply she states this in the synopsis, Glasheen was aware of the complexity of the telling of *Finnegans Wake* in her first preface, where she declared, "Nothing but Anna Livia's dying soliloquy comes to us direct" (*C* x). Glasheen borrows titles for chapters from publications of parts of "Work in Progress" or from references in manuscripts and letters. To head sections of the synopsis, she chooses relevant quotations from Joyce's letters and brief quotations from the *Wake*, particularly where they summarize character. References to characters named in the synopsis are cross-referenced to entries in the census, encouraging readers to move between these two approaches in her book.

Following the synopsis is Glasheen's most inventive and controversial approach to the *Wake*, a table called "Who Is Who When Everybody Is Somebody Else." Vertical columns list the five family entities that Glasheen introduces as the innkeeper and his family in the preface to her *Third Census* (HCE, Shaun, Shem, Issy, and ALP). A sixth column accommodates others, including male and female servants whom she attaches to the family. Read horizontally, we enter ninety-three sets of identities or roles from dramas, books, and myths that offer passing scenarios and structures to the *Wake*. The *Census* had the same six-part horizontal structure and offered forty-nine sets of identities vertically. Ellmann appreciated this "graphic presentation" of "how the characters change names and epochs . . . according to a system rather than caprice" (*C* v). Thus, Glasheen's *Census* is far more than a list of characters alluded to; it offers supplementary synchronic, diachronic, and allusive approaches to the *Wake*, encouraging and facilitating multiplicity of approach. There is a brief bibliography in *The Third Census*, now somewhat dated. The selected secondary sources number twenty-seven and carry publication dates ranging from 1929 to 1974. Additional works are cited within the main census listings.

In recent poststructuralist theory, character has been an unfashionable aspect of fiction. Roland McHugh finds a "novelistic approach" in all aspects of Glasheen's work (Atherton's as well), but particularly in the substrate of the pubowner's family cited in Glasheen's preface and implicit in the "Who Is Who" table. He finds that table inconsistent and seems to long for as many vertical columns as he has *sigla* in *The Sigla for "Finnegans Wake."*[17] The *sigla* studied by McHugh provide one way around traditional character analysis in the *Wake*, but McHugh himself complains that Glasheen's listing of them, particularly in "Who Is Who," is incomplete. Grace Eckley also longs for more columns in "Who Is

Who," but not because she resists a character-centered approach.[18] Glasheen does not resist her assignment to a narrative designation. In fact, she expresses some disappointment over a lack of narrative progress on the *Wake*: "In 1963 I hoped narrative progress, narrative connections would be looked at by other Joyceans. It has not been. I go on hoping" (*3d C* xxiii).

Another criticism is that Glasheen's census has certain problems endemic to guides of its sort. As Michael Begnal has noted, "concentration on specific allusions or thematic patterns has tended to draw attention to the detail, the part, rather than the whole of *Finnegans Wake*,"[19] though it should be recalled that Glasheen provides more comprehensive second and third approaches to the *Wake* in her synopsis and in "Who Is Who." Glasheen's *Census* does not completely assume the burden of proof, though we have noted some valiant efforts to register doubts with question marks preceding entries and to generalize about contexts where an entity is apt to appear. In the *Third Census*, some specific justifications do appear in parenthesis following the listing. But it might have been useful to set up a specific identification code (*s* for spelling, *c* for context with other names, etc.). Hans Walter Gabler offers a set of criteria for his choices made in the 1984 edition of *Ulysses*, and something comparable might have been developed here. In her preface, Glasheen classifies some characters as "archetypes" and historical characters that serve as *"leitmotivs"* and others as "proper tropes," local allusions that illuminate thought and mood and exist by the thousands (*C* xiv), but these classifications do not persist in her listings. Shari and Bernard Benstock developed a particularly intricate legend to immediately classify characters in Joyce's earlier works into such categories as Joycean characters, pre-existing historical figures, characters present, characters only mentioned, and so forth. But they also admit that they are census takers in a less labyrinthine world of character than that of the *Wake*.[20] Glasheen's form of listing conveniently provides the basic identification just above a citation, whereas in annotations of *Ulysses* by Weldon Thornton and Don Gifford it is necessary to thumb backward in the book for a first reference. In his study of Shakespearean allusions in *Finnegans Wake*, Vincent Cheng chooses to repeat information; I lost count of how many times he had identified Delia Bacon, for example. Glasheen is less convenient than Thornton, Gifford, and Cheng for reading straight through the *Wake*, as one has to search alphabetically for a name that may be a composite or a deliberately misspelled version of a listed entity in Glasheen. Here, Clive Hart's *Concordance* can be of help. Reference to it makes us grateful for the real information on every page of Glasheen, however. One does not read the *Concordance* for amusement or to engage in the transferral or transformation of ideas. Thornton provides much more biographical backing for his allusions and his descriptions, and the format of Atherton's *Books at the Wake*, with its separate sections for different classes of books and different intensities of usage, provides a richer range for complex, integrated discussion.

There are mistakes in each *Census*. The *Third Census* omits the heading for Book I, section ii, in its "Synopsis," for example, and the much-punctuated listings have much mispunctuation. To their annoyance, scholars who have published suggestions of additional identifications have not always found their materials integrated into successive censuses. Vivian Mercier tactfully suggested where Glasheen might find additional Irish materials after the first census but was distressed to find so few included in the third. I suspect from his experience and that of Bernard Benstock that new entries were more apt to reach Glasheen through her mailbox than through scholarly publication—the one exception to this being *A Wake Newslitter*, to which Glasheen was a consistent contributor.[21]

Students inexperienced with the *Wake* should not accept a Glasheen identification, emphasis, or summary of an event as gospel. It is not universally accepted that HCE was a Protestant, for example, though it is always good for a debate with Wakeians. I am not sure that "madelaine" is close enough to "Maggies" for Glasheen to find Proust in as many places as she does, though I am willing to suspect him where cakes are consumed. Glasheen's enthusiasm for the presence of Melville's "Billy Budd" has not been readily accepted. On the other hand, when assessing the merits of one of Glasheen's successors, a student should be most content where there is an inconsistent record of agreement with Glasheen rather than a blanket acceptance of her identifications. I am equally suspicious of scholars who are overly eager to use her as a straw woman.

To proceed with her project, Glasheen settled into an approach—character identification—that was practical and a bit of a compromise in the light of Joycean complexity, but hers was a game others could play and elaborate. Some of her practical decisions—including the choice of basic names to use in referring to family characters of the *Wake*—have stood. Years ago a colleague complained to me about Glasheen's popularization of the name "Issy." It is but one of many choices that could have been made for the daughter of the *Wake*, but it would be difficult to change now, as it has appeared regularly in scholarship of the 1970s and 80s. Two other identifiers now in common use, "Mamalujo" and "The Maggies," were probably made standard through scholars' use of the synopsis of the 1956 *Census*. In her multifaceted approach, Adaline Glasheen clearly intended to provide a basis for further researches and conceptualizations of *Finnegans Wake*. She said in her first preface,

"Whoever works on *Finnegans Wake* must be willing to expose his partial mind in the hope that others will complete it" (*C* xv). Frank Glasheen reports that "she spoke repeatedly of her moral obligation to be as much a help to beginning scholars as [her mentors, James Atherton, Thornton Wilder, and Phil Graham] had been to her."[22] The Benstocks felt no need to canvass character in *Finnegans Wake*, following in the wake of Adaline Glasheen. James Atherton omits from his account of the *Wake* writers who appear in name only, without substantial reference to their work; for these identifications, he refers readers to Glasheen.[23] Vivian Mercier took both the census and the "Who Is Who" chart as forms for further work. He praised "Who Is Who" for "stimulating the reader to fill gaps and find new parallels on his own."[24] Clive Hart also likes the table and would extend its horizontal listing to the inanimate contents of the book.[25] Glasheen admits to having an "eccentric conviction that *Finnegans Wake* is about Shakespeare" in a "Note to the *Second Census*" (*3d C* xxii). For his study of the *Wake*, Vincent Cheng subscribes to Glasheen's claim that "Shakespeare (man, works) is the matrix of *Finnegans Wake*,"[26] filling in that matrix in a more specialized study. Both Charles Peake and John Bishop have remarked to me on Glasheen's regular practice of suggesting questions and patterns for other critics to pursue. Bishop followed up Glasheen's suggestion under "ear": "If you have time on your hands, look up every 'ear' in FW" (*3d C* 81). The ear emerges at chapter length in Bishop's *Book of the Dark*, a work with much more defined physiological and dream-centered concerns than Glasheen's. I found the following worth investigating for my *Joyce and Feminism*: "Artemis is rarely named; but disguised as the Hen, Biddy Doran (q.q.v.; see also Leda), and disguised as the Moon, Artemis is all over the place. Like Hermes (q.v.) she is indicated mostly by her attributes, the forms of her cult, etc." (*3d C* 16). Students and scholars will continue to follow Glasheen's leading suggestions. A few that remain are: "I guess that Beckett's rejection of Lucia will be shown some day to be a fairly important part of FW" (*3d C* 26); "I think it will be found that there is a great deal of Apollo in FW" (*3d C* 13); "FW must be full of [Bridget's] legends. Such legends as I have come on were mostly unattractive and implausible" (*3d C* 39).

Several scholars have commented that Glasheen works in the spirit of *Finnegans Wake*. Ellmann said of the author of the *Census* that "she presents the information with a mixture of wit and conscience, ingredients appropriate to her author" (*C* iv). Clive Hart appreciates a "predictive" inclusion of Lord Haw Haw, whose treason was not tried until after the publication of the *Wake* but whom Glasheen includes in her census. Charles Peake liked her willingness to speculate and use her imagination.

Adaline Glasheen is irreverent, gutsy, enthusiastic, funny, all aspects of Joyce himself, and hence splendid company for him. Glasheen seems to have been attracted to certain qualities in Joyce that make her census taking understandable. "Like many of the Joyceans she came to know, she had always read rapidly and was able to recall details years later. It was obvious that Joyce, too, had read everything—classics and trash—and was transforming everything he'd read into a master work. Here was a game she could play."[27] Census takers must pay heed to all classes of people, and again the model is Joyce, who refused "to admit distinction of kind or degree between the mythical, the fictitious and the so-called historical person, or between the lowly and the great, the vulgar and the aristocrat" (*C* x). That Glasheen sensed the importance of marginal characters and genres so early in her analysis of *Finnegans Wake* may show a special wisdom learned from exercising scholarship on the supposed margins (both sexual and occupational) of the academic world. Glasheen also saw in Joyce the responsibility to be amusing. To use her own example, if Kafka or Matthew Arnold were to take us on the same circular tour of a "darkling plain" that Joyce does, the reader would emerge "near dead with discouragement." But Glasheen appreciates and imitates Joyce as tour guide. "Joyce is an athletic and exhilarating guide. He tells jokes all the night; he is brave without calling attention to his bravery; he finds struggles however ignorant, a sign of vitality" (*C* vii). Glasheen became our guide through a very long list; her struggle with both the ordering task and the identities never assumed an air of commanding pomposity or personal achievement and through its vitality encouraged the reader to list on.

NOTES

    1. Glasheen, Adaline. *Third Census of "Finnegans Wake"* (Berkeley: University of California Press, 1977), xiv. Subsequent references to this edition are cited parenthetically in the text, prefaced by the abbreviation *3d C.*

    2. Vivian Mercier lists Glasheen's as "the most useful book on the *Wake*" in an article that goes on to identify Irish sources for further identifications. See "In the Wake of the Fianna," in *A James Joyce Miscellany*, 3d Series, ed. Marvin Magalaner (Carbondale: Southern Illinois University Press, 1962), 226–38. Clive Hart places her second behind Atherton, but still an "indispensable source of information." See Clive Hart, *"Structure and Motif in "Finnegans Wake"* (Chicago: Northwestern University Press, 1962), 18.

    3. The first expansion, "Out of My Census" was "an appendage" to the first *Census* and appeared in the mimeographed publication of the Northwestern

University English Department, *The Analyst*, in 1959. One unique feature of this version is that Glasheen identifies her "donors," making it possible to detect what was supplied by TW (Thornton Wilder:, FS (Fritz Senn), RP (Ruth Von Phul), RE (Richard Ellmann), and eight others.

4. For a quick comparison of entries from the first through the third *Census*, see J. Mitchell Morse's review in *Comparative Literature*, 30 (Summer 1978): 278–30.

5. Frank Glasheen, letter to Bonnie Kime Scott, 3 Aug. 1987.

6. Ibid.

7. Richard Ellmann, foreword to *A Census of "Finnegans Wake"* by Adaline Glasheen (Evanston: Northwestern University Press, 1956), iii–iv. Subsequent references to *A Census* (i.e., the first edition) are given parenthetically, prefaced by the abbreviation *C.*

8. Frank Glasheen letter, 3 Aug. 1987.

9. Philip Lamar Graham, letter to Bonnie Kime Scott, 3 Sept. 1987. I am grateful to Mr. Graham for sharing samples of his correspondence with Adaline Glasheen.

10. Frank Glasheen letter, 3 Aug. 1987. For a sample acknowledgment, see James S. Atherton, *Books at the Wake* (Mamaroneck, N.Y.: Paul P. Appel, 1974), 16. Hugh Kenner dedicated his *Ulysses* to "Adaline and Fritz."

11. The original *Census* also had a "Joyce, James" entry, but not the deadpan, standard history.

12. Bonnie Kime Scott, *Joyce and Feminism* (Bloomington: Indiana University Press and Brighton: Harvester, 1984), 128.

13. Only the last two sentences were in *C*, 42.

14. Neither "Daedalus" nor "Dedalus" appears in *C.*

15. *C* already had six similar subaspects of Anna.

16. Most of the numbers I note here were in the *Census*, but the other unusual inclusions were not.

17. Roland McHugh, *The "Finnegans Wake" Experience* (Dublin: Irish Academic Press, 1981), 50–51.

18. Grace Eckley, *Children's Lore in "Finnegans Wake"* (Syracuse, N.Y.: Syracuse University Press, 1986), 107.

19. Michael Begnal, *A Conceptual Guide to "Finnegans Wake"* (Syracuse, N.Y.: Syracuse University Press, 1985), x.

20. Shari Benstock and Bernard Benstock, *Who's He When He's at Home* (Urbana, Ill.: University of Illinois Press, 1980), 1.

21. Vivian Mercier, "Evidence of Identity," *Times Literary Supplement* (June 17, 1977), 735. See also Bernard Benstock, "Three Generations of *Finnegans Wake*," *Studies in the Novel* (Fall 1977): 333–35.

22. Frank Glasheen letter, 3 Aug. 1987.

23. Atherton, *Books*, 16.

24. Mercier, "Evidence," 226.

25. Hart, *Structure*, 145.

26. Vincent Cheng, *Shakespeare and Joyce: A Study of "Finnegans Wake"* (University Park: Pennsylvania State University Press, 1986), 6.

27. Frank Glasheen letter, 3 Aug. 1987. Philip Graham remarked on Glasheen's "total recall of every book she had ever read" and the extensiveness of her reading, especially of novels. Graham letter, 3 Sept. 1987.

Suzette A. Henke

Exagmining Beckett & Company

The Incamination of His Factification

How does one conceal and reveal at the same time, leaving clues to "authorial intention" but obscuring the origins of a commentary that never allows itself directly to comment on the text or its origins? Doing so was a challenge to which Joyce rose with ingenuity and verve. In Eugene Jolas's journal *transition*, language was already fluid and in transition, implementing the avant-garde "Revolution of the Word" proclaimed by Jolas as part of his editorial policy. Joyce's "Work in Progress" began to appear serially in the inaugural issue of the journal and, from 1927 onward, represented the most innovative dimensions of Jolas's campaign for literary experimentation. "Over the next eleven years," Michael Finney observes, "Jolas published in *transition* all, or nearly all, of 'Work in Progress' and more than a hundred articles in which Joyce's work was discussed and defended."[1] Jolas's twelve-point proclamation of avant-garde verbal experimentation included the following statements: *"The literary creator has the right to disintegrate primal matter of words. . . . He has the right to use words of his own fashioning and to disregard existing grammatical and syntactic laws. . . . The writer expresses. He does not communicate. . . . The plain reader be damned."*[2]

Of the explicatory articles that had appeared in *transition* as glosses for Joyce's "Work in Progress" from 1927 to 1929, a handful were chosen, along with several commissioned pieces, for publication in *Our Exagmination round His Factification for Incamination of Work in Progress* — a collection intended as a "reader's guide" to a text that would not see book publication for another decade. Most of the contributors were avant-garde writers or critics interested in promulgating Jolas's "Revolution of the Word." The majority were, like Joyce himself, members of an expatriate artistic community exuberantly expanding twentieth-century aesthetic principles in the exotic environs of postwar Paris. In a 1929 letter to Valery Larbaud, Joyce confesses: "What you say about the

Exag is right enough. I did stand behind those twelve Marshals more or less directing them what lines of research to follow."[3]

As Richard Ellmann explains, "the spelling of Exagmination was to claim its etymological derivation from *ex agmine*, a hint that his goats had been separated from the sheep. . . . The book had twelve writers, like the twelve customers of Earwicker's public house, or the twelve apostles of Christ. . . . Joyce saw to it that one or another of the twelve answered the chief critics of the book, at that time Sean O'Faolain, Wyndham Lewis, and Rebecca West."[4] The twelve unwary disciples were marshaled by an author who, like Christ and Averroës, spoke in riddles and parables while destabilizing traditional cognitive formulas. Little did those first brave exagminers suspect that they were analyzing incaminated chapters of an oeuvre that would remain perpetually tessellated and fragmentary or that they themselves, as lexical archeologists, would be parodically inscribed into an encoded hieroglyphic text. They entered the progressive darkness of Joyce's rapidly progressing manuscript, searching for a (w)hole whose origins they believed they could, with patience, comprehend. They spun round the absent center of an ever-elusive textual matrix that always escaped their initial gropings toward mastery and understanding, if not their appreciation and celebration.

Joyce knew that the enterprise was in many ways futile, but he encouraged it and threw his lexical detectives the occasional scholarly vesta that would illuminate, at least, a space in the darkness. As a *sigla* for this group of ardent admirers, he used the zero, the nought of a "noughty . . . zeroine" (*FW* 261.24), with assurance that the disciples yearning for a handle on the whole would eventually tumble into the hole of saturnine ignorance. How could they not? They resembled the proverbial blind men describing an elephant, and in this case, more than half of the exotic beast was yet to be conceived by its creator. Published fragments of "Work in Progress" must surely have seemed "a miseffectual whyacinthinous riot of blots and blurs and bars and balls and hoops and wriggles and juxtaposed jottings linked by spurts of speed" (*FW* 118.28–30).

Those decentered disciples sent on a "wildgoup's chase across the kathartic ocean" (*FW* 185.6) foundered in a nexus of undecidability but made valiant efforts to resist the centrifugal forces that marginalized their critical enterprise. Joyce, as choreographer and puppet-master of this scholarly event, gave them just enough information to create the illusion of temporary mastery. HCE, that central signifying agent, remained present in the mode of absence but refused to provide a point of origin to explain the palimpsest of associations that makes up the web of the *Wake*. Exploring the illusion of philosophical or linguistic centeredness, the perplexed exagminers were hurled outward onto the margins of a subversive and decentered project.

The book, Beckett insisted, was about language itself—rooted in Dante, Vico, and Bruno, in a Renaissance obscurantism that whirled in spirals of oppositional history until its lexical exuberance exploded in the *"abnihilisation of the etym."* (*FW* 353.22). The essayists got *some* things right. They insisted that Wakean words become music. Lyrical laughter lilts over the ear of a jaded audience, resuscitating the aural/oral tradition of a race that appropriated a foreign tongue to laugh at its imperialistic colonizers and mock the yoke imposed on it. Appropriately, Joyce invoked the New World—expatriate American, Irish, and marginalized Europeans whose own deracinated lives gave them a kind of entrée into the rootless work they attempted to explain. Without a palpable center, these "noughty" exagminers turned inward and circled around themselves— around their own interests and preoccupations, the Sternian hobbyhorses that they found in the giant rebus that so fascinated and mystified them.

After successfully choreographing the work of his commentators, Joyce wrote these twelve apostles into the text of the *Wake* by adding to the galley proofs of "Tales Told of Shem and Shaun" in May, 1929, the following parodic commentary: "Imagine the twelve deaferended dumbbawls of the whowl above-beugled to be the contonuation through regeneration of the urutteratjion of the word in pregross" (*FW* 284.18–22). In a later, self-reflexive pose, he asked: "His producers are they not his consumers? Your exagmination round his factification for incamination of a warping process. Declaim!" (*FW* 497.1–3). Certainly, this exercise involves ingenious metafictionality. The act of literary consumption melds, quite literally, with the art of aesthetic production, so that the sons who consume the father/parent/author/host through mental mastication and explicatory elimination are, in turn, food for the voracious author's future literary parodies. What other writer could boast the pleasure of mocking his critics in the very text that they have essayed, somewhat ineptly, to clarify and interpret? Joyce was doubly exploitive of these innocent apostles. Offering them specific clues to the mysteries of his "Work in Progress," he refused, nonetheless, to valorize their partial theories with an authorial imprimatur. He then brashly subsumed the "twelve deaferended dumbbawls," together with their deaf and dumb bawlings, into the chaotic text of a progressing *Wake*.

Samuel Beckett, "Dante . . . Bruno. Vico . . Joyce"

Samuel Beckett's inaugural contribution is by far the most important in the collection and surely the most frequently read. Linda Ben-Zvi explains that the "intention of the title and the dots was to indicate the lineal descent from three Italians to the Irishman Joyce, inheritor of their traditions and ideas.... Beckett... had already developed a love for Dante, which went back to his youth.... The works of Vico and Bruno were probably unfamiliar to Beckett at the time of writing, although he had studied Italian in Dublin and was able to read them in the original when Joyce indicated the importance of the philosophers in the structuring of the *Wake*."[5]

Joyce, then, steered Beckett in the direction of Vico, whom the erudite Samuel judged a "practical roundheaded Neapolitan" worthy of the company of Hobbes, Spinoza, Locke, and Machiavelli. In Beckett's estimation, the utilitarian Vico simply appropriated the theories of Giordano Bruno and grafted them onto earlier hierophantic lore: "His division of the development of human society into three ages: Theocratic, Heroic, Human (civilized), with a corresponding classification of language: Hieroglyphic (sacred), Metaphorical (poetic), Philosophical, ... was by no means new.... He derived this convenient classification from the Egyptians, via Herodotus."[6] Joyce's masterwork in progress is elevated by Beckett to the highest ranks of modernist obscurantism: it embraces linguistic, mythic, and anthropological concerns, as well as Egyptian theology and Greek cosmological theory.

With Irish vaudevillian hat in hand, Beckett plays the innocent clown, a juggler balancing a "handful of abstractions" at Mr. Joyce's carnival. He proceeds to offer the uninitiated reader a condensed synopsis of Vico's *Scienza nuova:* "In the beginning was the thunder: the thunder set free Religion, ... Religion produced Society, and the first social men were the cave-dwellers: ... the cave becomes a city, and the feudal system a democracy: then an anarchy: this is corrected by a return to monarchy: the last stage is a tendency towards interdestruction: the nations are dispersed, and the Phoenix of Society arises out of their ashes" (5). Beckett's erudite trot sounds as if it had been written by an addled Polonius. "At this point Vico applies Bruno," and Joyce applies Vico— though each author "takes very good care not to say so" (5–6). Joyce, Beckett insists, is not a philosopher but a poet who draws on Vico's sociohistorical schema as a "structural convenience," a trellis on which to hang his linguistic "decoration of arabesques" (7).

As he does in all his work, Beckett deliberately plays Lucky to Joyce's Pozzo, Clov to a Hamm-master of English lexical buffoonery. In a masterful tour de force, he applies a minimalist reading to Joyce's maximalist text and treats this "collideorscape" (*FW* 143.28) as if it were a scientific treatise. He challenges the reader to see a perfectly intelligible pattern on the other side of the kaleidoscope—be it sociohistorical or lyrical-poetic.

Poetry, in Vico's world, is the "first operation of the human mind" and gives
rise to a language of fantasy and metaphor that antedates abstract thought.
Before language was "alphybettyformed" (*FW* 183.13), form and content
were inseparable in semiotic systems dependent on signifying gesture.

Joyce's "Work in Progress," Beckett tells us, is a modern poetic text of
"direct expression. . . . And if you don't understand it, Ladies and Gentle-
men, it is because you are too decadent to receive it" (13). Samuel
Beckett, the critic-magician, has taken us on a magical mystery tour of
the Viconian structure of *Finnegans Wake* only to lead us into a house of
mirrors and insist that if we cannot find a clear and direct representation
of a dazzling imaginary world, it is because we have lost the primitive,
childlike ability to enjoy poetic language. The clown has become, in the
wink of an eye, an impassioned preacher chiding an intransigent audience.
"You are not satisfied," he complains, "unless form is so strictly divorced
from content that you can comprehend the one almost without bothering
to read the other" (13). His exhortation becomes heatedly evangelical.
Arise, ye ignorant and lazy wretches (he implies) who refuse to feast on
the rich verbiage of the *Wake!* Would you be spoonfed Dickensian pap?
Would you live on an intellectual diet of curds and whey, a belly-buster
of sentimental drivel or a Zolaesque slice of belle-epochal sordidity? For
shame! "This rapid skimming and absorption of the scant cream of sense
is made possible by what I may call a continuous process of copious
intellectual salivation" reminiscent of "Monsieur Pavlo's [*sic*] unfortunate
dogs" (13). Would you respond to a "tertiary or quartary conditioned
reflex of dribbling comprehension" with canine cerebral chops? No,
forsooth! Renounce the devil and Rebecca West! Turn away from those
incredulous Joshuas who would snigger at Joyce's titillating prose.

Beckett has skillfully separated the goats from the sheep, the Wests
from the Egyptian/Viconian/Joycean elect. And with the enthusiasm of a
proselytizer, he calls us to the ranks of those saved by the new phenomenological imperative of postmodern literature: "Here form *is* content,
content *is* form." Joyce's writing, he tells us, "is not *about* something; *it is
that something itself*" (14). With one breathtaking rhetorical flourish,
Beckett ushers in the new age of Joycean apocalypse. By celebrating
a salutary language of gesture and poetry, of primitive sense and auditory
sensation, of mimetic lyricism and verbal arabesque, he unwittingly
inaugurates the era of postmodernism—of concrete poetry, absurdist
drama, and self-referential fiction. With Heidegger behind him and
Pynchon yet unborn, Beckett turns our attention to the textuality of a
nonreferential work of art. In so doing, he vindicates Joyce and Gertrude
Stein, Jean Cocteau and William Carlos Williams, and he announces a
new era for contemporary literature. Rediscovering the text in Joyce's

enigmatic rebus, he laughs at the puzzle embedded in this polysemous wonderwork and abandons a millenial literary quest for mimetic meaning. Beckett opens his critical tentacles to the "verb umprincipiant" of Joyce's masterly mélange of alphybettyformed language. Joyce, we are told, has "desophisticated" English and defamiliarized a failing mother tongue "abstracted to death" (15). He has revivified and resurrected a pallid, ghostly *parole:* "This writing that you find so obscure is a quintessential extraction of language and painting and gesture, with all the inevitable clarity of the old inarticulation. Here is the savage economy of hieroglyphics. Here words are not the polite contortions of 20th century printer's ink. They are alive" (15–16).

Dante is invoked as well, as the wordshaper who dared to synthesize his own artistic idiolect from a collage of vulgar Italian dialects and to offer his readers an ideal but unspoken Italian that shocked a Latinate intelligentsia. Let any "monodialectical arcadian" who fails to appreciate the "formal structure raised by Mr. Joyce after years of patient and inspired labour" (19) descend to the ninth circle of Dante's hell, forever to utter boring monosyllables of dull, Satanic iteration. Exhorted to join the Joycean elect, we are enticed by nothing less than perpetual purgation in a spherical narrative whose multidimensional and nondirectional movement excludes the possibility of aesthetic culmination. "There is a continual purgatorial process at work. . . . And the partially purgatorial agent? The partially purged" (22). In the conclusion to this ingenious essay, Beckett reveals more about his own stoic philosophy and future creative projects than about Joyce's "Work in Progress." With critical language creepycrawling through purgatorial spaces, can Belaquan bliss or the abode of *The Lost Ones* be far behind?

Beckett's essay is a dazzling tour de force, a feat of intellectual cunning inspired and embellished by that great scholarly pretender, Giacomo Joyce in his "joakimono . . . riding the high horse there forehengist" (*FW* 214.11–12). Joyce has pointed his exagminers to the most exotic and recherché of sources: Giambattista Vico, the father of modern sociology; Bruno the Nolan, a little-known Italian philosopher; the great Dante Alighieri; and the whole of Christian theology. "Latin me that, my trinity scholard!" (*FW* 215.26).

Certainly, Beckett's inaugural pronouncements have had a profound effect on *Wake* readers over the past half century. His emphasis on the book's self-reflexive strategy seems to emerge from the *Exagmination* like an epigrammatic diamond in a slag heap of erudition. His essay has become a *locus classicus* in Joyce scholarship and is frequently cited, selectively, in deconstructive discourse. At Joyce's behest, Beckett alerted early readers to the significance of Vico's historical, sociological, and poetic paradigms in the cognitive constructions of the *Wake*. But naive disciples seeking scholarly climax in Viconian thunderclaps or expecting to find a key to Joyce's "Work in Progress" in Vico's *Scienza nuova* must surely have felt titillated but unsatisfied.

Similarly, Bruno and Dante seem to have been introduced into Beckett's professorial argument largely to keep analogymongers busy for centuries. It is true that "the divine comic Denti Alligator" (*FW* 440.6) has a prominent place in the *Wake*, along with Lewis Carroll, Jarl Van Hoother, Humpty Dumpty, and a plethora of literary, historical, and fictional figures. Beckett, however, refrains from suggesting that his audience scrutinize the pages of *Alice in Wonderland*, learn nursery rhymes from their children, and delve into the symbolism of Grimms' fairy tales, even though such projects would have had as much relevance as a scholarly romp through early Viconian scribblings. Beckett had inherited a good groatsworth of his master's cunning, along with generous portions of exile and literary silence. He perspicaciously assessed his *transition*-al readers and knew how to win the hearts of early Wakeans. After Beckett's stirring diatribe, what self-respecting intellectual would admit to being so bigoted a "monodialectical arcadian" as to criticize Joyce's "Work in Progress"?

Beyond the era of *transition*, most of the other essays in the *Exagmination* faded into anachronistic oblivion. Joyceans frequently cite Beckett's essay as a kind of deconstructive, phenomenological, or intertextual landmark, though it is questionable whether the piece would have attracted so much attention were it not for its author's own reputation as a pioneer of avant-garde literature. It survives as a "curiositease" of Beckett's early critical career. Most of the other apostles in this volume have gone largely unnoticed—and, it seems, ubiquitously unread.

Marcel Brion, "The Idea of Time in the Work of James Joyce"

Few scholars, for instance, have ever heard of Marcel Brion's essay, "The Idea of Time in the Work of James Joyce," initially written in French and translated from *transition*. "Certain thinkers," Brion tells us, "have at times wondered if the essential difference existing between man and God were not a difference of time" (25). Here, in the inaugural sentence, is a philosophical appeal to all the existential verities—God, time, existence, essence, and the philosophy of difference (though not the Derridean notion of *différance*). "Space," we are assured, "is not concerned here" (25). Such Gallic seriousness, after Beckett's dazzling play of exegetical wit, is startling to the British or American *lecteur* who has not yet identified Brion as his intellectual *semblable*. We leap from the existential crags of time and existence to the mountains of mystical literature, the deity, and the laws of the cosmos. But where in all these meditations is Joyce's Wakean chaosmos? Joyce, Brion observes, follows in the footsteps of Proust as one of the "two greatest writers of our century, the only ones who have brought an original vision of the world to our epoch" (28).

The essay seems to lose something in translation. It helped justify Joyce to the French by comparing him favorably with Proust and Rabelais, but it tells us little about "Work in Progress." Paraphrasable as "Joyce . . . Proust . . . Rabelais . . . Einstein," the piece seems to have survived as an odd and unimaginative fossil of early reader-response criticism. The writings of Joyce, Brion tells us, are like those of Einstein: they "cannot be comprehended without a veritable initiation" (33). This essay, however, is hardly the initiation required.

Frank Budgen, "James Joyce's *Work in Progress* and Old Norse Poetry"

Rather than brushing up on seventeenth-century Italian, as Beckett suggested, the reader might well be advised to dabble in Old Norse and become acquainted with the marvels of the Eddas, filled with gods and hammer-hurlers celebrated in mellifluous kennings. Old Norse becomes a screen for Budgen's defense of Joyce's neologisms, and like Beckett, he puts the reader on the defensive: "For Joyce's purpose no word is unpoetic— none obsolete. Words fallen out of use are racial experience alive but unremembered. When in the poet's imagination the past experience is relived the dormant word awakes to new life and the poet's listeners are lifted out of their social grooves" (39).

According to Budgen, Joyce's Wakese is like the old Norse kenning, only more so. Language flows like a river. Images emerge out of the blurred, indeterminate landscape of the unconscious, as "vivid and unex- pected as those of a dream" (40). Joyce, Budgen believes, "has penetrated into the night mind of man, his timeless existence in sleep, his incommuni- cable experiences in dreams" (46). This notion of the *Wake* as a literary dream emerging out of the unconscious and charged with Freudian symbolism has haunted Wakeans ever since Joyce (via Budgen and others) suggested the analogy. Readers were quick to leap from the metaphor of dream to the precipitous conclusion that the entire book unfolds in the mind of a dreamer. Hence the half-century quest for an elusive dream narrator to give the work a familiar narrative/novelistic shape. Budgen admires the "glittering humour" of Joyce's composition and is eager to offer *Wake* enthusiasts a key to unlock the mysteries of this dazzling word hoard: "Whatever the elements brought together they have the rightness of a dream," he tells us, "in the pattern dictated by the dream's own purpose and logic" (45). Appealing to the "super reality" of nocturnal consciousness, he distorts and simplifies in order to encourage a potential cult of Freudened readers.[7]

The influence of Norse mythology on Joycean aesthetics certainly merits serious consideration, but the sculptor Frank Budgen was hardly the person for the job. Despite Joyce's own laudatory response to Budgen's efforts, the essay seems, sixty years later, little more than a sycophantic exercise. James Atherton's chapter on the Norse Eddas in *The Books at the Wake* owes little to Budgen, whose curious dabbling would probably excite a thunderous roar of horror from any true scholar of old Icelandic.[8]

Stuart Gilbert, "Prolegomena to *Work in Progress*"

Stuart Gilbert's pompous "Prolegomena" offers scant consolation to the uninitiated reader, and his titular evocation of Immanuel Kant signals a great deal of scholarly cant as well. The first page of the essay invokes G. K. Chesterton, Francis Thompson, Victor Bérard (in original French), Homer's *Odyssey* (in classical Greek) and, by way of a footnote, Joyce's "Work in Progress." Gilbert's contribution sounds very much like a parody of the arrogant asseverations of the *Wake*'s Professor Jones, and his scholarly treatise may have inspired some of the academic parody that peppers the completed oeuvre. While ostensibly encouraging his audience to persevere in the face of perplexity, he adopts a strategy of "oneupsmanship" and pummels the reader with footnotes reminiscent of Issy's marginal iterations in book II, chapter ii.

Gilbert cites Vico's *Scienza nuova* with the same enthusiasm that he earlier displayed for the Homeric parallels in *Ulysses*. Understandably, he meets with less success, since Vico's sociohistorical theories cannot be as readily applied to "Work in Progress" as Homeric parallels could to the odyssey of Leopold Bloom. Beckett's tongue-in-cheek parody of Viconian erudition is far more enlightening than Gilbert's somber, serious-minded synopsis. Whereas Beckett winks slyly at the reader, Gilbert continually shuts his eyes in reverential piety, insisting on the uniqueness of "Work in Progress" as a "constructive metabolism of the primal matter of language" that defies replication and "will in all probability remain a unique creation— once and only once and by one only. . . . A dangerous game, in truth, the *jeu de mots*, this vivisection of the Word made Flesh! But so, perhaps, was creation itself—the rash invention of a progressive Olympian with a penchant for practical jokes" (57). The implication is clear: God is one,

Joyce is one, and both are unique and incomparable in their jocoserious creations.

At least Gilbert can appreciate the humor of Joyce's Wakespeak, the "wonderland of perpetual surprises for every Alice of us" (57–58). Probably at Joyce's behest, he calls attention to Lewis Carroll and Humpty Dumpty, to the polysemic and polyglottic iterations of Joyce's jabber-wocking language. With Carroll and Vico as guides, he explicates several passages from "Work in Progress." Slithy territory, this. Gilbert happily wipes his glosses with what he does (and does not) know. He can draw on Lucifer, the Bible, Ben Franklin, and Prometheus, as well as Greek, Latin, German, and Malaysian roots. He concludes the essay with a "practical illustration" of Wakean exegesis culled from the portion of Jaun's sermon printed in *transition* 13. For contemporary readers familiar with Roland McHugh's annotations and Adaline Glasheen's *Third Census*, Gilbert's pronouncements seem a pallid reflection of Joyce's rich, polysemic perversity.

Eugene Jolas, "The Revolution of Language and James Joyce"

Eugene Jolas's essay "The Revolution of Language and James Joyce" is more to the point in its evocative echoes of *transition*'s own manifesto on "The Revolution of the Word." Jolas and his followers set the stage for current trends in critical speculation on grammatology and textuality, deconstructive theory and reader-response analysis. Sweeping away millenia of humanistic philosophy, Jolas contends that the "real metaphysical problem today is the word" (79). He counsels the deconstructive "disinte-gration of words and their subsequent reconstruction on other planes" (79), a process that takes into account the monumental discovery of the subconscious. Joyce, he claims, "has given a body blow to the traditionalists" and has stunned a "crumbling hierarchy of philologists and pedagogues" who are, quite simply, "afraid" (80).

Jolas defends "Work in Progress" by exposing the idiocy of its detractors. The Irish Sean O'Faolain gets a sound drubbing for defending the "immobility of English" in the face of Joyce's onslaught, for not being acquainted with Scandinavian linguistic roots, and for tenaciously cling-ing to romantic "*passé*-ism" (82). Calling Marcel Jousse and the aesthet-ics of abstract idealism to witness, Jolas insists that language should be infinitely tractable, malleable, and open to experimentation, deformation, amalgamation, and (though he does not use the term) defamiliarization. A member of the European intelligentsia, Jolas scorns the kind of British provincialism that tethers language to a unilingual base. He exhorts us to consider analogous experiments in France, Germany, and Italy: the astonishing neologisms of Léon-Paul Fargue, Gertrude Stein's "mysticism of the word," August Stramm's poetic experiments, and the "revolution of the surrealists, who destroyed completely the old relationships between words and thought" (84). One must call to mind, as well, Hans Arp's invention of "word combinations set against a fantastic ideology" and Marinetti's abortive futuristic theory of "words in liberty" (86).

Joyce, says Jolas, launched an independent aesthetic by inventing a texture of synthetic "neologies." "In his super-temporal and super-spatial composition, language is being born anew before our eyes" (89). Drawing on the mutations of Commonwealth dialects and anarchic American speech, Joyce jettisons the norms of syntax to reflect, mimetically, the mysterious world of dream narrative, "that a-logical sequence of events remembered or inhibited, that universe of demoniacal humor and magic which has seemed impenetrable" (91). Capturing the "broken images of a dream floating through a distorted film," he succeeds in fabricating a night language unintelligible to waking comprehension.

The problem with Jolas's impassioned defense is that Joyce was not a surrealist writer and did not claim to be one. Though publishing regularly in *transition*, he made a conscious effort to dissociate himself from surrealist poets like André Breton and futurist innovators like Marinetti. Words, for Joyce, were never free-floating and "at liberty"; writing was not an automatic stream welling up from the unconscious. As author of *A Portrait*, *Ulysses*, and *Finnegans Wake*, Joyce always remained a fabulous artificer, a Daedalian wordshaper who fashioned the labyrinthine linguistic mazes of the *Wake* with infinite skill and creative care. Godlike in his role as fabulator and linguistic fabricator, Joyce insisted that each word, phrase, sentence, and neologism be carved and crafted from a circumambient sea of floating linguistic signifiers. By presenting Joyce as an Irish surrealist, Jolas does him a disservice; and by doing an about-face to defend the mimetic dream quality of the text, he traduces his inaugural thesis of nonrepresentational art.

Like his fellow essayists, Jolas is eager to protect Joyce from Hibernian monolinguists as well as European sceptics. He hastily marshals any argument that comes to mind, citing similarities between Wakespeak and Shakespeare's *Cymbelline* while praising the book's surrealistic dreamscape. He does, nonetheless, make an excellent suggestion when he urges the novice to read aloud passages from "Work in Progress." By emphasizing the lyrical nature of the work, he alerts potential enthusiasts to the amazing linguistic/aural/oral pleasures of the text.[9]

Victor Llona, "I Don't Know What to Call It but It's Mighty Unlike Prose"

Taking his cues from contemporary cinematic experiments with the "*ballet mécanique*," Victor Llona praises "Work in Progress" as a *divertissement philologique*, a "glittering, mysterious show": "A vast company of actorwords . . . cavort here in a whirlwind dramatic ballet to a polyphonic orchestral accompaniment" (95). Llona announces in a footnote that he is preparing a biography of Rabelais, and the obvious similarities between Joyce's linguistic experiments and those of Master François clearly intrigue him.

Llona expresses the ingenuous hope that the ostensible dreamers dreaming the ur-narrative of "Work in Progress" will some day "awake and talk coherently." And he declares, like an evangelical prophet: "I feel that with the last fragments shall come the revelation" (102). Such eschatological expectations would, of course, eventually be shattered by an endlessly fragmentary revelation of sliding signifiers in the completed text of the *Wake*. Llona does acknowledge that his critical assessment is, by its very nature, brashly premature: "To me, one of the most striking and illuminating things in connection with *Work in Progress* is that it has managed to reverse the consecrated order of things. We commentators simply could not be kept in leash—we had to have our say in a volume which will grace the stalls in advance of the text under consideration" (102). This extraordinary reversal of critical practice is precisely what gives the *Exagmination* its unique status, a review volume published long before the text itself. "Thus the unfacts, did we possess them, are too imprecisely few to warrant our certitude, the evidencegivers by legpoll too untrustworthily irreperible" (*FW* 57.16–18).

Robert McAlmon, "Mr. Joyce Directs an Irish Word Ballet"

Robert McAlmon shakes Joyce's pantomimic style free of the strictures demanded of narrative storytelling and allies it with the language of gesture characteristic of dance and mime. "Prose too can possess the gesticulative quality" (106), he argues, and casts off the shackles of traditional meaning to invent an aesthetic theory linked with universal emanations of the subconscious. McAlmon sees in Joyce's "detestable genius" a fierce determination "to break through language to give it greater flexibility and nuance" in a medium "as free as any art medium should be, and as the dance at its best can be" (107).

This essayist performs an ingenious sleight of hand when he wrenches

"Work in Progress" free from traditional expectations of genre and narrativity. The work, he explains, is not a novel but a piece of music and mime, a "word ballet" expressive of the mysterious iterations of the subconscious. Like Jolas before him, McAlmon recasts the Joycean project in the image of surrealism and, in so doing, cozens the uncommon reader of *transition* into tasting the linguistic delights of the *Wake* by way of a word-music that releases "an esperanto of the subconscious" (110).

Though floundering uneasily through several slippery passages of "Work in Progress," McAlmon has definitely latched onto a useful strategy for grappling with Joyce's uncanny prose. Search not for meaning but for the *sensation* of meaning, he suggests. Let your heart stand open to a text that evokes "literary music, a ballet of dancing words" that pirouette in lilting arabesques evocative of a "sensual-sensitive esthetic response to prose music" (111). The book is a dance, a symphonic opera of Irish-Celtic-jesuitical extraction. Trance oneself and enjoy. After all, McAlmon promises (and here is the *coup de grâce*), Joyce has managed to "have it both ways": "Surely . . . he has broken into language and made it a medium much freer, more sensitive, musical and flexible, while retaining a subject content still meaty with psychologic, historic, and sociologic comprehensions" (116). Here is a prose packed with psychology, history, and sociology (i.e., narrative meaning). But don't try too hard to comprehend it. "His readers who take him with least effort are probably the younger generation, who . . . may demand less explanation about the meaning of meaning" (111).

Thomas McGreevy, "The Catholic Element in *Work in Progress*"

The Irish McGreevy briefly summarizes the Viconian paradigm of the *Wake* but devotes most of his attention to what he assumes are Dantesque structural elements. He depicts the author of "Work in Progress" as profoundly Catholic in sensibility, a man for whom "Catholicism is never a matter of standing on one leg. It is not a pose, it is fundamental. Consequently, it has to face everything" (121). McGreevy posits the hypothesis that *Ulysses* exposes the inferno of modern subjectivity and that the *Wake*, in turn, offers a contemporary Dantesque rendering of purgatory. "The purgatorial aspect of *Work in Progress* is most obvious, of course, in the purgatorial, transitional language in which it is written. . . . In *Work in Progress* the characters speak a language made up of scraps of half the languages known to mankind. Passing through a state of flux or transition they catch at every verbal, every syllabic, association" (124). The *Wake*, from McGreevy's Catholic perspective, becomes an ultrarealistic representation of purgatorial language, a stepmother tongue in transition (and in *transition*)—but toward what kind of utopian, polyglottic, panlingual paradise? Certainly, the *Wake* is steeped in Catholic theology and Dantesque allusion. McGreevy, however, without Virgil or Beatrice to guide him, seems to have gone astray in the dark wood of analogymongering.

Elliot Paul, "Mr. Joyce's Treatment of Plot"

One has to admire the courage of Elliot Paul's project to illuminate the "treatment of plot" in an essentially plotless work that defies traditional expectations of narrativity. "O ye of little faith!" cries Elliot Paul (or something to that effect): "With the precedent of *Ulysses* to suggest that Joyce is capable of construction in the grand manner, the majority of his former supporters have blandly assumed that the present book is confused and meaningless and that he is wasting his genius" (131). Joyce the word-master was probably delighted to find a disciple named Paul interpreting "with heartfelt timidity" (132) the scriptural message of "Work in Progress."

In fewer than two thousand words, Paul preaches the Joycean gospel to a would-be elect. He provides us with a basic primer, an ABC guide to the reading of *Finnegans Wake*. The "text is not nearly so puzzling" and "no violence is done to logic," he tells us, if one realizes that the book's "design is circular, without the beginning, middle and ending prescribed for chronological narratives" (132). Forgoing temporal prejudices, one has next to acknowledge that the treatment of space is elastic, so that the narrative can be located simultaneously in the Garden of Eden and in Phoenix Park. "The characters are composed of hundreds of legendary and historical figures, as the incidents are derived from countless events. The 'hero' or principal male character is primarily Adam, and includes Abraham, Isaac, Noah, Napoleon, the Archangel Michael, Saint Patrick, Jesse James, any one at all who may be considered the 'big man.' . . . His female counterpart, the river, is Eve, Josephine, Isolde, Sarah, Aimee MacPherson, whoever you like occupying the role of leading lady at any time or place" (134).

Paul, as scriptural exegete, patiently delineates the principal elements of Joyce's Viconian vision. He urges us to: keep in mind the "Fall motif" of the Garden of Eden, along with the Old Testament tale of Noah's ark; consult *transition* 6 for a list of *dramatis personae*; and look out for the eternal conflicts between Michael and Lucifer (both biblical and Miltonic), with Wellington and Napoleon sometimes substituting for Mick and Nick. To this recipe for a palimpsestic paradigm, add a dash of the "Irish ballad of Finnegan's Wake," a sprinkle of Humpty Dumpty, the fall of Satan, the birth of Isaac, the legend of Finn MacCool, the murder of Abel by Cain, and the romance of Tristan and Isolde. Remember that the "difficulties the individual words may present . . . have been much exaggerated" (136). Now you are ready to begin making progress in the extant text of Mr. Joyce's "Work in Progress."

One is tempted by Elliot Paul's impatient plot summary to imagine Joyce prompting this Pauline disciple to spread the Wakean gospel among a particularly obtuse audience. Paul speaks like a prophet and admonishes the faint of heart. He gives us all the clues and cues, all the practical hints and parallels needed to elucidate this puzzling text. Inadvertently, he prophesies the title of the progressive work but gets it a tittle wrong when he adds the infamous apostrophe suggestive of ballad rather than book. Here are the keys to the given narrative. We have only to take up our intellectual pallets (or ladders) and walk (or stumble) in an attitude of heartfelt timidity through this linguistic wonderland. The difficulties have, after all, been much exaggerated.

Joyce must have been metaphorically paring and biting his fingernails through every word of this Pauline epistle. In the guise of humble exegete, Paul attempts to supply a user's manual to Wakean disciples. William York Tindall's *Reader's Guide*, Campbell and Robinson's *Skeleton Key*, and Adaline Glasheen's *Census* would follow in Paul's wake. "It is to be expected that Mr. Joyce's enormous and incidental contribution to philology will be recognized in advance of his subtler aesthetic achievements but the latter is sure to follow and it may prove interesting to observe how, one by one, his former supporters try to creep unostentatiously over the tailboard of the bandwagon" (137). The sheep have, indeed, been separated from the goats.

John Rodker, "Joyce and His Dynamic"

Convinced that Joyce "is revitalising our language" and "will revivify our dying tongue" (145), John Rodker offers an assessment of "Work in Progress" that tells us little either about Joyce or his dynamic, other than that the text is dynamically progressive. Approaching unexplored psychoanalytic terrain, as well as the anthropological territory of Lévi-Strauss, Rodker observes that the "dynamic aspect of the work derives a large part of its importance from the fact that words are used so to speak 'in vacuo' by means of which they still preserve much of their ancient magic. Puns, klang words, mantrams are powerful because they are disguised manifestations of revengeful and iconoclastic impulses driven underground by fear; and because the violence of childhood inspires them, their underground life compacted, made sly, imparts to them an intense validity" (144).

Margot Norris devotes an entire chapter of *The Decentered Universe of "Finnegans Wake"* to a number of the suggestions outlined by Rodker. In this sense, the essay seems somewhat advanced in its allusion to dimensions of the text that would later be explored by more avid disciples of deconstruction and intertextuality. Rodker, however, fails to develop the tantalizing hypotheses seminally scattered in his adulatory prose. Echoing earlier Pauline pronouncements, he speculates that Joyce has made possible "a complete symbiosis of reader and writer; the only obstacle which now remains being the inadequacy of the reader's sphere of reference" (143). Rodker's object lesson is clear: we have been offered a uniquely polyphonic, multilayered text; it is up to us to make judicious and profitable use of the great tome. "Book here for eternity junction" (*U* 414).[10]

Robert Sage, "Before *Ulysses* — and After"

Addressing himself to the "general bafflement caused by those portions of James Joyce's "Work in Progress" which have appeared in *transition,*" Robert Sage enthusiastically points out that the graph of Joyce's literary career ascends toward ever more challenging explorations of "the magnificent universe that may be brought into being by language" (153). He praises the *Wake*'s revolutionary, Einsteinian, "four-dimensional" perspective and reminds us that in this "unprecedented creative work there is, properly speaking, no plot, no character development, no action, no narrative sequence" (155–56). Sage, however, gratuitously feels compelled to locate Joyce's entire chaosmos "in the slumbering mind of a capricious god" (156). Suggesting that "Work in Progress" could be explained as an unstructured, surrealistic narrative emanating from the mystical consciousness of a divine narrator, he promulgates the "single-dreamer" theory now largely discredited by *Wake* scholars.

"Work in Progress," Sage admits, is rife with legend and myth, technical innovation, cosmic comedy, and boundless humor. He finds therein the joy of biblical inspiration, an "inexhaustible promise of new revelations. . . . But to everyone it should represent a cyclopean picture of humanity and the gods as viewed across the aeons" (169–70). Why, one might wonder, does he feel compelled to drag in the gods? This penultimate essay in Joyce's original dozen provides a somewhat tedious *ricorso* in a potpourri of idiosyncratic reader responses.

William Carlos Williams, "A Point for American Criticism"

And now, at last, a word from the Americans. At Joyce's behest, William Carlos Williams embarks on a wrathful refutation of Rebecca West's essay in *The Bookman* condemning the author of *Ulysses* and "Work in Progress" as sentimental, tasteless, obscene, narcissistic, and, worst of all, a Manichean masquerading in Homeric clothing.[11] Unwittingly chauvinistic, West fears that such experimental writing might explode like a mine and radically threaten the sanctity of "each theory of the universe that we have built for our defence" (177). As an American outsider, Williams does not hesitate to criticize such entrenched bigotry and xenophobia. No deconstructor she, West cannot appreciate the gaps and subversive slippage in Joyce's audacious oeuvre: "She cannot say that it is the break that has released the genius—and that the defects are stigmata of the break" (178).

Williams launches enthusiastic defense of the avant-garde impulse erupting in "Work in Progress": "Forward is the new. It will not be blamed. It will not force itself into what amounts to paralyzing restrictions. It cannot be correct. It hasn't time. It has that which is beyond measurement, which renders measurement a falsification, since the energy is showing itself as recrudescent, the measurement being the aftermath of each new outburst" (179). Williams indicts West for a panicky retreat to Freudian categories that seem to him not only unfair and illogical but the sign of a disorderly mind. What does Joyce's narcissism, he asks, have to do with his literary production? "It is stupid, it is narrow British to think to use that against him" (180). Williams's own peculiar American revolutionary cry insists that genius transcends its material. He predicts, with some accuracy, that Joyce will find a more enthusiastic audience in the New World: for "this is the opportunity of America! to see large, larger than England can" (180). The British are reduced to Lilliputian status in this war of literary giants—a war largely to be fought on the soil of continental Europe and the United States.

Williams is writing fervidly in the American grain, and he thinks that Joyce is doing so as well. The cloacal insularity of Britain is doomed and dying, he tells us; whereas the younger American culture, "in full vigor, wishes for a fusion of the spirit with life as it exists here on earth in mud and slime today" (181). Rebecca West may dismiss the Irish Joyce as a foul, obscene, narcissistic fool, but the "true significance of the fool," says Williams, "is to consolidate life" (182). Joyce is "breaking with a culture older than England's" (183), and, like Wilhelm Meister, he has "found his America" in the daring experiments of "Work in Progress." Williams praises Joyce as a literary redeemer trying to "save the world" by resuscitating and reinvigorating a "static, worn out language" (183). The "dementia of Wyndham Lewis" and the protestations of Rebecca West are merely symptoms of a dying British culture. Only America can offer Joyce the kind of acclaim he deserves.

Williams's essay is well intentioned and sincere, but somewhat muddled. The father of concrete poetry admired Joyce's lexical freshness, his experimental style, his radical deracination of etymological roots, and his shocking defamiliarization of linguistic signifiers. But this exaggerated diatribe lacks the critical sophistication needed to rescue Joyce from a set of infamous detractors. Both Lewis and West get a more expansive rejoinder in the hilarious satire of Joyce's own Wakean counterattack. Williams's fraternal defense of a brother poet and his indictment of West as a "scared protestant female" probably pleased Joyce, despite (or even because of) its misogynist rhetorical ring. Notwithstanding the infelicities of this essay, Williams did succeed in introducing "Work in Progress" to a clamoring American audience; and, by depicting the *opus* as a New-World endeavor, he prepared the way for a more positive reception of what many considered an essentially unreadable text.

Letters of Protest

So insisted G. V. L. Slingsby, the "common reader" who confesses to "definite disappointment" over the "maze of printing that Mr. Joyce would evidently have us regard as a serious work" (189). If Joyce's words are to be read as music, it should understandably prove "extremely difficult for a reader in the folk tune stage of development to be faced with a literary Sacre du Printemps for full orchestra. One can but struggle" (190). "Is Mr. Joyce's hog latin making obscenity safe for literature?" he asks (191). Or is Joyce merely "an enormously clever little boy" trying to fool a gullible public with an exhibitionistic display of lexical acrobatics?

Most contemporary critics believe that Joyce himself authored Slingsby's piqued communication to the uncommon reader of "Work in Progress." He loved to play the pierrot artist inverting critical caprice in a Shem portrait of the forging penman writing himself in the furniture of critical self-parody. This, surely, is Joyce sniggering in the hellhole "known as the Haunted Inkbottle, no number Brimstone Walk" (*FW* 182.30–31), playing Freudian games of jocular hilarity and fashioning squirts of squid ink out of his wit's waste to sling at his own toughened integument.

The timorous Slingsby pronounces himself fearful of "a temperature risen to meningital heights" and of joining, in consequence, the company of "coverlet pickers" (191) reminiscent of May Dedalus, and of Mary

Jane Murray Joyce, in the last stages of a terminal illness, pathetically picking fantasied buttercups from shabby bedcovers and calling the doctor Sir Peter Teazle. Such deflections of black humor by way of private jokes and involuted self-mockery betray the signature of joky Jacob writing himself into this unique collection of critical exagminings.[12]

Vladimir Dixon, once assumed to be another incarnation of Shem-Jimmy, has now been identified as a genuine historical person and bona fide Russian emigré, an American-educated scientist who, in his "litter" to "mysterre Shame's Voice," adopts the persona of a slavic ingenue thoroughly perplexed by the *Wake*'s linguistic polyphony.[13] Bakhtin and Nabokov stand back! Dixon's booming (and shameless) voice resounds in punning parody of all the detractors of "Mister Germ's Choice" and his astonishing "Work in Progress." Here, embedded in the text, are Averroës and "kismet" from *Ulysses* (from "Nestor" and "Circe," respectively); Biddy the hen, unable to comprehend her own letter's significance; and the "Coveryette" alluded to in Slingsby's complaint. Such startling coincidence of internal allusion suggests that Joyce must surely have collaborated in the composition of at least one of these comic diatribes. Two epistolary endpieces were, of course, imperative. Otherwise, the collection would have stood at an unlucky thirteen submissions. For anyone as superstitious as Joyce, the twelve disciples had to be trailed by a double pastiche of detraction to bring the number up to a safe, suggestive fourteen.

The *Exagmination* as a whole, composed so precipitously and with so little awareness of the chaosmic (w)hole to follow, remains a startling example of a new genre of metacriticism that few authors have chosen to emulate. Although none of the pieces has contributed significantly to our understanding of *Finnegans Wake*, they occupy their own special *museyroom* in the history of a half-century of critical inquiry and remain of great archeological interest to Joycean paleontologists sifting through the bones of earlier interpretive mastications. Part of the *Wake*'s wonder has always been its insistent refusal to be described, pinned down, categorized, or clearly explained. The exagminers' sometimes arrogant efforts to offer a key to Joyce's lexical mysteries taught a second generation of readers to tread more carefully—to avoid all-encompassing philosophical generalizations on the one hand and plodding linguistic exegeses on the other. Of all the marshaled apostles, only Samuel Beckett managed to capture the fun, the hilarity, and the pedantic self-parody of the text under exagmination, and it is largely because of Beckett's own reputation that the collection has endured as a modernist classic. After the publication of *Finnegans Wake* in 1939, Joycean scholarship struck out in new, unforeseen directions, exemplified by James Atherton's source studies in *The Books at the Wake* and Adaline Glasheen's meticulous

Census. Those dozen intrepid pioneers who first dared to respond to the challenge of semiotic *différance* have survived in literary history as critical anomalies. Baffled, the twelve disciples nonetheless read on, without ever becoming "out of patience." And it was their faith, more than their understanding, that bequeathed a valuable legacy to future explorers of Joyce's tantalizing Tower of Babel.

NOTES

1. Michael Finney, "Eugene Jolas, *transition*, and the Revolution of the Word," in *In the Wake of the Wake*, ed. David Hayman and Elliott Anderson (Madison: The University of Wisconsin Press, 1978), 39.
2. Eugene Jolas, *transition* 16–17, (June 1929); quoted in Finney, "Eugene Jolas," 44.
3. James Joyce, *Letters of James Joyce*, 3 vols., vol. 1 ed. Stuart Gilbert (New York: Viking Press, 1957; reissued with corrections 1966) 1:283. Vols. 2 and 3 ed. Richard Ellmann (New York: Viking Press, 1966).
4. Richard Ellmann, *James Joyce*, rev. ed. (New York: Oxford University Press, 1982), 613.
5. Linda Ben-Zvi, *Samuel Beckett* (Boston: Twayne, 1986), 22–23.
6. Samuel Beckett, et al, *Our Exagmination round His Factification for Incamination of Work in Progress* (1929; rev. ed., London: Faber and Faber, 1972), 4. All additional references to this collection will be cited parenthetically in the text.
7. Joyce himself was one of the principal sources of the dream theory proposed to explain the perplexities of "Work in Progress." He frequently described the experimental text as a "book about the night" and in December, 1926, wrote to Harriet Shaw Weaver: "One great part of every human existence is passed in a state which cannot be rendered sensible by the use of wideawake language, cutanddry grammar and goahead plot" (Ellman, *Joyce*, 2:584–85).
8. Budgen's essay was first published in *transition* 13 (Summer 1928): 209–13. On 27 May 1928, Joyce wrote a note of appreciation to Budgen: "On my return from a holiday in Toulon and Avignon I found your article here.... Many thanks. I like it very much. I am sure it will make a good effect. It is all to the point" (*Letters* 3:177). After the essay's publication, Joyce again penned a compliment: "Many thanks for your article which Giorgio has just read to me. It is nice and hard like the nuts of Knowledge" (ibid., 184). James Atherton acknowledges Budgen's early recognition of the influence of Norse mythology on the *Wake* and declares at the beginning of his own chapter on "The Eddas": "Frank Budgen was the first to write about Joyce's use of the Eddas.... Joyce must have thought well of this essay for he told Miss Weaver that he hoped to have it translated and published in a Danish or Swedish review" (Atherton, *The Books at the Wake*, rev. ed. [Carbondale: Southern Illinois University Press, 1974], 218).

9. Jolas's contribution was first published in *transition* 11 (February 1928) and was clearly intended as a defensive tract implicating Joyce in the "Revolution of the Word." Michael Finney believes that Jolas's "remarks contain no real information about the language of 'Work in Progress,' but they do create a kind of messianic vision of Joyce as the redeemer of fallen language" (Finney, "Eugene Jolas," 42). In summing up his discussion of Joyce's relation to *transition*, Finney concludes: "I suspect the truth is something like this: Joyce agreed with some of the things Jolas had to say about reconstructing language, and he was indulgent of any philosophy or approach which would justify his linguistic and literary experiment. But whatever the truth, the fact remains that until its publication as *Finnegans Wake* in 1939, 'Work in Progress' was intimately associated with the Revolution of the Word—physically and ideologically—in the pages of *transition*" (ibid., 52).

10. Jonathan Culler, in discussing the 'reader-response' theories of Roman Ingarden, Wolfgang Iser, and Umberto Eco, tells us that "some works—those Umberto Eco describes in *L'Opera aperta* as 'open works'—provoke a general revaluation of the status of reading by inviting the reader or performer to play a more fundamental role as constructor of the work. . . . One can maintain, for example, that to read *Finnegans Wake* is not so much to recognize or work out for oneself connections inscribed in the text as to produce a text: through the associations followed up and the connections established, each reader constructs a different text" (Culler, *On Deconstruction* [Ithaca, N.Y.: Cornell University Press, 1982], 37).

11. Joyce had West's essay, "The Strange Necessity," read to him and was particularly annoyed that the author should couch her criticism of *Ulysses* in a meditative ramble that described shopping for hats in Paris. Bonnie Scott notes that such "mixing of bonnets with books is so Joycean a representation of thought processes, that one wonders at Joyce's being affronted. Joyce's supposed revenge was to allude to West throughout *Finnegans Wake* with references to bonnets" (Scott, *Joyce and Feminism* [Bloomington: Indiana University Press, 1984], 118). For instance, "she sass her nach, chillybombom and forty bonnets, upon the altarstane" (*FW* 552.29–30) is undoubtedly a reference to West, as is the implicit swipe at "robecca or worse" (*FW* 203.4–5). See Patrick Parrinder's article "The Strange Necessity: James Joyce's Rejection in England (1914–30)" in *James Joyce: New Perspectives*, ed. Colin MacCabe (Sussex: The Harvester Press, 1982).

12. Richard Ellmann gives a poignant description of the summer of 1903, when James Joyce watched "his mother slowly die. She had not been out of bed since early April, and Josephine Murray nursed her with boundless devotion. . . . Mrs. Joyce had tried to be lighthearted; she nicknamed the dapper doctor 'Sir Peter Teazle,' but sickness frayed her temper, and in the summer her vomiting grew worse" (Ellmann, *Joyce*, 2:135). Buck Mulligan's taunting swipe at Stephen Dedalus in *Ulysses* expands on the mother's helplessness and distraction: "And what is death, he asked, your mother's or yours or my own? . . . To me it's all a mockery and beastly. Her cerebral lobes are not functioning. She calls the doctor sir Peter Teazle and picks buttercups off the quilt" (*U* 7).

13. In an explanatory note appended to the Dixon letter of 9 February 1929, Richard Ellmann comments: "This letter, obviously composed if not written by Joyce himself but never acknowledged by him, was delivered by an unknown hand to Sylvia Beach's bookshop. The address was that of Brentano's bookshop. Joyce urged her to include it in *Our Exagmination . . .* where it duly appeared as the last word" (*Letters* 3:187). In a 1979 article entitled "Who Was Vladimir Dixon? Was He Vladimir Dixon?" Thomas A. Goldwasser gives evidence of the "true identity" of Dixon, a Russian-born emigré educated at MIT and Harvard University and, from 1923 until his death in 1929, an employee of the Singer Company in Paris. Goldwasser verifies Dixon's authorship of "A Litter to Mr. James Joyce" and notes that, with the exception of "this one piece, the last published during his short life, Dixon wrote exclusively in Russian. And, although he was an American citizen, he published in Russian expatriate periodicals. Perhaps this is why he has been overlooked for so long" (*James Joyce Quarterly* 16, 3 [Spring 1979]: 219).

Fritz Senn

Rereading *The Books at the Wake*

James Stephen Atherton lived all his life in Wigan, a coal mining town in the north of England, as a teacher at a technical high school; he never had a university appointment, except in 1965 and again in 1970, when he was invited by Thomas F. Connolly to the summer session of the State University of New York at Buffalo as a visiting professor. He wrote many articles and one of the most useful books we have on *Finnegans Wake.* He discovered Joyce almost on his own, when Joyce was not yet a subject for British universities. Atherton was a recluse, a scholar in the closet who received relatively little help, but he corresponded with other Joyceans, mainly and extensively with Adaline Glasheen. We owe him for many insights, discoveries, and valuable findings.

Atherton's book, the result of many years of patient labor and still an indispensable, reliable companion on our journeys through the *Wake,* was the first full-length study of its kind devoted exclusively to *Finnegans Wake.* Before it, *Our Exagmination* dealt only with the fragments of a work yet to appear in its entirety; David Hayman's comparison of Joyce and Mallarmé was highly specialized; and Adaline Glasheen's first *Census* took a lead in the many lists that were yet to follow. Only Campbell and Robinson's *Skeleton Key* was there as a central support, admired and criticized, unavoidable and often frustrating. All of these were original contributions. They had to be: in the fifties, it was not yet possible to fill a book by reprocessing the work of previous scholars. There was not enough material; authors were very much dependent on their own meticulous research.

Atherton chose a simple task, and he did it well. The task was simple in the sense that it could be described and reasonably delimited; the aim was clear. The execution, of course, was far from simple. Literature grows, Atherton held, out of an author's life (Joyce's life then meant Gorman's biography; Ellmann's was not yet in print during the years when Atherton went through his sources, though some early articles were available and one volume of *Letters*). It grows also out of other books, and *Finnegans Wake*, which depends more than any other work of literature on its multiple predecessors, in some way tries to encompass them all. Atherton set out to trace and discuss the relevance of these intertextual transfusions in a first panoramic look. It is a huge area; he knew he had not covered it fully, and yet it turns out that he had staked out the territory remarkably well. His results have become part of our standard mainstream knowledge. If Atherton's book is ever to be replaced, it will be by a communal effort. Our further endeavors will always be complementary, a filling of the gaps that Atherton knew remained. Some gaps already have been filled; supplementary studies on Dante, the *Book of the Dead*, Shakespeare, Vico, and Ibsen have yielded entire books. All of them were helped by Atherton's early pioneering work.

Atherton investigated Joyce's printed sources. His classification separates the "Structural Books"—those from which Joyce took ideas or principles—from "Literary Sources," the major part of the book. An appended "Alphabetical List of Literary Allusions" makes it easy to find the multiple specific attributions. The section on "Structural Books" is the shortest one—authors like Vico, Quinet, Nicholas de Cusa, Giordano Bruno, Freud, and Jung turned out to be more important or pervasive than Atherton could uncover in a first attempt. Toward the end of the section, Atherton tabulates "what appear to be the main axioms of the *Wake*," eclectically derived from the structural books. The list is unpretentious, wholly pragmatic, and effective: the axioms can still serve as our basic equipment for the odyssey through the *Wake*'s idiosyncrasies. A similar list, a much expanded and more systematic version of Atherton's, with up-to-date theoretical backing, has recently been offered by George Sandulescu in *The Language of the Devil*, whose "Axioms," "Principles," "Maxims" and "Rules" by now take up seventy pages.[1]

Atherton's "Literary Sources" is full of discoveries. He was the first, I believe, to point out and document a view that Joyce might have picked up in Vico, as well as in the *Book of the Dead* (or heretically derived from his own religious instruction): the notion that God's creation is also original sin, the creator's sin. HCE's creativity and sinfulness coincide. Similarly, an author like Joyce or Shem sins himself into his work. As usual, Atherton does not make a systematic fuss about it; he simply presents what he has observed clearly and persuasively, with textual evidence, and lets it go at that. He also was one of the first to work out that *Finnegans Wake* is about itself and its elaborate genesis (a reprocessing of former literary selves), that it comments on itself and its own creation—features that have since been pushed, with abundant abstract conjecture, into necessary but fashionable prominence.

Each *Wake* reader has to deal with doubtful glosses, and Atherton offers some references as possibilities to be considered. He also gives us some sound and cautious indications, what I privately term Atherton's Law, which is useful for the sifting of one's prima facie fumblings but which is nowhere explicitly formulated. Atherton comes closest to phrasing it when he writes that "Joyce did not usually insert single details but groups. A writer's name is likely to come fairly close to allusions to his work, and numerous as are the quotations which Joyce makes, he seems to have tried to give a key to the source of each one by including the name of its author in the same passage."[2] The better kind of *Wake* glossing has stuck to this rule of thumb: we hardly ever find isolated "allusions" or "references" (Atherton's favorite and somewhat unreflected terms) in *Finnegans Wake*; Joyce usually gives a clue, he names or suggests his source (or a language) in multiple ways. To be satisfied with an ascription, Atherton looked for reinforcement, for patterns, a cluster or a constellation—sheer common sense, but some later scholiasts have on occasion been less demanding.

Chapters like "Lewis Carroll: The Unforeseen Precursor" are a wholesale application of this principle of multiple reinforcement. It sets out with the reading of a passage in which Joyce acknowledges Carroll's work; it goes on to compare literary techniques, gradually unfolding into a mapping of references and borrowings from *Alice in Wonderland* and *Sylvie and Bruno*, as well as from Carroll's strange, divided, paradigmatic life, which included a penchant to take photographs of young girls. This kind of presentation—perceptive, readable, with many peripheral glosses along the way—has become a model reading, a particular, specific, inroad to the *Wake* that some of us have tried to emulate.

Atherton made more worthwhile discoveries than perhaps anyone else, such as his notice of Joyce's use of Rowntree's *Poverty*, the detailed study of the *Book of the Dead*, and the *Diary of the Parnell Commission*. He was helped by his extraordinary knowledge of literature, including minor and forgotten writers of the nineteenth century, but above all by his surprising recall of the *Wake* itself at a time before Hart's *Concordance*, which later on was to facilitate mechanical research. On a smaller scale, *The Books at the Wake* is full of minor illuminations that deepen our understanding and enjoyment of a phrase or passage. It is not so much the range of the findings that makes the book valuable but the subtle applications: a feeling that the *Wake*, though mysterious and in part forbidding, is a "real, live" book by a human author (an author, moreover, who is fallible and prejudiced); a book that can reach out to us, delightful and worth reading; a verbal challenge that we *want* to read or reread.

Atherton also pointed out what is not in *Finnegans Wake* (since not everything is). In particular, he attempted to define the limits of Joyce's reading. He saw it as much narrower than what was generally assumed, which was that Joyce's education was as encyclopedic as Joyce might have wanted us to believe at times—including, for example, many of the voluminous Fathers of the Church—all in all, much more reading than would have been possible in one life. Joyce did not read every book to which he alluded (that he perhaps ought to have done), nor had he necessarily read from cover to cover all the books he did read. Again, this sounds truistic, but it had to be shown. In a very matter-of-fact way, Atherton shows that Joyce did not know much about, say, Nicholas de Cusa. So his negative advice is useful, too, for it allows us to take short cuts. "It does not follow that Joyce himself had this wide reading," he suggests about Newman, "although he did read, of course, a great deal; but all the passages which Stephen quotes from Newman's works in *A Portrait* are given in a one-volume anthology, *Characteristics from the writings of John Henry Newman*, William S. Lilly, London, 1875."[3] Such hints may save us a lot of unnecessary work; the blanks Atherton drew need not be repeated by us, we do not have to rummage the same drawers. Of course, we can never be sure; but for us early readers there was a trust that Atherton in his reservations was generally right. He also freely admitted his failures to trace certain sources or his continuing puzzlement. Atherton never tried to oversystematize, a danger of interpretative superimposition. Observing a pattern, he would try to tack it down, to unravel it as far as it would go, but would also mention his doubts.

Many notes in the *Wake Newslitter* later on began with a complaint that Atherton had missed something (as though he had ever aspired to complete coverage); they thereby testified to a widespread expectation that he had been able (or had claimed to be able) to cover the whole area in a comprehensive sweep.

That this indispensable source study was allowed, within a few years, to go out of print is indicative of British neglect both of Joyce and of *Finnegans Wake* in particular. The book was reissued in an unauthorized paperback (unauthorized in the sense that the author never heard of it) and then in an "Expanded and Corrected Edition" in 1974. The expansion comprised an updated introduction and a much amplified appendix of the "Alphabetical List of Literary Allusions," an unsurpassed treasure among reference books to which we add our own notes. Atherton's original handicap can be seen in the "Additional Bibliography (1957–72)," which documents all the now standard works he had to do without.

Every contribution must be taken for what it can still offer, not for what will inevitably become dated through changing cultural and ideological priorities. Atherton provides many pertinent insights and detailed information. In his time, *Finnegans Wake* was not yet a mythical TEXT but a text to be looked at and figured out as best as one could. Much of what we now take for granted about the internal workings was to evolve slowly in our understanding. In our enlightened age, three decades after Atherton did his research, during which time *Wake* studies and theories have been proliferating, some of his premises may appear naive and unsophisticated. He never pretends to be metaphysical or systematic, he reports on what he has discerned in an honest, unassuming manner. Wakean reading experience has no doubt made us more alert to the shakiness of all foundations. Atherton's introduction (which suitably begins with "Perhaps") says that "final literary evaluation must follow and be based upon a complete understanding of the book. No such understanding has yet been reached and none seems to be in sight" (11). We would nowadays use a term like "complete understanding" a bit more cautiously or reject it outright, but with a remote ideal of such an understanding as a utopian goal, Atherton has significantly increased our practical "understanding" of details. He showed us ways of approaching the *Wake* when few readers undertook the challenge. His emphasis on (or rather, tacit assumption of) a sound philological foundation was perhaps mistaken: paradoxically, evaluations of *Finnegans Wake* are possible with almost no understanding of its textual actuality. Enough of the nature and dynamics of the *Wake* is generally known for theorizing (either inspired or tiresome). Atherton, perhaps more than anyone, has helped us toward this plain and modest kind of understanding, a basis for all subsequent critical work.

Atherton occasionally may have confused the author's voice with that of some fictional distortion; he speculated on Joyce's "opinions" on Lewis Carroll and Oscar Wilde, to whom he found "hostile references": "It seems as if Joyce, who wrote wittily of sexual misconduct, could not forgive people who were actually guilty of it; and he treats Wilde with contempt and loathing to an extent which makes allusions to him conspicuous in a book where the general atmosphere is one of kindliness and good humour" (95). We are less ready now to extract Joyce's own involvement and attitudes by direct quotation. Authors have become less important and less visible—and also more intrusive and conspicuous—since the fifties. Sometimes a Joycean phrase, not sufficiently accounted for, was dismissed as just a joke or an oversight ("perhaps Joyce simply forgot" [21]). And a few statements came out with more assurance than Atherton himself professed: "The French Symbolistes, for example, are quoted but never named. But when one reflects that a major tenet of their creed was '*Nommer est détruire,*' one sees that this was the purest politeness on Joyce's part" (20–21).

In the manner of most Anglo-Saxon criticism of his time, Atherton did not focus on language as a separate concern; he was not particularly interested in the choreography of signifiers, in the processes of semantification, how meaning (whatever that is) comes about. The pendulum has now swung the other way, and yet ironically, language, though given generous lip service, tends to be bypassed now for different reasons. At first it was not seen at all. Now that it has become Language (or its upstart twin, Discourse), it is abstracted out of our focus again.

It is a pity that Atherton (who of course was one of Roland McHugh's main sources for *Annotation*) did not write more out of the unique store of his knowledge, which extended to the whole culture in which Joyce grew up. Atherton was an English Catholic who had received in part the same education. He knew about the kinds of echoes that we latecomers (or foreigners) may find in *Brewer's Dictionary of Phrase and Fable* — if we are lucky (the *Wake* renders our luck very chancy). He had so much at his fingertips that we may never find in print: the terminology of the turf, of sport, of early radio, of songs and ballads, of many jokes current among public schools. In conversation we asked him specific questions, and he often came up with revealing answers in a matter-of-fact tone suggesting that this was familiar to everybody and therefore not worth recording, the kind of things no doubt that everybody once knew and that now may have gone out of a live oral tradition.

Jim Atherton was therefore the ideal person to have on hand when it was a question of simply knowing what some cryptic item on the page might mean. In the summer of 1975, the German translation of *Ulysses* was ready in typescript and had been revised, except for that most rebarbative chapter, "Oxen of the Sun." Hans Wollschläger, the translator, Klaus Reichert, editor-in-chief of the whole edition, and I convened in Unterengstringen, near Zürich, for a final recension. As it happened, Atherton was on holiday in Switzerland and allowed himself to be exploited; the four of us spent a long Sunday going through the final pages, a medley of voices, mainly nonstandard English tongues in various dialectal or vernacular guises. It was extreme good fortune for the translators to have the best-qualified expert at their elbow, willing to supply a running commentary, far beyond what was at that time already in print.

Atherton's situation did not allow him to take part in the many Joyce conferences of the late sixties and in the burgeoning Joyce Symposia. But he attended the one in Paris in 1975 and in a sense met in person the new developments in Joyce studies that we might conveniently date from that symposium. He reported about it in the *Times Literary Supplement* (July 4, 1975):

> At one scarifying moment during my week in Paris for the James Joyce symposium which has just taken place there I found myself, at a cocktail party in the Avenue Foch, being introduced by Jacques Lacan to Roland Barthes as the man who would tell him what *Finnegans Wake* was. I stammered something, wondered, just how one *would* nod good-bye to La Rochefoucault, then mumbled "Un livre . . . un dédale où je suis perdu," and was not surprised when M. Barthes walked away. (Had he misheard *dédale?*)

It must have been a strange non-encounter between two worlds, almost like the one between Proust and Joyce of mythic alternative memories, also in Paris. On the one side, the solid, honest, painstaking scholar, facing, on the other, those who would soon become the new leading lights. In an odd sort of way, it was appropriate that the two French philosophers—who are obviously not to be blamed for the blight that would yet be caused by some of their disciples—should have chanced on an embarrassed, out-of-place James S. Atherton. For ultimately, the kind of poststructuralist mass that Lacan celebrated in the Sorbonne at the august inauguration of the Symposium in June 1975 would not have been possible, Joyceanly speaking, without the preliminary spadework of a devoted laborer in Wigan, Lancashire. Jacques Lacan needed—and quoted with appreciation ("monsieur Ass-er-ton")—James Atherton when he meditated on Joyce *le Symptôme* and on *Finnegans Wake*. When Atherton meditated on *Finnegans Wake* he needed only *Finnegans Wake*.

A personal afterword: When a young reader who wanted to find his way into the *Wake* through some of the infrequent early articles approached Atherton from Zürich about his essays and their location, Atherton wrote back to the enthusiastic student that, since he lived in that city, he might investigate allusions to Zürich in *Finnegans Wake*. So, starting out as a reader and consumer, I did go through the book (gingerly, with cold feet) and gleaned what allusions I could find or invent; I thus became, over the years, a producer of Joycean notes and a fairly active commentator— something that in the course of Joycean contagion would have happened anyway. But it happened before I ever thought of it as a possibility, and I took the step from reader to what they call critic much sooner, more precipitately, and I was drawn into the early circle of correspondents that included James Atherton, Adaline Glasheen (a superb letter writer), Thornton Wilder, Nathan Halper and, later, Clive Hart, Bernard Benstock, and many others. Out of this early circulation of epistolary notes the *Wake Newslitter* arose, for which James S. Atherton was one of the most valuable contributors.

NOTES

1. C. George Sandulescu, *The Language of the Devil*, (Gerrards Cross: Colin Smythe, 1987), 105–78.

2. James S. Atherton, *The Books at the Wake* (1959; rev. ed. Carbondale: Southern Illinois University Press, 1974). Other references to this work are made parenthetically in the text.

3. Not in *The Books at the Wake* but in Atherton's notes to *A Portrait of the Artist as a Young Man*, intro. and annotated by Atherton (London: Heinemann, 1964), 249.

*Morton P. Levitt**

Harry Levin's *James Joyce* and the Modernist Age: A Personal Reading

It was at the suggestion of James Joyce that Harry Levin wrote *James Joyce*. The story is well known to Harvard students and to readers of Levin's pioneer study. Levin recounts the events, which transpired shortly after *Finnegans Wake* first appeared in 1939, as follows:

> [I] was one of the disappointingly small number of reviewers who treated the work at the length and with the respect that it should have been able to take for granted. Though I held some reservations and made some wild guesses and missed only Joyce knew how much, somehow I must have met his mind here and there; for he kindly registered his response in a note which gave Mr. Laughlin the notion of putting me down for the volume on Joyce in his newly projected series, "The Makers of Modern Literature." I agreed to that proposal in the happy thought that my subject would be living longer and writing more, and that this summary essay on his life-work would be a distant holiday for a young scholar then professionally immersed in Elizabethan drama.[1]

The story is told only in the 1960 revision of *James Joyce;* in the original edition (1941), Levin speaks only of his debt to the innovative publisher of New Directions: "To James Laughlin IV, I owe the original suggestion for this volume" (ix).[2]

This is one of the few substantive changes in the revised text. Looking back over his youthful work from the perspective of nearly two decades, Levin concludes that there is little point in trying to bring *James Joyce* up to date: "there has been so much more to say," he comments in mid-June

---

*I would like to acknowledge the assistance of Carmen Carrasquillo, who did much of the research for this essay.

1959, "and . . . so much of it has been or is being so well said by so many others." For himself, therefore, he says he "would rather read about Joyce than continue to write about him" (xii). He speaks here with characteristic understatement: rereading *James Joyce* nearly three decades later still, in June 1987, I perceive how well it holds up and begin to recognize how much I—perhaps all readers of Joyce—owe to this Renaissance scholar.

I'm not quite sure when it was that I first read Levin on Joyce. I know that it wasn't in 1958, when I first read *Ulysses,* sandwiched among *The Magic Mountain, Swann's Way, The Sound and the Fury,* and eleven other modern novels in a fifteen-week undergraduate course (not at Harvard). It was hard enough to read the novels; I could not possibly have read any secondary studies, even had I known of them. And I suspect that it was not in 1961, either, when I reread *Ulysses* in a graduate course: I read at that time, I'm quite certain, some of the (then) obvious sources—Gilbert, Gorman, Ellmann, Kain, even Tindall—but I was too caught up in the excitement of discovering the text to be much concerned with the comments of others about the text.

But at some point I did read Levin's study of Joyce, or perhaps I read a few of his chapters and skimmed the others (I was not much involved in the *Wake* in those years). I took no notes—at least, I can find no notes, and I tend to keep good records of such tasks. I know for certain only that I came to this work some time after I had encountered *The Power of Blackness: Hawthorne, Poe, Melville* (1958) and *The Gates of Horn* (1963), Levin's wonderful reading of French realistic fiction of the nineteenth century. I suspect—I hope—that when I did read *James Joyce* it was the original edition, without the 1960 postscript, "Revisiting Joyce." I am grateful that I did not reread *James Joyce*—both editions this time—until shortly after my book *Modernist Survivors* was published. It is difficult enough to know what we have assimilated from our predecessors and made our own over the years. It would have been distressing to discover while I was still writing how much of my reading of Joyce, of modernism, and of the novel's tradition and growth is first spoken of or hinted at or implicit within Harry Levin (especially in his postscript). To read him today, my own new book perched safely on the mantle alongside my desk, is somehow affirming. I cannot tell now, never will be able to tell, precisely what it is that I—that we all—owe to Levin. With time, though, it becomes increasingly evident that our debt is substantial. And we have been repaying it, perhaps unwittingly, for years, as we have learned to look not simply to the mysteries of the Joycean text (as we may be tempted to do) but also to the humane vision of life that informs it. Ever diligent in advancing the cause of his art, Joyce chose more wisely than he could have known in writing to Laughlin about Levin.

Joyce, of course, did not live much longer or write any more works after *Finnegans Wake*, and so Levin "all too soon" (xii) began his work on Joyce. He had published an edition of Ben Jonson a few years earlier and would publish an edition of the Earl of Rochester the following year. There would be editions and studies of Shakespeare and Marlowe in years to come, *The Myth of the Golden Age in the Renaissance* (1969), further work on nineteenth-century American and French and twentieth-century comparative literature, studies on the forms of literature and the state of criticism, and the influential and popular *Portable James Joyce* (1947). Levin remains today a forceful and creative critical presence. He may well be our foremost comparatist. But he could hardly have foreseen such a career when he started *James Joyce*, seemingly so far out of his field, "amid circumstances of general distraction" (xii)—near the start of the most horrifying decade of human history. Looking back to his early work, at the end of the following decade, in the midst of our own era, Levin concluded that it might best "be characterized by the subtitle attached to its last chapter in Spanish translation: *"un epitafio"* (xii). The mood and tone are clearer still in his 1960 postscript, a self-conscious epitaph of sorts to Joyce and his great generation of modernists: "as modernism recedes into the background, as we settle down into what Arnold Toynbee would classify as the post-modern period, Joyce assumes a predominating position in any retrospect of the moderns in English" (243).

1960 was also the year in which Levin wrote "What Was Modernism?" the seminal essay that at the same time announced the passing of the age and gave it its name. At once regretful and celebratory— a true epitaph to what even then seemed a golden literary age—Levin's essay stakes out new critical and historical grounds, building on his reading of Joyce, looking both backward and forward in time, an indispensable tool for modernism's admirers and detractors alike. A quarter of a century further on, with distraction more general still and barbarism become our characteristic mode, as nations practice genocide almost as mundane behavior and novelists decry the day and their inheritance, Levin's measured, humane, admiring vision may help us to rethink modernism, Joyce's role in the movement, and our literary inheritance in a so-called postmodernist time.

Levin has the advantage in approaching Joyce of not being a Joycean. He seems incapable of reading Joyce out of context and falls back consistently on the broad and deep literary background he shares with his subject. He never makes the mistake that some of us—admirers and detractors alike, ignoring the evidence of the texts—may be tempted to make: to read Joyce as if he were truly unique, *sui generis*, cut off from his contemporaries and aloof from his ancestors, connected, at best, only to those who follow in his wake and even then somewhat tenuously. Levin sees connections everywhere—as Joyce does and as he seems to want us to do. Levin is perhaps the first to recognize fully that Joyce is, in a very real sense, the most traditional of novelists (for the novel's tradition demands movement), announcing his fictional debts on almost every page he wrote. Levin begins with the late nineteenth-century literary background (3) and offers one of the earliest discussions of the modernist *Künstlerroman* (41–43). When he speaks of internal monologue we understand that he has read both Dujardin and his predecessors (90–93); when he sets out the fruitful antagonism of naturalism and symbolism within Joyce's fictions—and he is surely among the first to do so—he brings in not just Ibsen and Zola, Mallarmé and Huysmans, but Hawthorne (141), the medieval morality play (109), and Milton and Rabelais (219–20). He has read Vico and understands his importance to Joyce (142ff.); he is at ease with the eighteenth-century background as well, both Continental and English (pp. 209–12), and recognizes the centrality of Swift in Joyce (166–67); and he anticipates Northrop Frye's discussion of the anatomy as form and sees the tradition at work even in *Finnegans Wake*. At a time when most spoke of Joyce's uniqueness, Levin says of Joyce that "his real originality is firmly grounded in literary tradition" (93).

In a time of increasing specialization (even in literature, even in Joyce studies) and of increasing commitment to the increasingly new, it is a renewed pleasure to read a critic who knows too much and sees too broadly to specialize and who has too much respect for literary history simply to forget the past. This is not to argue that all of Levin's judgments on Joyce hold up today or that I approve of every aspect of his approach. Blessed by the heightened vision afforded by distance, it is easy enough in 1987 to find fault with specific readings in *James Joyce* and with some of its larger themes. What is surprising is how sound so much of it still seems today.

On the simplest, textual level, I am convinced that Levin is mistaken when he suggests that Simon Dedalus "may have been one of the lovers of Molly Bloom" (122); this is to agree with Bloom—so, at least, it would seem—that Molly has had lovers other than Boylan. Few readers today believe that she has, and her view of Simon—"such a criticizer" (*U* 632),[3] "always turning up half screwed" (*U* 636): a proud, pompous man turned comic figure—makes it clear that he could not be among them. Levin also too readily accepts Eliot's mythopoesis as being identical to Joyce's (208), and he has surprisingly little to say about Jews in *Ulysses:* they provide, after all, not only its protagonist but also its most prevalent—and, arguably, most important—pattern of imagery (and perhaps its central myth as well).[4] These are all readings more consistent with their time than with ours, the result of accepting the text of *Ulysses* and its early critics at more or less face value.

Something similar happens with *Finnegans Wake*, both more recent in 1941 and less accessible. Levin gives us a good deal of Buckley (164) but little of Berkeley; he has some problems with narrative technique and may fail to recognize the shifting points of view of Shem and Shaun as a cause of their divergent presentations ("Shaun . . . , unlike his 'cerebrated brother,' is treated with a proper respect" [162]); his overall view of the novel (quite sensible and sound on the whole, especially when we consider the lack of a critical context in 1941) is at times a bit simplistic: "The plot is little more than a series of verbal associations and numerical correspondences. Relationships are often clearer than significances" (146).

On another level, I cannot accept all the implications of Levin's conclusion that Joyce's "subject broadens as his style darkens" (168). Surely the *Wake* is broader in subject than is *A Portrait*, but I am not convinced that its style (or tone or vision of life) is appreciably darker. Distant, daytime, humorless young Stephen Dedalus is both less and more than avatar of the Romantic artist-hero in *A Portrait;* he offers both an epiphany of artistic promise and a callow, incomplete view of humanity: dark enough in its narrowness. And where middle-aged, failing HCE exists in a night world resonant with tragedy in *Finnegans Wake* and wakes to a day without promise (other than the promise offered every day to all men by the sunrise), he also offers a model that is wonderfully funny and even perhaps—if we can see him in a certain light—inspiring. This is a view easier to accept at fifty than it would have been at thirty, of course, and it assumes that HCE is in this respect a further development of Bloom. For Joyce's themes are consistent throughout his canon, but his humanity (understanding, acceptance, compassion) deepens as he and his heroes mature.

But Levin's reactions to Bloom and to HCE are rather different from my own: he exaggerates Bloom's predicament, as I see it (a "future on the dole" [207]) and underestimates his stature ("*Ulysses* is totally lacking in the epic virtues of love, friendship, and magnanimity. . . . Mr. Bloom . . . is the sorrier exile. A mute inglorious Shakespeare, a rejected Messiah, he has nothing to offer Stephen but a pathetic object lesson" [131, 133]). We may need the perspective of the postwar, post-Holocaust, post-Vietnam world to perceive it, but to me at least—and I suspect, to many other readers as well—Bloom may well turn out to be not just a decent provider but even a hero of sorts: the lesson he offers to Stephen includes dignity, perseverance, and empathy, the breadth of human possibilities for modern heroism. HCE, too, may be more than he seems, is surely more than Levin—taking Joyce, really taking Stephen, too literally at his wor(l)d—can acknowledge: "Joyce shows no more concern for his hero," he says of the *Wake*, "than a geneticist for a fruit-fly; he happens to be interested in the peculiarities of the *genus* earwig. Indifferent, he pares his fingernails, having reached the stage of artistic development that passes over the individual in favor of the general" (193). Such a conclusion would be harder to reach today; there is more ambiguity here than Levin could possibly have seen a few months after his subject's death, not much more than a year after the appearance of that final novel.

Similarly, Levin misjudges Joyce's concern for his audience because he cannot distance himself sufficiently from Joyce and because he can see little distance between Joyce and his creation: "Joyce's case history [in *Finnegans Wake*], subtly and painstakingly analyzed by himself, is the exception to prove the rule that literature cannot exist without an audience" (217). Perhaps the young Stephen of *A Portrait* would applaud such a view, but in "Scylla and Charybdis" he demonstrates his own powerful need for an audience, and Joyce, I sense—without much specific textual proof but in the conviction that he did not do all that work, undergo all that turmoil, simply because he liked or needed to spend a few calm hours each day writing at his desk—Joyce wanted and expected a wide audience of dedicated readers. His model, I guess, was Dickens, the greatest and most popular novelist of his age, but he would be a Dickens who would educate his audience not only how to read its world but also how to read. The only artist who can (theoretically) thrive without an audience is the Romantic artist, always suffering for his art, in all ways isolated from his society. The young Stephen might believe that such an artist can function convincingly, but the mature Joyce did not.

Underlying my several disagreements with Levin is his insistence that Joyce's life is central to his art, that life and art are largely indistinguishable in Joyce, "the most self-centered of universal minds" (11). "He lived his work and he wrote his life" (215). Levin reads *A Portrait* as autobiography ("based on a literal transcript of the first twenty years of Joyce's life" [45]); finds the failure of *Exiles* in its dependence on the dramatist's life ("Joyce's characterization is far too subjective to be dramatic" [38]); and identifies Stephen Dedalus with Joyce, Richard Rowan with Joyce, HCE and his artist son, Shem, with Joyce, at once father and son and archetypal creator. But never, interestingly, does he link Joyce with Bloom, who shares hardly at all in the facts of the artist's life but shares profoundly in sensibility, a sign of Joyce's humanity that Levin simply misses. In the 1960 postscript, "Revisiting Joyce," however, Levin tones

down his rendering somewhat: "Precisely because his career was trans-
muted into his works, biographical knowledge is a necessary tool for the
understanding of his creative process." And now he offers us also Stanislaus
Joyce's "useful caveat": " 'A Portrait of the Artist is not an autobiography;
it is an artistic creation' " (234). James Joyce offers only a brief introduction to its subject's life (and in its postscript praises Richard Ellmann's
forthcoming biography).[5] Levin himself does not search obsessively for
biographical sources or parallels; his interest, despite his insistent theme,
is in the art and not in the life.

There is nothing inherently pejorative in labeling Joyce's fiction
"autobiographical," but it is needlessly limiting. It shifts our attention to
the essentially trivial, undercuts the act of creation, hints shamelessly
that experience and memory in art are as meaningful as imagination and
discipline. ("I could have written those stories," I have several times
heard Dubliners say of Joyce's Dubliners. "I knew those people. I had
those experiences. I could have written those stories if only I had wanted
to.") Almost from the first, Joyce was able to pick and choose and
transcend the facts of his life—even to subvert the facts of his life for the
sake of his art. (Witness Stephen the outsider on the playing fields of
Clongowes: good Romantic art and poor autobiography.) I, too, was
taught that Joyce was the most autobiographical of novelists, and I read
avidly through Ellmann's James Joyce when it first appeared, searching
out the sources and données of the art, happily assuming that I was
thereby learning its secrets. Those notes have faded; I now read through
my text of Ulysses without noticing them. Given time and greater distance,
any reader of Joyce can learn to note and then bypass the artist's often
trivial life and go on to the real life, his art.

So much for disagreement. Considering the almost half-century that
has passed since the initial appearance of Levin's James Joyce, remembering
that it was the first critical study to attempt to examine the whole of
Joyce's career, with major emphasis on both Ulysses and Finnegans Wake
(which, after all, had only recently been published), such complaints
seem few, unsurprising, and, on the whole, rather minor. I am impressed
not by my differences with Levin but by how easily he can usually
persuade me and how often we agree, meaning, perhaps, how often I
have adopted as my own, without always knowing the source, perhaps
filtered through my teachers, critical positions that he was the first to
advocate. I increasingly suspect, as I reread and reconsider James Joyce,
that my entire generation of students of Joyce—thus, the teachers of the
next—is similarly indebted to Harry Levin, in ways that we cannot
always calculate or even perceive.

His appeal is not to those who specialize in the narrow, if necessary, areas of Joyce study: philologists, local historians, those who delight in the wordplay and tropes of the *Wake* without much concern for wider contexts, those who can see single theories as solutions to a single great puzzle, whether *Ulysses* or the *Wake* or the work of Joyce as a whole. Although he himself reads the texts well and convincingly, it is not simply as a New Critical reader of the ultimate modernist fictional texts (for which the New Criticism was developed, after all) that he exerts his influence. His appeal is to those who are drawn to the "cultured allroundman" (*U* 193) Joyce, encyclopedist, humanist, exemplar of the modernist age. His autobiographical emphasis aside, Levin appeals always to balance: of measured judgment and intuitive leap, of criticism and scholarship (a major issue of the time), of text and source—in the best and most customary New Critical tradition. He has from the start understood Joyce's primacy in the modernist age; he has consistently been sensitive to the modernist experience—even when announcing its passing—despite his own intellectual roots in the Renaissance.

Yet today some of his judgments, despite their judiciousness, seem rather daring in the context of their time: on Homer, for example. Following Joyce's lead, early teachers of *Ulysses* invariably began their courses with his charts of analogues and correspondences to the *Odyssey* (and, by extension, to the *Iliad* and related myths). This was my introduction to Joyce (interspersed with keys of lesser sorts to Proust and Faulkner). Anyone who looks closely at the Gilbert-Gorman and Linati charts and at the novel they allegedly describe will discover soon enough, however, that most of the listed characters and episodes have no real parallels in Joyce and that most of the others operate on the most superficial of levels. The practice undoubtedly continues, but I assume that most teachers of Joyce today recognize that the charts really do not function significantly. Some must have noticed it in Joyce's time as well, but few seemed willing to contradict the master about his own work.

Levin does briefly recount the Homeric parallels in *Ulysses*, for "they reveal, more graphically than further discussion or second-hand summary, how the myth of the *Odyssey* is superimposed upon the map of Dublin, how the retelling of an old fable is absorbed into the cross-section of a contemporary city" (76). But he adds a proviso: "The reader of Joyce who turns back to Homer is more struck by divergences than by analogies" (72); and he warns us further that while "in some respects, the Homeric parallel is a useful contrivance for the reader" and even the "plethora of other symbols" (organs, arts, techniques) may sometimes work,[6] they actually serve a far different purpose: "They are not there for us, but for Joyce." Myth and symbols alike, Levin goes on—and he is perhaps the first to make the now obvious point—"may well have served as a scaffolding, while Joyce constructed his work" (75–76). To beginning readers of *Ulysses* in courses in which they are not expected to delve very deeply, the schema can be comforting. I certainly was happy to know as an undergraduate in a survey course that there was apparently an order after all to this immense, demanding, seemingly chaotic work. But in other cases in which a crutch is not needed, the convenient charts simply get in the way and keep us confined to the surface. (It is, after all, the wrong order that they provide.)

How tactful and full of potential Levin's compromise is: to paraphrase the charts for our beginners' use, to warn us against taking them too literally, and to make the imaginative leap and suggest that they may have been of far more value to Joyce than they can possibly be to us. Levin does not pursue his insight further, but he enables us to envision a still young Joyce engaged in his first major modernist undertaking, its goals only distantly in sight, perhaps himself in need of assurance—in spite of his pride in his powers—that his goals are attainable: to see for the first time the possibility of a Joyce beyond his own myth. Ironically, and appropriately, this Joyce whom Levin makes possible for us is directly at odds with the Stephen-Joyce of the biographical myth. We can begin to see him in ways that Levin, in 1941, could not, but we do so in large part because of Levin's insight.

Levin is farsighted in other respects as well, but his vision develops always out of close reading. He notes, for example, the lack of visual imagery in *Finnegans Wake:* "Joyce's imagination, as his light is spent, concentrates on the 'mind's ear'" (175). Here the biographical fact— Joyce's increasing blindness—is placed at the service of the text.[7] It reveals what may prove a major flaw of the *Wake* and underlies a major pattern of its imagery that Levin does not detail—can we call it visual? —the imagery of near blindness, become part of the older (but still Romantic) artist's necessary baggage. Shem the Penman is as callow as Stephen, but his isolation is not simply self-created: he has suffered in ways that in Stephen—in anticipation of the artist he intends to become— remain merely potential. Levin speaks not so much of Shem, however, as of his father. It is Earwicker's "dream vision," he notes, that "lacks visual imagery"—no suggestion yet that others may share in the dream; but "Words are the stuff that Earwicker's dream is made on. The darking shadings of consciousness, the gropings of the somnolent mind, the states between sleeping and waking—unless it be by Proust—have never been so acutely rendered. But Joyce's technique always tends to get ahead of his psychology." The problem is one of verisimilitude. Many of the dream-word images of the *Wake* "cannot be traced, with any show of plausibility, to the sodden brain of a snoring publican. No psychoanalyst could account for the encyclopedic sweep of Earwicker's fantasies or the acoustical properties of his dreamwork" (175).

The implicit question that Levin poses here—at least, the question that I infer from his observation, beyond the questions of imagery or psychological verisimilitude—is whether Joyce's narrative technique is thereby flawed or whether it can in practice be consistent. And the question as posed may, as I see it, contain its own answer: how else to reproduce dream images on the page except in words? Dreams are inherently filled with visual images, of course, even the dreams of an author going blind; but *Finnegans Wake* is neither a dream nor a series of dreams, however interconnected: not one man's dream, or one family's dream(s), or the universal dream in which we all potentially share. It is a literary effort—the most elaborate of literary efforts—not to create such a dream but to suggest one, and to do so not in the depths of the mind but on the flat surface of the physical page. That this is a truism does not deny its truth or its relevance. The puns or portmanteau words or constructs of history and consciousness that make up *Finnegans Wake* are not a representation in the same sense as are the shared images of Bloom and Stephen in "Circe" or Molly's stream of consciousness in "Penelope." Those are words meant to represent words, sometimes common, always comprehensible, words that may hint at deeper forces, but words nonetheless. Visual (or other) imagery in *Ulysses* is exactly what it seems: seen or remembered or imagined objects and events, at times with undertones of metaphor and symbol, but recognizable always by their viewers (usually at first glance) and by the reader as well.

The language of the *Wake*, on the other hand, is intended to suggest not merely the multiple images present in dream but also the states of mind and culture that may lie beneath them. It is never immediately recognizable in full; its meaning is, for lack of a more precise term, entirely metaphoric. Some of the images that Levin finds most disruptive may, in fact, be Shem's and not his father's—a partial answer to the question of verisimilitude. And the fact that so few of these images are overtly visual may be the result not of Joyce's near-blindness but of the necessary limitations and challenges of his task. Few are auditory or tactile or gustatory or olfactory. Few, indeed, are images at all, in the usual sense of the term. It may also be that Joyce's psychology is at times flawed, as it may be flawed in *Ulysses*. But not his narrative technique: if we can suspend disbelief long enough to investigate the truism, then point of view in the *Wake* may appear wonderfully consistent.

Such a reading, in which point of view is a natural concomitant of language and image, of state of mind and state of the world, of the accretions of history and of immediate observation, without the intervention of some outside narrator (whether God, the omniscient author or one of his puppets, or the reader's own agent, the Victorian or some other *paterfamilias*), relayed directly to the reader who may experience it as the characters do—such a reading of the *Wake* is implicit within Levin's discussion of point of view in *Ulysses*:

> The imitation of life through the medium of language has never been undertaken more literally. *Ulysses* ignores the customary formalities of narration and invites us to share a flux of undifferentiated experience. We are not told how the characters behave; we are confronted with the *stimuli* that affect their behavior, and expected to respond sympathetically. The act of communication, the bond of sympathy which identifies the reader with the book, comes almost too close for comfort. The point of view, the principle of form which has served to integrate many amorphous novels, is intimate and pervasive. Joyce's efforts to achieve immediacy lead him to equate form and content, to ignore the distinction between the things he is describing and the words he is using to describe them. In this equation, time is of the essence. Events are reported when and as they occur; the tense is a continuous present. (87)

Blessedly unaware of contemporary theories of "narratology" (an ugly word for what may well be an unneeded concept), innocent of the jargon that has been spread like a compost heap on the modernist novel by some of its recent critics, Levin in 1941 is forced to fall back on the language of Henry James and his early followers, who first developed point of view as a topic for critical discussion. Their language, on this most complex of subjects, is simple, even simplistic, without much pretension or claim to near-scientific precision, using a few straightforward terms that most of us can readily understand. (Hence the obvious academic temptation to improve on their example.) And so Levin, because he cannot name, is compelled to describe. He provides no secret language of geometry or apocrypha, or narrative theory; seeks no disciples who alone can speak such a language; makes no effort to assume mastery over his subject, like some preliterate tribesman, by giving it its name. His discussion, then, is not very precise. It lacks totally in pretense. And it remains as lucid and revealing a general description of what actually happens in the narrative of *Ulysses* as we have had. (I omit here, as Levin does, those few specific examples of true narration by a character, as in "Cyclops," as well as those cases that require a more complex, perhaps less realistic explanation, as in Stephen's and Bloom's shared visions in "Circe." But these problems too, I am convinced, lend themselves to such an approach.)

Levin makes available a comprehendible way of reading narrative in *Ulysses* and, in the process, places its author much closer to the center of the great narrative tradition of the novel than most critics of the time could realize. We need no secret key or arcane language to follow this narrative, only attentiveness to the text and a strong sympathy with the actors, some help perhaps, some patience, and much goodwill. (Accepting such a view, F. R. Leavis could never have excluded Joyce from his canon.) Levin may also point the way to a later generation of readers, who have less need to be impressed with their status as a self-proclaimed "elite" (since *Ulysses* may now be accessible to more than a few). It is a vision of Joyce and a Joycean audience that I find particularly appealing: an accessible Joyce writing for a broad audience, intending to make demands on his readers, expecting to reward them for their efforts, but surely not planning to appeal to a select few only. Such a view of Joyce seems to me to be implicit throughout Levin's *James Joyce*. It is a central reason for my great admiration and respect for the work.

Once again, I have been using Levin as affirmation of my own reading of Joyce. (Here, incidentally, I feel no possible anxiety over his possible influence. I know unequivocally that my reading of point of view in *Ulysses* long antedates my reading of Levin. But I am delighted to find support for my views in his.) The danger of such an approach, of course, is that the critic of the critic may write solely about his or her own work and not truly about the subject, or else use the subject for self-justification. I hope I have honestly avoided the trap, perhaps following the example of Levin, who is so expert a judge of other Joyce critics: perceptive, judicious, never—so far as I can tell—grinding some personal axe. Not surprisingly, I find myself agreeing with many of Levin's individual judgments ("William York Tindall . . . has jeopardized his efforts [as editor of *Chamber Music*] by appending a naïvely Freudian commentary" [233]); applauding his warning about "subjective over-reading" (238) and his indictment of the narrowness of English reactions (under-reading) to Joyce (240–41);[8] and admiring his ability to stand back from his own time and measure it dispassionately: "A generation of critics lived in [*Ulysses'*] shadows, terrified at the prospect of a sequel, and secretly convinced that anything short of the millenium would be an anticlimax" (139). Levin's experience with Joyce's reputation prior to 1941 foreshadows my own in the early 1960s, when occasional older colleagues continued to insist, albeit less strongly than they might have twenty years earlier, that Joyce was obviously a fraud. "It is ironic and pitiful," Levin writes, that Joyce "left himself open to attack—from venal and vulgar writers—as an enemy of literary standards. His introverted traditionalism was mistaken for irresponsibility. In an irresponsible time, on the contrary, the responsible artist is a lone custodian of tradition" (218).

The measure and balance of Levin's critical judgment are echoed always in the grace and balance of his prose. *James Joyce* is filled with apt illustrations: "Joyce at best is a merely competent poet, moving within an extremely limited range. The poetic medium, narrowly conceived, offers him too little resistance.... His real contribution is to bring the fuller resources of poetry to fiction" (27); Molly "is the compliant body as Stephen is the uncompromising mind, and as Bloom—torn between them—is the lacerated heart" (125); "Bloom is an exile in Dublin, as Stephen is a Dubliner in exile" (84); the lyric description of the bird-girl who leads Stephen into art in *A Portrait* "is incantation, and not description" (52); and, at the other end of Joyce's career, with the *Wake*, Levin in 1965 "must admit that [he is] slightly discouraged—not so much by the complexities of the work as by the shortness of human life" (240).

Joyce's own death appears to Levin as the end of an era: "With Joyce's death, in the second year of the present war, a year or two after the deaths of Yeats and Freud and Trotsky, and a month or two before the deaths of Bergson and Virginia Woolf and Frazer, we realize how bare the cultural horizon has become, and how suddenly we are stepping into another age" (221). Twenty years later, "What Was Modernism?"[9] rounds out the subject, sees Joyce as modernist exemplar, and strongly suggests that the new age holds little appeal for the Renaissance scholar. Although he is here announcing modernism's demise, Levin does so with evident regret, even with a certain nostalgia, and it is clear that his affinities remain with it and not with its putative successor.[10]

When *James Joyce* first appeared, it was widely if erratically reviewed. Some reviewers took the opportunity to comment negatively on Joyce, largely ignoring his commentator.[11] Others, more positive toward Joyce, were more concerned to advance their own readings of his work and significance, at some times faulting Levin for believing otherwise, at other times largely ignoring him.[12] Still others saw *James Joyce* as "the best [book] we have had yet" on the subject.[13] And that is where matters have pretty much remained. The parochial dissenters have been forgotten over the years, and Levin's work has stood as one of the best early introductions to this demanding century's most demanding writer. But we have largely taken it for granted in recent years, as a sort of period piece. Levin has been better known among Joyceans for the *Portable James Joyce* and even for the exemplary Joyce of "What Was Modernism?" *James Joyce* has been judged historically important but perhaps no longer very useful, or at least not very useful except to beginning readers of Joyce. I held much the same view myself when I agreed to undertake this reconsideration. But Levin's rendering of Joyce seems to me to hold up very well indeed, less obviously out of date than I had expected, much further ahead of its time than readers of the time could realize. He makes some inevitable mistakes, and we have our disagreements, some of them fairly serious. But Levin's *James Joyce* seems to me not merely one of the best of the early books on Joyce but still one of the best general studies of Joyce that we have. We might all take the opportunity to reconsider it.[14]

Some of the early writers on Joyce we remember solely because of their work on Joyce. But we would know and respect others had Joyce never left Dublin or published a word except in the *Irish Homestead*: Edmund Wilson, Joseph Campbell, Samuel Beckett, of course, and Harry Levin. *James Joyce*, written at the beginning of Levin's career, appears in retrospect to provide a modernist thread that would run throughout the career, a paradoxical emblem of revolution and tradition, of receptivity to (even creation of) the new age, and of understanding (and imaginative use) of the old. Looking back on Levin's work as a Joycean, we can see much of the history of Joyce criticism and trace the novelist's evolving reputation. "When we condemn Joyce," Levin says in 1941 of the early detractors of Joyce, "we are condemning ourselves" (216). But Joyce's reputation is so secure today that he needs no defending; I suspect that younger critics today can hardly imagine a time when he did. Today we may wish to adapt Levin's comment and suggest instead that in praising Joyce—his humor and perception, his encyclopedic approach to fiction, his exquisite and moving prose, his profound humanist impulse—we are also praising ourselves, our receptivity, our own humanism. It must have been difficult to imagine such a state in 1941. But we have had good teachers, and we have learned. "May I now say," Levin concludes in his 1960 afterword "Revisiting Joyce," "that the Joyce for whom I would bespeak your continued admiration is the learner and teacher?" (246). It is the early learner and long-time teacher Harry Levin for whom I would seek ours.

NOTES

1. Harry Levin, *James Joyce: A Critical Introduction* (New York: New Directions, 1960), xi–xii. All additional references to this work are cited parenthetically in the text. Since pagination is identical in the two editions (except, of course, for the new preface and postscript), I cite this text even when I am referring to the 1941 edition.

2. As Levin later explained, "'The authors whom I have tried most to follow are those who have done the most to develop the ranges and artistic techniques at their command—notably James Joyce, who prompted my little book about him by writing a friendly note to my publisher after I had been rash enough to review *Finnegans Wake*. My ultimate hope is for a kind of criticism which, while analyzing the formal and esthetic qualities of a work of art, will fit them into the cultural and social pattern to which it belongs.'" Quoted

in *Twentieth Century Authors: A Biographical Dictionary of Modern Literature*, ed. Stanley J. Kunitz (New York: H. W. Wilson Co., 1955), first supplement, 574.

3. All references to *Ulysses* are to the Gabler Random House edition (New York, 1986).

4. See my essays "The Family of Bloom," in *New Light on Joyce from the Dublin Symposium*, ed. Fritz Senn (Bloomington and London: Indiana University Press, 1972), 141–48, and "A Hero for Our Time: Leopold Bloom and the Myth of *Ulysses*," in *"Ulysses": Fifty Years*, ed. Thomas F. Staley (Bloomington and London: Indiana University Press, 1974), 132–46.

5. "And the emergent personality," Levin predicts of Ellmann's Joyce, "with his alcoholic lapses, his financial irresponsibility, the tragedy of his daughter's mental illness, his neurotic obsesion with betrayal, his self-centered unconcern with people he could not use, counterweighed by the single-minded exertions of his artistry, will impress and perplex us even more than the embattled artist did in his lifetime" (235–36). In fact, I think, something rather different has happened. Although some problems with the life remain of interest—some of them relating to Ellmann's biography (even in revision)—the generations of readers of Joyce who did not know of the artist in his lifetime, given the time to assimilate this portrait, have been drawn away from the life and back to the life's work.

6. "We find ourselves approaching [them] gingerly," Levin writes, "like Charlie Chaplin chewing a pudding in which a coin has been embedded" (75).

7. I have myself suggested elsewhere, not entirely true to the principle of separation of text and life, that Joyce's lifelong preoccupation with the theme of martyrdom in his art may somehow have affected the facts of his life. "'Shalt Be Accurst?' The Martyr in James Joyce," *James Joyce Quarterly* 5 (1968): 128–34.

8. As for the modern English novel, Levin concludes that "its distinction has been borrowed from three outsiders—the American, James; the Pole, Conrad; and the Irishman, Joyce" (215). I am inclined to agree, while disagreeing with Levin's assessment of Woolf as a writer of "bloodless grace" (215)—and with his passing view of Proust's identification with Marcel (127).

9. First published in *The Massachusetts Review* (1960), "What Was Modernism?" appears also in *Varieties of Literary Experience*, ed. Stanley Burnshaw (New York: New York University Press, 1962), and in Levin's collections of essays entitled *Refractions: Essays in Comparative Literature* (New York: Oxford University Press, 1966).

10. A recent, unsympathetic critic—and not a very judicious one, I fear—complains that Levin's essay has acted to stultify interest in "postmodern" writers in favor of dissertations "done under the direction of scholars like Mr. Levin. . . . [H]is own position, if taken seriously, can have only two consequences: to breed more laudatory criticism of the past and to paralyze the creators of our own time." Joseph A. Buttigieg, *A Portrait of the Artist in Different Perspective* (Athens: Ohio University Press, 1987), 4. Buttigieg will surely not like my recent book, *Modernist Survivors* (1987), which does precisely what he seems to deplore or even worse: to go beyond Levin and argue that what is best about contemporary

fiction is what it owes to the modernists; in short, that modernism may well survive in an allegedly postmodernist age. Levin himself stands by his judgments in *Memories of the Moderns* (New York: New Directions Press, 1981).

11. See, for example, the review in *Punch* signed "H.K.," CCVI (9 February 1944), 124, or "J.C.R." writing in *Kenyon Review* 4 (1942): 430–32.

12. Lionel Abel's review in *Partisan Review* 9 (1942): 259–60, ably illustrates this tendency.

13. Herbert J. Muller, "Harry Levin: *James Joyce,*" *Accent* 2 (1942).

14. The day after completing this essay, while preparing to teach Thomas Mann's *Doctor Faustus*, I came across a most revealing comment by the great German modernist, writing in 1945: "I read with careful attention a book that was not directly pertinent, but whose keen analysis stimulated me to consider the situation of the novel in general and where I myself stood in its history. This was *James Joyce*, by Harry Levin. Since I cannot have direct access to the linguistic structure erected by the Irish writer, I have had to depend upon the critics for elucidation of the phenomenon he presents. Books like Levin's, and Campbell's and Robinson's major commentary on *Finnegans Wake*, have revealed to me many an unexpected relationship and—given such vast difference in our literary natures—even affinity. I had held the prejudice that alongside Joyce's eccentric avant-gardism my work was bound to seem like lukewarm traditionalism.... There are sentences in Levin's book which touched me with a strange intensity. 'The best writing of our contemporaries is not an act of creation, but an act of evocation, peculiarly saturated with reminiscences.' And this other one: 'He has enormously increased the difficulties of being a novelist.'" Thomas Mann, *The Genesis of a Novel*, trans. Richard and Clara Winston (London: Secker & Warburg, 1961), 75–76.

Richard F. Peterson

A Reader's Guide
to William York Tindall

In his introduction to *James Joyce: His Way of Interpreting the Modern World*, William York Tindall composes a portrait of the critic as a young man newly graduated from Columbia University.

Tindall recalls that, after completing his undergraduate degree in 1925, he took up an offer from his parents and set off for Paris to see something of the world. Having heard talk of *Ulysses*, in spite of the efforts of Columbia's professors to shield their students from the lure of contemporary literature, he hurried to the rue de l'Odéon and "bought the blue-covered volume."[1] Although acknowledging that he now reads *Ulysses* with more understanding, Tindall fondly remembers that June 16 in the gardens of the Luxembourg when his misunderstanding of Joyce's book "did little to interfere" with his satisfaction and delight (2). That memory of his first reading of *Ulysses* led Tindall to his premise for writing his book on Joyce and also to the conclusion that "*Ulysses* is suitable for the common reader" (2). As for *Finnegans Wake*, the seasoned reader, once through the book, will have "the feeling that there is nothing better—or, indeed, more necessary—to do than to read it over again" (2).

Once establishing his audience and, at least by implication, his own role as the reader's guide, Tindall moves from modest proposal to lofty claim for his subject. For Tindall, Joyce "seems to have understood everything," and, because he invented the perfect forms for what he understood, his effect on the modern mind "has been almost as pervasive as that of Einstein or that of Freud" (2–3). Joyce, however, was the artist, and through the power of words—Tindall later praises him as the "master of all verbal effects" (96)—he influenced, unlike the scientist, both feeling and thought. Lord of language, Joyce gave voice to our desire to absorb and comprehend our world and to express our understanding of its complexities in intelligible form. To make Joyce accessible, while a humbling task for Tindall, will require nothing short of guiding the uninitiated reader through a maze of complex words, rhythms, and structures to find the symbols that reveal Joyce's radiant and moral vision of the modern world.

Not surprisingly, Tindall begins the body of *James Joyce* with "Daedalus," a chapter in which he claims that Joyce, inspired by the original labyrinth of Daedalus, composed "an elaborate design" (5) in his work. Using the streets of Dublin as a labyrinthine setting, Joyce dramatized the complexities of human nature, ranging from the artistic temperament to the mind and soul of the common Dubliner, while creating appropriate but ever-elaborating forms out of his own imagination. Also discovering, like his "fabulous artificer," the necessity of learning the art of escape, Joyce converted Daedalean flight into the literary theme of exile and the aesthetic strategy of detachment. His art, however, accomplished no less than a portrait of the emotional, moral, and spiritual paralysis of the modern city and the artist's need for freedom from that corrupting influence, as well as a final vision of the human family struggling with guilt and alienation but capable of acceptance and reconciliation.

Tindall's Joyce, then, is the fabulous artificer of our age, the modern artist who creates labyrinthine works out of his own fears and desires, his inherited history, and the vast range of his cultural knowledge and creative imagination. Appropriately, Tindall's role now becomes more sharply defined as the reader's guide through the Joycean labyrinth. Preparing for the journey, he provides a brief outline, or map, of the Joycean landscape, especially its domestic, nationalistic, and religious features, and identifies the cast of characters who embody Joyce's central preoccupations. His main responsibility, however, is to find a way through Joyce's elaborations to his central meaning, and, for Tindall, the way to understanding Joyce is through the symbolism of his works.

Before the encounter with the forest of symbols, however, Tindall finds it necessary to school the reader on Joyce's understanding of the human condition and his affirmation of the human spirit. Through his greatest creations, Leopold and Molly Bloom, Joyce rendered humanity complete, but with both irony and compassion. At once comic and pathetic, Bloom, through Joyce's multiple techniques, emerges as a flawed, modern everyman but, because of his "patience, courage, and freedom from self-pity," becomes, at the end, "one of the greatest representatives of human dignity" (35). Tindall's claims for Molly Bloom are equally ambitious, if not more so. Not just everywoman or fundamental, she becomes, in her interior monologue, "the essential being of everywoman"

(36). Nevertheless, she, too, appeals as the most human of characters: "Nowhere is Joyce's understanding more apparent and nowhere his mixture of humor, irony, and compassion" (38).

Affirming Molly's "yes" to be a sign of Joyce's own affirming spirit, Tindall sees Joyce broadening his vision of humanity in *Finnegans Wake* to include the family cycle. Tindall proposes that Joyce, borrowing from Giambattista Vico's philosophy of historical recurrence in *La scienza nuova* (1725), developed a structure or "revolving stage" for the human family that spins, with a push from myth, history, and language, through the divine, the heroic, and the human ages. Led and misled by a patriarch who is both the local publican Humphrey Chimpden Earwicker and the historical and mythic Here Comes Everybody, Joyce's family performs the eternal drama of the rise and fall of all families, beginning with Adam and Eve and their contentious children and running to HCE and ALP, their warring twins, Shem and Shaun, and their flirtatious daughter, Issy. With added insight from J. G. Frazer's *The Golden Bough*, the Egyptian *Book of the Dead*, Giordano Bruno's coincidence of contraries, and "the post-Newtonian universe of Einstein and Planck" (91), Joyce finally found, in his understanding of the recurring conflicts of the family, "the absolute in time and reconciled it with eternity" (93). *Finnegans Wake*, because it exists in its formality and completeness both in and out of time, "is a symbol of eternity" (94).

The idea that Joyce forged vast and intricate symbolic forms out of his words and works becomes the key to Tindall's conclusions in *James Joyce*. Tindall sees symbols as a way of both knowing and giving shape to what we know. Since our greatest concerns and insights are often beyond the direct statement or simple analogue, we use symbols to represent "something too large, complex, unspeakable, or ideal for expression" (106). The only way for Joyce, who saw both correspondence and paradox everywhere, to express himself was as a symbolist, and the only way for the reader to know Joyce's work is by recognizing and understanding the symbols.

Dismissing the critical view of Joyce as a follower of the naturalist school of Zola, Tindall evokes the French symbolists as the literary pioneers who showed Joyce "ways of expressing what he wanted to express" (110). Mastering words and myth, the French symbolists scorned the imitation of nature and created symbols to suggest deeper insights into the nature of things. While no literary landscape is more solid or soiled with reality than Joyce's Dublin, his works construct "an elaborate structure of analogies, parallels, or correspondences" (113). Possessed of a "queer mind," Joyce approached life and art indirectly and expressed himself, at his best, through the literary methods of the symbolist.

Greatly admiring the symbolic systems of Dante and the symbolic power of Flaubert and Ibsen, Joyce developed his art from the symbolist indirection of *Chamber Music* and the aesthetics of *Stephen Hero* and *A Portrait* to the elaborate symbols of *Ulysses* and *Finnegans Wake*. Circling around the human failings of pride and guilt, *Ulysses* and the *Wake* are composed of their own symbolic structures that allow the reader to separate life from art, to gain the necessary distance for understanding and acceptance: "Reappearing in art, the horrors of life have become elements in a joyous, impersonal structure" (125). Tindall, who began his *James Joyce* with the remembrance of his innocent delight on first reading *Ulysses*, concludes his book with a vision of Joyce as the master symbolist, building an imaginary world that, while corresponding to reality, liberates the reader from desire and loathing so that he or she may join in the celebration of the human comedy. For Tindall, Joyce, recognizing comedy as the greatest of arts, embraced the comic spirit and wrote genial books "of brightness and gaiety" (125). Like Shaw, however, Joyce, writing in a desperate age, "was most serious and most profound when at his gayest. His humor is the proof of understanding and the sign of equanimity" (126).

Initial critical reaction to *James Joyce* anticipated Tindall's major influence on the reading of Joyce's work, especially among beginning readers. Reviewers found Tindall the ideal reader, genial and expert, of Joyce's most complex books, though they also expressed concern about his zealousness. Richard Kain, for example, thought Tindall had "the dexterity of the adept," but, placing Tindall in the hermetic school with Joseph Campbell, he also thought that *James Joyce* went too far in its search for correspondences: "At times the disciple seems to outdo the master in the quest for analogy."[2] Nathan Halper believed *James Joyce* to be among the best books on Joyce because of Tindall's "ear for feeling" and "eye for meaning."[3] He also praised Tindall for convincing his audience that although reading Joyce is hard work, it can be "lots of fun. Tindall shows us that the fun is worth the work."[4] Like Kain, Halper complained about Tindall's enthusiasm but saw the problem more in terms of Tindall's celebration of Joyce's humanity. For Halper, *James Joyce* emphasizes Joyce's affirming spirit to the extent that Tindall portrays Joyce as "the Artist as a Kindly, Sweet Old Man" while ignoring Joyce's "Nay to all that stifles life."[5]

The most interesting review of *James Joyce*, however, and the most insightful in recognizing the inevitable role Tindall was to play in Joyce scholarship, was written by Vivian Mercier. Not overly concerned with the enthusiasm in Tindall's search for Joyce's symbols or humanity, Mercier preferred to stress Tindall's admirable geniality. Unfortunately, in an age of academic specialization that divides the scholar and the gentleman, a critic "with no axe to grind" becomes vulnerable to those looking for something less openly personalized and generous in tone. Tindall "never attempts to crush the reader with the weight of his learning, nor forces upon him any particular theory, whether artistic, political, or scientific. It is almost certain that he will be branded as a gentleman."[6]

In the 1950s, with the publication of his edition of *Chamber Music* (1954) and *The Literary Symbol* (1955), Tindall reinforced his interpretation of Joyce with symbolic readings of the early lyrics, the short stories—especially "The Dead"—and *A Portrait of the Artist as a Young Man*. With *Forces in Modern British Literature* (1956), he added his portrait of Joyce as the ubiquitous figure in the symbolic landscape of modern literature. With Tindall now well traveled as a guide through Joyce's works, Marvin Magalaner and Richard Kain attempted to assess his contributions to the understanding of Joyce in *Joyce: The Man, the Work, the Reputation* (1956), their review of the critical patterns and tendencies in Joyce scholarship. They ranked Tindall with Hugh Kenner and Stuart Gilbert as one of the major contributors to the symbolic interpretation of Joyce's work and saw his view of a humane Joyce coalescing with those of Kain and Frank Budgen. They also claimed that the books by Tindall and Harry Levin were the "most completely documented studies of Joyce" and "his intellectual affinities."[7]

In their consideration of Tindall's distinctive role in Joyce criticism, Magalaner and Kain reminded their readers of Tindall's grassroots work in his graduate seminars—Magalaner had written his own dissertation in 1951 under Tindall's direction[8]—and "the intensive communal reading of *Finnegans Wake*" that "should be highly productive of future scholarship."[9] They also praised Tindall for remedying the lack of knowledge of the French symbolists' influence on Joyce and for insisting on the importance of the epiphany in understanding Joyce's early work. For Magalaner and Kain, Tindall's large influence and reputation rested, however, on his study of symbols, especially his development of the fullest document of the symbolic design of Joyce's art—though they restated Kain's complaint that Tindall went too far in searching for symbols and quoted from James Johnson Sweeney's review of *James Joyce*, in which Sweeney described Tindall as "a goodnatured, somewhat roly-poly puppy rushing now here for a sniff, now there."[10] Nevertheless, preferring Tindall's geniality and his sometimes overextended analysis, for which "Joyce is as much to blame as Tindall,"[11] to critical puffery and superficiality, Magalaner and Kain offered this early tribute to Tindall's contribution, especially with *James Joyce*, to the advancement of Joyce studies:

Professor Tindall begins his book on Joyce with the remark that the
works of this Irishman "compose an elaborate design." The distinctive
contribution of this critic to the understanding of Joyce is his ability to
point out insistently this pattern of development from work to work. There
is no trick to identifying the obvious extension of plot from *A Portrait* to
Ulysses, but to show wherein *Chamber Music*, let us say, and *Finnegans
Wake* are complementary jewels in the same general setting advances
considerably the student's appreciation of Joyce's literary labyrinth. . . .
Rescuing this design from the critical chaos that threatened permanently to
engulf it has been this critic's valuable and practical gift to readers of
Joyce.[12]

Tindall's practical role as guide for the reader of Joyce became even
more obvious and perhaps somewhat official with the publication in
1959 of *A Reader's Guide to James Joyce*. In the preface to *A Reader's
Guide*, Tindall reaffirms his belief, essential for a work of this nature,
that Joyce, a master of language, is difficult, demanding, but not impossible for the common reader. He also restates his general position on
Joyce's work—he "wrote one great work in several books"[13]—and Joyce's
humanity—his particular subject "became mankind everywhere at every
time" (ii).

Seeing his earlier *James Joyce* as general introduction to Joyce's world
and broad survey of his later works, Tindall describes his *Reader's
Guide* as a specific examination of all the major works and their key
parts. His "job," like that of the New Critic, is to point out details
and relationships within and between the texts. Not concerned with
Joyce the man, *A Reader's Guide* is "centered on the text" (ii). Nevertheless, Tindall also asks the reader to share in the puzzlement as well
as the attraction of studying Joyce, to join in "asking questions, hazard-
ing guesses, and, sometimes, when almost sure of something, announcing
it" (ii). For Tindall, great literature is inexhaustible, and therein lies
the fun. Rephrasing Mercier's earlier judgment of Tindall's eventual
contribution to Joyce studies, Tindall now judges himself in almost the
same terms: "Not as critic here, still less as scholar, I think of myself
as teacher" (ii). And for the teacher, as for Beckett's Moran, there is
nothing more delightful than studying a subject always beyond complete
understanding.

After expressing his gratitude for the help of other Joyceans, including
several former students, Tindall takes up *Dubliners*, *A Portrait*, *Exiles*,
Ulysses, and *Finnegans Wake* in chronological order. His approach to
Dubliners is story by story, whereas *A Portrait* and *Exiles* require a
broader stroke. *Ulysses* demands the most attention—Tindall's discussion fills more than one-third of the pages in *A Reader's Guide*—but

Finnegans Wake comes in for an annotated outline and a close reading of selected parts and passages.

No more than sketched in *James Joyce, Dubliners* receives a complete reading by Tindall in *A Reader's Guide*, including some scrupulous symbol hunting. He sets up his discussion by pointing to paralysis as Joyce's major theme and then preparing the reader for an understanding of the text as "moral censure, ambiguous portrait, and charitable vision" (6). The book's first level of interpretation distinguishes between misjudging *Dubliners* as didactic and correctly perceiving its moral intention of mirroring the failed life of its characters. Although Tindall states in the preface that he is not interested in looking for Joyce in the text, his second-level approach to *Dubliners* argues for an interpretation of it, especially its stories about adults, as "a collection of private horrors" (6) in which Joyce creates "Joyces who might have been" (6) had he remained in Dublin. Tindall's final view of *Dubliners* is similar in nature to his earlier interpretation of *Ulysses* and *Finnegans Wake*, in which he claimed that irony and affection lead to a hard but compassionate vision of modern man.

Once further establishing *Dubliners* as structurally determined by its characters' progressive ages from childhood to adulthood, its parody, preceding and anticipating *Ulysses*, of Homer's *Odyssey*, and its use of the seven deadly sins for analogy, Tindall makes it clear that his purpose in reading the stories is to make the case for Joyce's writing in *Dubliners* as symbolic rather than as naturalistic fiction. Tindall justifies his strategy by drawing support from Joyce's theory of epiphany as expounded by Stephen Dedalus in *Stephen Hero*: "Plainly Stephen's epiphany or radiance, a shining out or shining forth, is what we call symbolism and his radiant object a symbol" (10–11). And since Joyce had already developed his theory of epiphany by the time he was writing his *Dubliners*, Tindall finds it profitable to read each story "as a great epiphany and the container of little epiphanies, an epiphany of epiphanies" (11).

Once Tindall becomes intent on the text, he finds symbols in the key words "paralysis," "gnomon," and "simony" on the first page of "The Sisters;" "unassigned," or indefinite, symbols in Father Flynn and his sisters; and the story's epiphany in the boy's nightmare vision of the priest. "An Encounter" and "Araby," read on this level, join "The Sisters" as archetypal quests for God, Church, or "something at once theological, ecclesiastical, and moral" (19). Accordingly, Tindall interprets the stories of adolescents as aborted or failed journeys, while, beginning with Lenehan in "Two Gallants," seeing each adult character as "pitiless self-portrait" and "Joyce's own epiphany—or one of them" (25).

"The Boarding House" and "Counterparts," described, if not dismissed, as naturalistic by symbolist Tindall, are briefly sketched, but the remaining stories are closely scrutinized for symbolic devices, analogies, epiphanies, and even multiple epiphanies involving character, author, and reader. In "Clay" Maria becomes witch, Blessed Virgin, and Ireland on Joyce's eve of All Saints' Day. "A Painful Case," because it is the eleventh story in the collection, becomes the moment in *Dubliners* when the narrative, Joyce apparently having experienced an author's epiphany, becomes less mean and more understanding: "to Joyce, attentive to such matters, eleven was the number of renewal" (33). "Ivy Day in the Committee Room" brings forth Dublin's political epiphany; "A Mother," its cultural epiphany; and "Grace," with its Dantean analogies, Dublin's religious epiphany. After the three stories on public life, "The Dead," both climax and summary, brings all characters and correspondences to the Morkans' annual dance for a "triumph of dramatic impersonality and the radiance of 'distant' harmony" (48). More than this, "The Dead," concerned with "the conflict of pride with love, of ego with humanity," is also Joyce's "first major presentation of what obsessed him" and "not only the epitome of *Dubliners*, but a preface to *A Portrait*, *Exiles*, and *Ulysses*" (49).

In his chapter in *A Reader's Guide* on *A Portrait of the Artist as a Young Man*, Tindall places Joyce's autobiographical novel within the tradition of the *bildungsroman* and compares the book with other modern novels of adolescence or apprenticeship, including Samuel Butler's *Way of All Flesh*, D. H. Lawrence's *Sons and Lovers*, Somerset Maugham's *Of Human Bondage*, and Thomas Mann's *Magic Mountain*. Tindall's own interest, however, is more with the actual character of Stephen Dedalus and the conflict between Stephen's artistic temperament and his ordeals as child, adolescent, and young man. Although Stephen's reactions and perceptions are recorded impressionistically, the events or crises in his development determine the structure of *A Portrait*. Yet the economic, political, and moral horrors that paralyzed the characters in *Dubliners* affect the character of the artist differently: "Stephen, increasingly impatient with what has shaped him, resolves at last upon escape and exile. Unlike Eveline and Little Chandler, fellow creatures of Dublin, he has the enterprise to act on his resolve" (56).

Tindall's own judgment of Stephen Dedalus, however, is negative, in spite of Stephen's early struggles with Ireland and his determination to escape its nets. Pointing to the full title of the novel, Tindall sees Joyce's ironic distance from Stephen in the last chapter of *A Portrait* confirming that Aristotelian Stephen is very much a young man in actuality but qualifies as the artist only in potentiality. Joyce's irony exposes Stephen's moral failure, evident in his excessive pride, arrogance, and fears, and allows the perceptive reader to discover the fraudulence in Joyce's self-proclaimed artist: "Deceiving himself maybe and the simpler reader, he does not deceive ironic Joyce" (67–68).

While judging Stephen as a forger in the worst sense, Tindall does, however, read Stephen's fascination with signs, especially in the last two chapters, as an important clue to Joyce's own "method of correspondence, analogy or symbol" (82) and as reason enough for a symbol hunt through *A Portrait* that makes much of birds, water, roses, and other image clusters. Tindall also speculates on the relationship between Stephen's aesthetic theory and Joyce's own views on art—"we know that Stephen's aesthetic theory was Joyce's once" (95)—but concludes that theory serves Joyce to expose Stephen's "aloof humanity again" (96). Tindall further warns that critics who read anything more into the theory do so at the risk of assuming Stephen is Joyce and of becoming indifferent to the text.

Before returning to the fallen Stephen Dedalus in *Ulysses*, Tindall offers a brief comment on *Stephen Hero*—"a kind of footnote to *A Portrait* now" (101)—but a fuller discussion of *Exiles*, "one of the more difficult of Joyce's works" (104). For Tindall, Joyce's play is not dramatic enough, in spite of its well-made structure and its properly Ibsenian domestic problem, because Joyce did not achieve the objectivity with Richard Rowan that he had with Stephen Dedalus. Treating Rowan with seriousness rather than irony and humor, Joyce, perhaps too personally involved with the play's hero and theme, "failed to embody his insights and obsessions in an object for an audience, something standing by itself without the aid of notes or comment, on a stage" (115). Although admired by Joyce, *Exiles*, with its emotional uncertainties and heavy seriousness, "seems his most painful case" (115).

Disposing of *Exiles*, Tindall now goes to the heart of the matter in *A Reader's Guide*, his close reading of *Ulysses*. His approach is to reestablish the general view of *Ulysses* expressed in *James Joyce*, then take the reader through a chapter-by-chapter account, enhanced by an annotated listing of the more formidable allusions, of plot, theme, and method. The great theme of *Ulysses* "is moral" because "Joyce condemns pride, the greatest of sins, and commends charity, the greatest of virtues" (125). Joyce's narrative, in spite of its painstaking attention to the external details of a day in Dublin, creates a symbolist world through Homeric correspondences, numerous motifs, and recurrent images, and through its play on allusion, quotation, and symbolically charged language. Joyce also devised a special narrative technique to fit the perspective and concerns of each of the eighteen chapters. All that Joyce's book lacks then is a "wakeful reader with a past" (133) and perhaps a watchful guide who apprehends the radiant harmony of *Ulysses* and the humane vision of Joyce.

Tindall's jaunt through the chapters of *Ulysses* is as much a revelation of the attitude and style of the critic as it is an explication of the text. Using the Stuart Gilbert chart, Tindall fills in the narrative, stressing its parallel with the Son's search for and atonement with the Father, identifying the methods and arts of each episode, and adding copious notes. Yet, while fulfilling his responsibilities as reader's guide to the text, Tindall insists on sharing in the fun of reading *Ulysses*. He calls "Ithaca" his favorite chapter and finds Joyce's "reduction of humanity to inhumanity in a celebration of humanity is not only unexpected and amusing but a commentary on our times" (226). Rarely faulting Joyce for narrative excesses in *Ulysses*, Tindall does, however, admit his frustration with "Oxen of the Sun" and warns that in identifying parodies the reader may lose sight of the narrative. Frustration, however, is rarely a problem for Tindall, who clearly enjoys playing the reader's guide as he puzzles over allusions, riddles, and parables and delights in the richness and profundity of the book. This personal delight is nowhere more evident than in Tindall's offering of Molly Bloom to the reader of *Ulysses*:

> There great Molly lies, evading all habits and ideas, exceeding them. There she lies, an offering to Boylan, Bloom, and Stephen, and to our sensibilities. To understand her is to understand all, and to understand that, as the Frenchman said, is to forgive. I accept Molly as the American lady accepted the universe—and I should be a fool not to. Nevertheless, born on Depot Street, reared on Main Street, onetime scholar of two Sunday schools (one Episcopalian, the other Congregationalist), member of a poor but decent profession, I am glad not to be married to this embodiment of everything. Maybe everything is good for everybody, but, as the Englishman said, there can be too much of a good thing. (232)

Filled with the abundance of humanity in *Ulysses*, Tindall now turns his attention to *Finnegans Wake*. He begins with a comment on the self-reflexiveness of the text—"*Finnegans Wake* is about *Finnegans Wake*" (237)—that could warm the heart of the poststructuralist, just as his comments on Molly Bloom might well chill the soul of the feminist. Self-reflexiveness, however, becomes little more than a refrain for symbolist and morally minded Tindall, who takes the more encompassing view that the *Wake* "not only is but says" and that the book speaks "with understanding and compassion to our deepest concerns" (239).

Before beginning to read and understand the *Wake*, however, the reader, hears some practical advice from Tindall. He recommends a working knowledge of *Ulysses* as a prerequisite to the *Wake* and a minimum commitment of one hundred hours to a first reading of the text itself. He also urges the reader not to despair at the thought of becoming lost in the Wakean maze: "Enjoy what you can follow, and if you do not understand it all, be comforted; for you are one at last with all the scholars, one with all but Joyce, who understood everything, even himself" (263). The reading of the *Wake*, after all, is communal, an activity in which each new reader adds something to everyone's understanding of the book, while sharing in the general fun—and, considering its world of multiple puns, allusions, parallels, and correspondences, the *Wake* offers lots of fun to compensate for its difficulties and confusions.

Tindall's account, with annotations, of what happens in *Finnegans Wake*, though much briefer than his summary of *Ulysses*, is meant to provide an informed context, both general and specific, for the new reader. Acknowledging that no summary of the story in the *Wake* is sufficient for the reader's understanding of the text, Tindall presents his own as a starting point or "wave of the hand" (241) but also as a guard against "free-wheeling interpretation" (265). Borrowing heavily from Vico for headings of parts and chapters, Tindall walks or perhaps jogs with the reader through key fables and parodies, through games and homework, catalogs and signs, trials and inquest, only to discover that behind it all is the same old business of humanity at its best and worst, rising and falling through all time and space, merely as preparation for starting all over again. As for the poor reader, if he or she has any doubt or question about the guide's tour, then Tindall has the right advice: "Turn back to the first page, now, and see for yourself" (296).

With *A Reader's Guide to James Joyce*, Tindall marked a simple but clear path, which he would later widen with *A Reader's Guide to "Finnegans Wake"* (1969), through Joyce's major works. Whereas *James Joyce* introduced Joyce's world, *A Reader's Guide to James Joyce* takes the reader through the Joycean maze of words, symbols, and structures. Balancing a genial practicality and humor with an insistence on attention to the text and to the major influences on Joyce's work, Tindall wrote books with a general appeal and practical application for students of Joyce. With his sympathetic understanding of Joyce and his efforts to interpret Joyce's books as great symbolic texts, he also became a major voice in Joyce studies and a strong influence on Joyce scholars.

Once the Joyce industry moved into the productive 1960s, Tindall's contributions went through a period of respectful reappraisal. In "Joyce Scholarship in the 1960's," Thomas Staley ranked Tindall among the major contributors of the 1950s and stated that his criticism was still acknowledged.[14] This attitude of proper respect for Tindall's work but with a hint or suggestion of its temporary or superficial value is even more strongly reflected in Clive Hart's essay on *Wake* scholarship in *James Joyce Today* (1967). Hart acknowledged Tindall's annotated outline of the *Wake* in *A Reader's Guide* as "sane, amusing, commonsensical, and often illuminating, but of insufficient weight to oust the *Key* from its position in the mind of the average graduate student."[15] This view of Tindall, anticipated by Vivian Mercier in his review of *James Joyce*, was stated more clearly and critically by Staley, a decade later, in his essay on Joyce scholarship in *Anglo-Irish Literature: A Review of Research* (1976). Once again acknowledging Tindall's contributions in the 1950s, Staley nevertheless concluded that Tindall's "studies have been more popular with students than scholars, for his interpretations, while often clever and interesting, lack evaluative quality, placing nearly equal stress on both minor and major points—the stress being determined by the richness of symbolic dimensions rather than by their immediate importance within the fabric and structure of Joyce's work itself."[16]

Staley's judgment of Tindall's studies as large in influence but superficial in interpretation reflected a concern, expressed as early as the reviews of *James Joyce*, that Tindall's search for symbols lacked the balance, depth, and theoretical perspective necessary for it to have a permanent impact. The essays in *A Companion to Joyce Studies*[17], however, published several years after Staley's review of Joyce research, offered a different perspective by drawing attention to Tindall's major role in defining and establishing the key debates in Joyce scholarship. Chester Anderson, another former Tindall student, Morris Beja, James Carens, and Sidney Feshbach pointed out Tindall's guidance in opening the way for meaningful critical discussion of the lyrical arrangement in *Chamber Music*, of the epiphany in *Dubliners*, of Joyce's ironic detachment in *A Portrait*, and of the symbolic and archetypal patterns in *Ulysses* and *Finnegans Wake*. Rather than drawing attention to Tindall's limitations, Anderson and company preferred to remember Tindall as a worthy guide and genial companion for students and scholars.

With the shift from the "age of criticism" to the "age of theory" in Joyce studies,[18] Joyce scholars obviously have turned much of their attention to understanding and broadening the theoretical approach to Joyce's works. And this trend also means that practical criticism now seems out of key with a time that defines a close reading of the text quite differently from Tindall's earlier readings of Joyce. Yet Tindall's work in mapping out the territory for Joyce students and scholars has been of great service in giving the study of Joyce its early credibility. Even beyond the historical importance of Tindall's studies is the role readily accepted and played by Tindall. Perhaps more than any other Joyce critic, Tindall has been the understanding guide to Joyce for the beginning reader and the informed teacher for many students of Joyce. While current theoretical debates appear to range beyond Tindall's discoveries and gentle inquiries, students looking for plain talk and common sense will still find a helpful voice crying encouragement and pointing the way in his reader's guides.

NOTES

1. William York Tindall, *James Joyce: His Way of Interpreting the Modern World* (New York: Scribner's, 1950), 2. All additional references to this work are cited parenthetically in the text.

2. Richard M. Kain, "Mythic Mazes in *Finnegans Wake*," *Saturday Review of Literature* 33 (March 4, 1950): 19.

3. Nathan Halper, "The Anatomy of James Joyce," *New Republic* 122 (March 27, 1950): 19.

4. Ibid.

5. Ibid.

6. Vivian Mercier, untitled review, *Commonweal* 52 (June 2, 1950): 204.

7. Marvin Magalaner and Richard M. Kain, *Joyce: The Man, the Work, the Reputation* (New York: New York University Press, 1956), 149.

8. The following is a list of students who wrote their dissertations at Columbia University in the 1950s and 1960s on Joyce:

Marvin Magalaner, "James Joyce's *Dubliners*" (1951)

Robert Ryf, "A Study of James Joyce's *A Portrait of the Artist as a Young Man*" (1956)

Leonard Albert, "Joyce and the New Psychology" (1957)

Kevin Sullivan, "Joyce's Jesuit Schooling" (1957)

Virginia Moseley, "Joyce and the Bible" (1958)

Norman Silverstein, "Joyce's Circe Episode: Approaches to *Ulysses* through a Textual and Interpretative Study of Joyce's Fifteenth Chapter" (1960)

Philip Handler, "Joyce in France" (1961)

Richard Madtes, "A Textual and Critical Study of the 'Ithaca' Episode of James Joyce's *Ulysses*" (1961)

Chester Anderson, "*A Portrait of the Artist as a Young Man*, by James Joyce" (1962)

Avel Austin, "*Ulysses* and the Human Body" (1963)

Dounia Christiani, "Scandinavian Elements of *Finnegans Wake*" (1963)

Robert Hurley, "The Proteus Episode of James Joyce's *Ulysses*" (1963)

James Card, "A Textual and Cultural Study of the 'Penelope' Episode of James Joyce's *Ulysses*" (1964)

Edmund Epstein, "The Ordeal of Stephen Dedalus: The Father-Son Conflict and the Process of Maturing in James Joyce's *A Portrait of the Artist as a Young Man*" (1967)

Ulysses Keener, "Joyce's 'Scylla and Charybdis' " (1969)

Gordon Lameyer, "The Automystic and the Cultic Twalette: Spiritual and Spiritualistic Concerns in the Works of James Joyce" (1969)

9. Magalaner and Kain, *Joyce*, 252.

10. James Johnson Sweeney, "Out of the Joycean Maze," *The New York Times Book Review*, 19 Feb. 1950, p. 5; quoted in Magalaner and Kain, *Joyce*, 203.

11. Magalaner and Kain, *Joyce*, 203.

12. Ibid., 254.

13. William York Tindall, *A Reader's Guide to James Joyce* (New York: Noonday, 1959), i. All additional references to this work are cited parenthetically in the text.

14. Thomas F. Staley, "Joyce Scholarship in the 1960s," *Papers on English Language and Literature* 1 (Summer 1965): 279–86.

15. Clive Hart, "*Finnegans Wake* in Perspective," in *James Joyce Today: Essays on the Major Works*, ed. Thomas F. Staley (Bloomington: Indiana University Press, 1967), 141.

16. Thomas F. Staley, "James Joyce," in *Anglo-Irish Literature: A Review of Research*, ed. Richard J. Finneran (New York: Modern Language Association, 1976), 387.

17. Zack Bowen and James F. Caren, eds., *A Companion to Joyce Studies* (Westport, Conn.: Greenwood, 1984).

18. See Staley's remarks in his review of Joyce scholarship in "James Joyce," in *Recent Research on Anglo-Irish Writers*, ed. Richard J. Finneran (New York: Modern Language Association, 1983), 181–202.

Clive Hart

Frank Budgen and the Story of the Making of *Ulysses**

Frank Budgen was very much at home in the physical world, visually and tactilely sensitive, as plastic artists must be, to all that was going on around him and always keen to be physically in touch. The cosmos was, for Budgen, a real and solid place, and, although he was capable of extended abstract thought, it was never in abstraction that he wished to live. In these and in many other important respects he was Joyce's opposite. Joyce, too, savored the physical world, but he did so at something of a remove. Sinewy, though hardly tough, Joyce liked to have things done for him rather than to do them himself. Budgen was very much "the other." A man self-taught since the age of twelve provides a sharp contrast to a Jesuit-trained artist with a university degree. Temperamentally, too, there were great differences: Joyce disliked water, dogs, lightning; Budgen had been a sailor, loved and had a natural affinity for animals, was awed but not at all frightened by spectacular natural phenomena.

Budgen sometimes spoke of himself, deprecatingly, as having been a Shaun to Joyce's Shem, but the pattern was more complex than that; despite his awareness of Budgen's otherness, Joyce recognized that his friend could never be reduced to a simple antiself. For Budgen was also an artist, and an artist in a medium that Joyce never claimed to understand. That kind of otherness could not be written off as Joyce sometimes tried to write off the otherness of his brother Stanislaus. Budgen commanded

*This essay is a modified version of my introduction to the revised edition (1972) of Budgen's *James Joyce and the Making of "Ulysses"* (London: Oxford University Press, 1972). It is reprinted here by kind permission of Oxford University Press.

respect, and he did so not only because of the complete seriousness of his approach to his art but also because he was never in the least inclined to be subservient to Joyce. In Joyce he recognized a master of words, and this he admired and enjoyed. But, being self-taught, he belonged to no schools, had no time for cliques, cultural fashions, or critical movements, and was totally without affectation of any kind. For Budgen, James Joyce was not only Joyce the writer, to whose work one paid due homage, but also Joyce the man, with many faults as well as many virtues. Furthermore, Budgen, the self-taught man, had taught himself remarkably well. He had spent some years painting in Paris in the great days before World War I, and he was quite as much at home among writers and artists as was Joyce. He was a rare and interesting mixture of artist and practical man, in some respects a more complete person than Joyce could ever be.

Although Budgen was pleased to be of assistance to his sometimes purblind friend, he also had a very full life of his own to lead, and the idea of devoting himself almost body and soul to Joyce and Joyce's art, as Paul Léon was to do for a time, would have been wholly repugnant to him. It was partly because Budgen respected Joyce and was prepared to help, as one helps any intimate friend, but had no intention of being subjected to Joyce's will that Joyce found him so refreshing and valuable a person. Budgen had resilience and a kind of toughness that must have proved attractive to Joyce (also in his own way resilient) and that must have been still more highly prized in later years when Joyce was surrounded, as was so often the case, by yes-men. In addition, Budgen's attitude to the arts, though less experimental than Joyce's, less intellectual, was at bottom not so very dissimilar. The thought in Joyce's works was, by his own admission, always (or almost always) simple. His novels, though superficially avant-garde, were composed on a groundwork of accurate realism, both physical and psychological. In their fundamentals, *Ulysses* and even *Finnegans Wake* are artistically and aesthetically utterly unlike the dadaist, surrealist, *transitional*, revolution-of-the-word works that they sometimes superficially resemble. And because they are so positivist, so grounded in common sense and cause and effect, they are much more clearly understood in principle, if not always in detail, by a Frank Budgen than, for example, by a Eugene Jolas.

Among the visual artists, Budgen's heroes were, as he himself used to say, the impressionists, and he continued to paint in that now unfashionable mode until, in his last years, his eyes began to fail. His canvases, which are almost always full of light, are representational in a suggestive rather than a denotative way, and the best of them shimmer with multicolored sunshine and shadow. On the surface, they seem to have little to do with Joyce and his books, but both men, although going beyond simple representation, made it the essential structural basis of their work. As Budgen himself says at the end of "Further Recollections of James Joyce"

> When I met Mrs. Joyce in Zürich after the war, she told me that during the day preceding the sudden onset of his fatal seizure Joyce had been to an exhibition of French nineteenth-century painting. Somehow there seems to me to be an affinity there, I mean between French nineteenth-century painters and Joyce, in the sense that all the work of his imagination and intellect was rooted, as was theirs, in a natural sensibility.[1]

Neither Budgen nor Joyce had much patience with abstract art; neither of them was interested in automatic creativity, which short-circuits the connection between spirit and hand; each believed in the artistic value of hard work and the rational application of technique. (Budgen once said that he would like to be able to paint the way Brahms wrote symphonies.) But above all it was in their conception of the relationship between the artwork and the rest of the universe that they were alike: although their creations might depart from the day-to-day reality of ordinary people, they were rooted in it and ultimately responsible to it.

Bloom is preeminent in *Ulysses* not only as the most important center of consciousness, the most important character, but also as the bearer of the central values and the perceiver of the central percepts. He is near to being, as Joyce wanted him to be, "a complete man, a good man," and while *Ulysses* transcends him aesthetically, it celebrates him morally. Furthermore, although the art of *Ulysses* goes beyond anything of which Bloom could conceive, it is based on his own *Weltanschauung*. Among other things, this is, as Hugh Kenner has said, a novel of "cups and saucers, chairs and tables, sticks and stones,"[2] a novel in which the physical world, perceived as real through the simple act of knocking one's sconce against it, counts for a great deal. The moral and psychological problems of *Ulysses*, which are explored with such sensitivity, are the problems of men and women who live in, and respond to, a real, physical environment. Without that environment, the problems, and the characters, would simply fade away.

Budgen, a far more substantial figure than Bloom, did not share either Bloom's or Joyce's sexual obsessions, but, allowing for differences of scale and of important detail, Joyce could recognize in Budgen a man who understood the Blooms of the world from the inside. Again, whereas Joyce had managed to shake off the chains of a mighty religious organization and emerge into common life fairly unscathed, if necessarily conscious at all times of his Catholic background, Budgen had quietly slipped, with no great effort, from a sometimes fanatical but ultimately low-powered evangelicism that left him, for most of his life, an orthodox agnostic, indifferent to the claims of religion, though not disposed positively to deny the existence of a god—some god—and an afterlife. Budgen's personal disinterest and his natural respect for the spiritual and emotional value that belief may provide for others made him, once again, similar to the kindly, doubting Bloom. Indeed, Budgen might almost have been speaking of himself when, describing Bloom's reactions at the funeral, he wrote: "His mind is proof against the pathos of religion, but, seeing that some rite is necessary, as well this as another."[3]

Criticism of *Ulysses* over the first half-century and more of the novel's existence has shown that it can be all books to all men. Some read it as strenuously Catholic—a cry from a man eternally shut out; others see it as bitterly antireligious. For some, it is a celebration of the virtues of the bourgeois; for others, an indictment of urban civilization. Budgen's view of the general tenor of *Ulysses* was undoubtedly influenced by Joyce, who had consciously tempered his comments on the book to the personality and taste of his friend. Budgen reports:

> Joyce's first question when I had read a completed episode or when he had read out a passage of an uncompleted one was always: "How does Bloom strike you?"
>
> Technical considerations, problems of homeric correspondence, the chemistry of the human body, were secondary matters. If Bloom was first it was not that the others were unimportant but that, seen from the outside, they were not a problem. (106–7)

At other times and with other interlocutors, Joyce was capable of suggesting other emphases, but the version of the truth he both implicitly and explicitly conveyed to Budgen comes closest to the spirit of the book as I read it. Budgen concludes that the novel as a whole is amoral but accepting, contemplative but skeptical:

> It seems to me that Joyce neither hates nor loves, neither curses nor praises the world, but that he affirms it with a "Yes" as positive as that with which Marion Bloom affirms her prerogative on the last page. It is not to him a brave new world, about to set forth upon some hitherto unattempted enterprise. Rather is it a brave old world, for ever flowing like a river, ever seeming to change yet changing never. The prevailing attitude of *Ulysses* is a very humane scepticism—not of tried human values necessary at all times for social cohesion, but of all tendencies and systems whatsoever. There are moods of pity and grief in it, but the prevailing mood is humour. (73)

Budgen was able to adopt this point of view because he was content to let the book mean what it says. Although he was widely read in literature and philosophy of all kinds (more widely read, I believe, than Joyce), he was not disposed to treat *Ulysses* as allegory, to search for recondite meanings, to translate its plain sense into something else. Reading a book was for Frank Budgen both a simpler and a more arduous matter than that: he wanted to understand the surface. *James Joyce and the Making of "Ulysses"* was the first attempt to provide a reading of the novel in those direct terms, and it is still one of the very best. The length and complexity of *Ulysses* make the shaping of a complete commentary a singularly difficult matter. Budgen found for his book a most satisfying rhythm and structure, matching biography to criticism in a way that not only allows each to illuminate the other but shows their fundamental interdependence.

Joyce's response to Budgen's suggestion that he write the book is summed up by Budgen himself in the preface to the 1960 edition, reprinted in the revised Oxford text: "Joyce's attitude . . . changed from that of benevolent scepticism to one of enthusiastic approval. During my short stay in Paris he gave me many suggestions for improving and enriching my text and when I moved on to Ascona letters dictated to Paul Léon followed in the same strain. Some of these are incorporated in the text of the present book."[4] Despite its accuracy, this statement is insufficiently detailed to convey the full flavor of Joyce's participation in the writing. Though by far the greater part of the book stems from Budgen alone, in 1932 and 1933 Joyce sent sheet after sheet of suggestions which, when adopted, turned some parts of it into a collaborative effort.[5] In the beginning, it did not prove difficult to incorporate new material, but, as Budgen's book went to press, changes became increasingly troublesome to make. Joyce, who was merciless to publishers and printers, had no hesitation in suggesting that Budgen should act in the same way as he himself had done in 1921 when seeing *Ulysses* through Darantière's in Dijon. At the end of a sheet of suggestions called "les dernières des dernières," Paul Léon wrote, on Joyce's behalf: "Revise proofs: What you do not get in on the galleys you can add on the revise. He advises you to get in all these small points and if the expense exceeds the usual six shillings per sheet-page he will defray the cost himself but by cheque coming through you, so long as the publication is not retarded." The suggestions on that sheet, which Budgen incorporated, were followed by at least one further batch, headed "les Toutes dernières des Dernières (leaving only one other possibility which is les toutes dernières des toutes dernières)." Most of the material consists of additions to passages of local color, autobiographical details and corrections, and explanations of parts of "Work in Progress." Sometimes Joyce would simply list items under various rubrics without further comment, as he did, for example, on four sheets headed "Zurich Figures," written out for him by Lucia:[6]

Metzger Lenz. A more than Velasquez figure meat warrior. He occupied all the tram platform.

The King of Oil's daughter, born Edith Rockefeller, ill favoured, malsaine fantastic distinguished and benevolent, she stalked about the town distributing charities houses and jachts. Rossen [Rawson] taught her husband Mc Cormick to whistle the song it ain't gonna Waltza no more.

Oom Paul Of Niederdorf Ministre de la Grille, Dutch interior mais où sont les Bifteks D'Antan?

L'homme qui rit. He had a lion's mouth from ear to ear and walked about the bourse with a copious english newspaper held up to his face.

Budgen made use of these passages in various ways, toning down the aggressive description of the recently deceased Edith Rockefeller (and omitting altogether a sardonic marginal addition written by Joyce himself: "She is the daughter of one Rockefeller / Whose oil brought more death into our / World and much of our woe"):

> Mrs. MacCormick has a suite of rooms there. She is daughter of a king, an oil king, born Edith Rockefeller, and one of the richest women in the world.... Fantastic, distinguished, benevolent, she walks the town scattering right and left charities, houses and yachts.... Mr. Rawson, a friend of Joyce, taught Mr. MacCormick to whistle "It ain't gonna waltza no more."
>
> Here and there about the town one sees a tall bearded man of royal carriage. An exiled king? They are becoming common. No, a reigning monarch. His realm is called the "Meierei," a grill-room in Niederdorf.... His name is Oom Jan.... I heard with grief of the death of that great Dutchman. Où sont les bifteks d'antan?
>
> ... Butcher Lenz, in girth surpassing Velasquez's actor, takes up all the platform of a tram designed for five and a conductor. L'homme qui rit walks round the bourse with a copious English newspaper held up to his face. He has a lion's mouth that stretches from ear to ear. (28–9)

Joyce's suggestions fitted very effectively into Budgen's extended collage of Zürich life in wartime.

Most of Joyce's notes, although lively enough, are set down without noticeable intrusion of the linguistic experimentation and mythico-symbolic grotesquerie in which he was by 1933 so immersed. Occasionally, however, he indulged his love of wordplay, and in such cases Budgen used or discarded as seemed appropriate. Joyce's comment on the Zürich figure Sigmund Feilbogen, for example, is taken over only in part:

> *Sigmund Feilbogen* Ear trumpet which he oriented and occidented night and day to catch rumours of peace anywhere at any hour. The slings and arrows of outrageous fortune had hit him hard. Said to have lost his proffesorship in the higher school of Commerce in Vienna because his wife (Rubens type with one eye gone West) urged by female curiosity half

consumed the host the pope gave her in St. Peter's and then spat it into her handkerchief.

No doubt sensing that this colorful passage was not entirely in keeping with the tone of his context, Budgen reduced it to: "One time professor in the higher school of commerce in Vienna, Sigmund Feilbogen haunts the Café des Banques, with an eartrumpet which he orients and occidents night and day to catch rumours of peace anywhere at any hour" (29). "Orients and occidents" exemplifies a kind of wordplay that Budgen found natural to his own linguistic temper (potential nonposters of letters were warned against leaving them in "poche restante"). Frank Budgen was not, however, the sort of man to relish the last part of the story.

Where the tone was appropriate, Budgen was quite capable of using late Joycean methods himself. In the "dernières des dernières," Léon wrote to Budgen to say that Joyce had inquired about the motto of the city of Zürich:

> He wrote to prof Fehr for the arms and motto: ... The latin motto is: Nobile turricum multarum copia rerum. The version on the gate is phonetic: it means Noble Zürich abounding in all manner merchandise. Turricum for the Zuricher in war time meant only a boot polish and the abundance in merchandise could be worked in about the butter cards.

The passage about the butter cards occurs on page 31 of Budgen's book, but he chose, instead, to work in Joyce's suggestion at a point more convenient for the printer, in the last paragraph of chapter 2, where, like the Joyce of "Work in Progress," he leaves it to his reader to recognize the hidden allusion to the Zürich motto crowning his celebration of the city: "noble Turricum, in spite of rationing, abounded in all manner of goodly merchandise" (38).

Special mention should perhaps be made of the long set piece on women's underclothing on pp. 213–14. Although Budgen, looking on Bloom's obsessions with kindly interest but without involvement, could not share Joyce's intense concern with the paraphernalia of sex, he responded to a plea from Joyce, sent through Léon in a letter dated 30 March 1933: "As a personal favour he would like you when treating the subject of the Nausikaa episode to reconsider the way you have dealt with the mysteries of ladies' toilet and to remember that some words are too sacred to be either said or written." Joyce later repeated his request in a further letter, dated 7 May 1933.[7] The disquisition on underwear and Budgen's illustration for the Nausicaa episode, among those reproduced in the first edition of his book, were included as gestures of friendship.

As Budgen points out in "Further Recollections," he felt no obligation to accept those suggestions of Joyce's that were alien to his temperament. He made annotations on several of the note sheets indicating his opinion of the offerings. One of Joyce's notes, quoted in part in "Further Recollections," is headed "*BIRTH–NIGHT* chez J.J.": "We did not sing either the Wearing of the Green or And Shall Trelawney Die? in honour of our respective Irish and Cornish forebears . . . but the evening was sure to close with a rendering by Ruggiero and J. of the Greek National Anthem —Χάιρε, Χάιρε, 'Ελέυθερία (Hail Hail oh! Liberty!)." Against this this Budgen wrote, at various times, three notes: a bold "Left Out"; "Don't remember" (in "Further Recollections" he is more positive: "we didn't"); and "don't like quoting Greek." Under the heading "*TENOR*," Joyce, via Léon, writes about what is now *Finnegans Wake* 427.10–13:

> W i P Pt II sect. 1 and 2 contain frequent lyrical reminiscences of count MacCormack's voice. He is alluded to in J.J.'s letter to S published in the New Statesman as the tuning fork among tenors. W i P part I almost closes with a suspired rendering of the famous recitative E lucean le stelle by a pipe smoking Cavaradossi beginning: "And the stellas were shining" and breaking into the moving romance measure with the version: O dulcid dreamings languidous! Taboccoo!

In the margin of this illuminating paragraph Budgen, never a particularly musical man, adds the simple remark: "Can't write about music."

A great many of Joyce's suggestions concern, as this one does, his real love of the moment, "Work in Progress." Mentioning Chapelizod, which Budgen had recently visited at Joyce's suggestion, he invites Budgen "to work in actual names of persons there, from your visit"; he is particularly concerned with the Blake parallels, duly emphasized by Budgen toward the end of his last chapter; and there is one highly interesting passage about the fundamental principles of "Work in Progress" (paraphrased in "Further Recollections"):

> Yeats's defence & definition of magic: a) The borders of our minds are always shifting tending to become part of the universal mind b) The borders of our memory also shift and form part of universal memory c) This universal mind & memory can be evoked by symbols
>
> It should be pointed out that Mr. J. lived amidst all this (including Yeats) and his library was full of theosophicle works though he did not use any of the recognised symbols—using instead words trivial and quadrivial and local geographical allusions (Trivial meaning litterally—carrefour—where three roads meet).[8]

Some valuable remarks of Joyce's had to be omitted altogether from the book. Among the most interesting is a reference to Bloom's bath, in Lotus Eaters: "Does your reader realize what a unique event this was in the Dublin I knew up to 1904." Another refers to the *"King* v. *Humphrey"* sequence of "Work in Progress": "You say this is a difficult case [Budgen 307] but some years ago I read a court in India had to try a case of a hindu goddess (who was allowed to plead by proxy) versus Rabindranth [*sic*] Tagore."

Although Budgen's book is the only extended account of any part of Joyce's life written by someone who knew him intimately, in matters of detail it is not, and was never intended to be, everywhere literally true. Budgen himself gives a hint in his preface to the 1960 edition:

> With a number of false starts in front of me I began to wonder if Joyce's confidence in my original method of approach were not a little too optimistic. Then out of the fog I was moving in I saw emerging the shapes of a man, a book, a place, a time. I was able to begin at the beginning and my memory was set free. It is remarkable how much hindsight it takes to perceive the self-evident.[9]

Both the portrait of the man and the book as a whole are shaped by Budgen the artist. Time also, as he implies, is consciously shaped, molded, adapted to the overall design. *James Joyce and the Making of "Ulysses"* is a partly fictionalized biography, the general impression of which is as true as Budgen can make it, but the details of which are often manipulated in the interests of a greater truth—*Dichtung und Wahrheit*, in fact. Many, perhaps most, of the remembered conversations—"We were walking down the Rämistrasse when, the Uetliberg before us suggesting a giant, Joyce said . . . "—are worked up from comments in letters and note sheets. Budgen was not content merely to set down recollections of his day-to-day contacts with Joyce. Memory being fallible and fragmented, he deliberately fictionalized to approach truth indirectly.[10]

Joyce was well aware of the creative element in Budgen's book, and he was at pains to encourage its development. A decade earlier he had clearly recognized a parallel between Budgen and his hero, Ulysses. Budgen, absent from home for some years, had returned to London after the war; Joyce wrote to him on 10 December 1920:

> A point about Ulysses (Bloom). He romances about Ithaca (Oi want teh gow beck teh the Mawl Enn Rowd, s'elp me!) and when he gets back it gives him the pip. I mention this because you in your absence from England seemed to have forgotten the human atmosphere and I the atmospheric conditions of these zones.[11]

In 1933, Joyce continually urged Budgen, another Ulysses-Bloom, to include in his book more material about himself: "Speaking of the importance of the landscape more should be worked in about your art"; "Curtail quotations or insert short explanatory sentences less of J. more of yourself." And in a note about Shaun the Post he made the importance of the Budgen-*Ulysses* parallel explicit: "A passing allusion to your work in the GPO especially if you did any nightwork would not be amiss in this connection. The more bewildered the reader is as to whether you are painter, sculptor, civil servant, sailor, postman etc. the better as the same applies to Ulysses." Budgen's book retells the story of *Ulysses* just as *Ulysses* retells that of the *Odyssey;* it was written by a similarly accretive method, with last-minute changes, and the two characters who figure most prominently in it, Joyce and Budgen, are often shown leaving aside their real many-sidedness to play the roles of Stephen and Bloom.

That Budgen's book is such a happy mixture of clear-sighted exposition and sympathetic personal understanding is due mainly to the quality of the human relationship that he and Joyce were able to establish. With many people Joyce was, in minor ways, something of a poseur. As Budgen subtly indicates both in the scene of their first meeting and throughout the biographical passages, he was never taken in by the poses, which, except on rare occasions, Joyce seems wisely to have abandoned after the development of their intimacy. Although the most direct and unaffected of men, Budgen knew how difficult it is to attain complete sincerity and thorough self-knowledge. His comments about self-portraiture—the artist being condemned to paint himself in the act of painting himself, inevitably watching himself act to himself—contain some of the wisest things ever said, directly or by implication, about the relationship of writer to subject in Joyce's basically autobiographical art. But Budgen was more than the ideal commentator: he was, as Joyce realized, the successful embodiment of that desired fusion that never occurs in *Ulysses* —the spiritual marriage of Stephen and Bloom.

Entering the novel himself in conversation and in imagination, Budgen focused above all on its felt life. Although fully sensitive to its linguistic richness, he responded to it as, above all, a book about the concerns of living people. Many important aspects of *Ulysses*, not touched on in his study, have been explored with profit by others. Later generations of critics and readers have nevertheless always been well advised to temper their findings with the warm good sense of *James Joyce and the Making of "Ulysses."*

NOTES

1. Frank Budgen, "Further Recollections of James Joyce," *Partisan Review* 33 (1956): 366.

2. Hugh Kenner, "Homer's Sticks and Stones," *James Joyce Quarterly* 6 (1969): 298.

3. Frank Budgen, *James Joyce and the Making of "Ulysses,"* 1st ed.

(London: Grayson & Grayson, Ltd., 1934), 89. All additional references to this work are made parenthetically in the text.

4. Frank Budgen, *James Joyce and the Making of "Ulysses,"* 1st American ed., independently set (New York: Harrison Smith and Haas, 1934; reprint, Bloomington: Indiana University Press, 1960); rev. ed., (includes "other writings"), ed. Clive Hart (London: Oxford University Press, 1972), 5.

5. Joyce's note sheets, found among Budgen's papers after his death, are with one or two exceptions unpublished. In what follows, I have had space to quote only a small portion of the material. Except for a few words written by Joyce himself, everything was taken down by Lucia and Paul Léon at Joyce's dictation. Some of the notes are in the hands of the amanuenses; others, generally the more interesting, are in typescript. Many were annotated by Budgen as he worked on them, a few containing, in the margins, drafts of sentences for his book. Most of the note sheets are undated. They are quoted here by permission of the Trustees of the Estate of James Joyce.

6. The notes printed here reproduce the sometimes idiosyncratic spelling of the amanuenses.

7. Richard Ellmann, ed., *Letters of James Joyce*, vol. 3 (New York: Viking Press, 1966), 279–80.

8. Budgen, *Further Recollections*, 361.

9. Budgen, *James Joyce and the Making of "Ulysses,"* 1st American ed., 4.

10. In chapter 8 of *Myselves When Young* (London: Oxford University Press, 1971), Budgen includes other recollections of Joyce, generally more factual in character. In a book written so long after the deaths of Joyce and Nora, Budgen felt able to deal with certain aspects of Joyce's life and personality in a more direct manner than would have been possible in 1934.

11. Stuart Gilbert, ed., *Letters of James Joyce*, vol. 1 (New York: Viking Press, 1957), 152.

Melvin J. Friedman

Ellmann on Joyce

Time that with this strange excuse
Pardoned Kipling and his views,
And will pardon Paul Claudel,
Pardons him for writing well.

(W. H. Auden, "In Memory of W. B. Yeats")

In 1969 a dispirited Irving Howe, unhappy with Carlos Baker's *Ernest Hemingway: A Life Story*, made this observation: "During the past few decades, when our professors have been composing a large number of Definitive Lives, often on the premise that truth is a by-blow of bulk, we have had only one major work in this genre, Richard Ellmann's *James Joyce*, a book endlessly pleasing for its ability to evoke the spiritual history of a great novelist without slipping into pedantry or cozy sentimentalism."[1]

Katherine Frank, in assessing the generic possibilities of literary biography, couples Ellmann's *James Joyce* with Leon Edel's *Henry James* as "two of the greatest modern biographies."[2] She locates "the distinctive voice of Richard Ellmann" and finds that "the success of *James Joyce*, for all its thematic acuteness and historical breadth and soundness, derives from this voice" (502).

Such statements suggest that *James Joyce* occupies a position in the history of modern literary biography corresponding to the place of Erich Auerbach's *Mimesis* in the history of modern literary criticism and theory. Ellmann's "voice" as a biographer-critic and Auerbach's "voice" as an unerring reader of texts seem to have determined the contours for two types of literary discourse. The ambition of both enterprises is stunning, Ellmann's perhaps in a less obvious way than Auerbach's. *Mimesis* closely examines texts from Homer and the Old Testament through Virginia Woolf, whereas *James Joyce* treats a single literary life — but one that engaged and refashioned many of the texts Auerbach discusses. Ellmann charts the circuitous course that the "myth-hopping" Joyce (words he later used in *Ulysses on the Liffey*) took as he wandered across the literary terrain from Greek antiquity to French symbolist expression. To sound the litany of Joyce's sources and forebears, from Homer and Aristotle down to Dujardin and Mallarmé, passing by Dante, Vico, Goethe, Flaubert, Tolstoy, and Ibsen, is to engage in something quite as elaborate as Auerbach's schema.[3] Yet neither Ellmann nor Auerbach limits himself to a single method, neither falls victim to a single approach. Ellmann, for example, is quite aware of the seductions offered a biographer by Freud, but unlike Leon Edel "in his search for the figure under the carpet" (Frank 501), he keeps a respectful distance. Ellmann, in fact, concludes his "Freud and Literary Biography" somewhat equivocally: "That Freud makes biography difficult does not mean that he should be put aside. Biographers need a depth psychology, and Freud, with his followers and deviationists, offers one. . . . Perhaps we should be gingerly in applying Freud's theories, for it is when they are most ostentatious that they awaken the most uneasiness. . . . For all this Freud remains a model, though no doubt a tricky one."[4] Auerbach also eschews any kind of narrowing critical persuasion. Thus he remarks in his epilogue:

> The method of textual interpretation gives the interpreter a certain leeway. He can choose and emphasize as he pleases. It must naturally be possible to find what he claims in the text. My interpretations are no doubt guided by a specific purpose. Yet this purpose assumed form only as I went along, playing as it were with my texts, and for long stretches of my way I have been guided only by the texts themselves.[5]

Indeed, "the texts themselves" seem to be what matter to both Ellmann and Auerbach, who seduce their readers through the clarity and elegance of their language and devotion to literary study rather than through any kind of ostentatious, doctrinaire theorizing.

Katherine Frank rightly points out that *James Joyce* was published "before the recent flurry of biographical criticism" (501). It is a work conceived, as she indicates, before biography "lost its critical innocence" (499). Ellmann brought out *James Joyce* in 1959, a year after his edition of Stanislaus Joyce's *My Brother's Keeper*.[6] It began the second phase of his scholarly career, which brought him from Yeats to Joyce. Not only did the Joyce biography win the National Book Award, but it kept attracting the adjective "definitive," a word that survived into Walter Goodman's obituary of Ellmann in the May 14, 1987, *New York Times:* " . . . his 1959 biography that is considered the definitive work on the Irish novelist. . . "[7]

This time of "critical innocence" about the nature of biographical art was also one of relative scholarly innocence about Joyce's work. The early, seminal criticism of Harry Levin, William York Tindall, Hugh Kenner, and Richard M. Kain was already in place, but the scholarly paraphernalia was still awaiting the editorial skills of Richard Ellmann, Robert Scholes, Richard M. Kain, David Hayman, Phillip Herring, Michael Groden, and Hans Walter Gabler, among others. *James Joyce* appeared at that restless moment in Joyce commentary when the early critical soundings were about to give way to more substantial and sophisticated scholarship. Many of the works that passed for scholarship before Ellmann's biography were "authorized" and even orchestrated by Joyce himself, including *Our Exagmination round His Factification for Incamination of Work in Progress* (1929), Stuart Gilbert's *James Joyce's "Ulysses"* (1930), Frank Budgen's *James Joyce and the Making of "Ulysses"* (1934), and Herbert Gorman's *James Joyce* (1939). Stuart Gilbert's 1957 edition of the letters was the last of the works that seemed to carry Joyce's own signature of approval.

Ellmann's biography removed many of the cobwebs that were accumulating about the life and the work, especially those placed there by Gorman's *James Joyce.* The final sentences of Ellmann's introduction express with clarity and eloquence what he is about:

> Implicit in his work there is a new notion of greatness, greatness not as an effulgence but as a burrowing that occasionally reaches the surface of speech or action. This kind of greatness can be perceived in his life, too, though camouflaged by frailties. To be narrow, peculiar, and irresponsible, and at the same time all-encompassing, relentless, and grand, is Joyce's style of greatness, a style as difficult, but ultimately as rewarding, as that of *Finnegans Wake.* [8]

Ellmann's is emphatically a "critical biography" in that it mixes life with letters in a most intriguing and original way. There is no formula for what he has done. Details of the life play off commentary on the work in a kind of seamless fashion; one tends to reinforce the other at every turn. As Katherine Frank remarked, it is the "voice" of Ellmann that gives shape to his biographical-critical enterprise, rather than any theoretical predispositions.

Ellmann is faithful to chronology. On each left-hand page are the inclusive dates of the chapter, on each right-hand page Joyce's age. The critic in Ellmann occasionally takes over for the biographer, with something of an entr'acte effect. Such a sustained critical interlude occurs when Ellmann abandons his narrative and offers twenty-five incisive pages on *Ulysses* (see chapter 22, 367–390). Richard D. Altick interestingly explains Ellmann's rhythm on this occasion:

> He described the origins of *Ulysses'* characters, places, and events in the order in which Joyce encountered them as a child and young man. Then, having reached the year 1914, Ellmann stopped the film and in a retrospective chapter reran the reels with a different filter, this time drawing out from the chaos of events a leading theme previously undiscussed: Joyce's artistic development, the emergence of peculiarities of technique which were destined to make *Ulysses* so revolutionary a work of fiction, and the slow formation of an over-all plan for the book. Once Joyce was seen to be prepared for the great work of his life, Ellmann resumed the narrative and watched the author putting his long-meditated plans into execution.[9]

Ellmann simply does not conform to what Leon Edel called, writing of *James Joyce* and two other biographies, "the old-fashioned Victorian chronological manner." Ellmann's own critical urgencies break in on the narrative, unsettling, even undercutting, its forward movement, giving *James Joyce* a secure place among works that Edel classifies as "the more experimental kinds of biography in our century."[10]

To look more closely at Ellmann's chapter 22, which is not what one usually expects from "old-fashioned Victorian" biography, is to see relatively few biographical details and a great many critical insights. Ellmann discusses such matters of technique as Joyce's use of interior monologue (inspired by Dujardin, George Moore, Tolstoy, and Stanislaus's journal), his flirtation with literary counterpoint, his positing of "undependable narrators," his blurring of the line separating fact and fiction. He also discusses characters, sources, themes, and events in convincing and vigorous new ways. The significance of Homer, Dante, and Shakespeare to Joyce's enterprise is given fresh emphasis. Ellmann moves back and forth through the oeuvre, showing how *Ulysses* profits from earlier Joycean techniques and anticipates those of *Finnegans Wake*. Chapter 22, in breathtaking, telegraphic fashion, offers a showcase for the biographer's critical skills. It has firm ties to Ellmann's two more recent Joyce books, *Ulysses on the Liffey* (1972) and *The Consciousness of Joyce* (1977).

In these two later studies, Ellmann fleshes out matters he could only suggest in *James Joyce*. The patterning of *Ulysses*, with its "triadic organization" (space/time/space-time), resulting in six sections of three chapters each, is the basis of Ellmann's schema in *Ulysses on the Liffey*. Homer is made to wrestle with Aristotle and David Hume for ascendancy, as Ellmann rarely restricts his discussion to Odyssean parallels. Indeed, he finds help from an enormous number of literary texts, both ancient and modern, insisting on the importance of *The Divine Comedy, Faust, Candide*, and the *Argonautica* of Apollonius of Rhodes, among many other works, in illuminating various sections of *Ulysses. Ulysses on the Liffey*, a short book of barely two hundred pages, has something of the large lines and epic sweep of Auerbach's *Mimesis*. Ellmann proves, finally, how textually complex *Ulysses* is by mounting evidence of the staggering number of literary and mythical echoes sounded in its pages — a contribution of the same order as David Hayman's justly applauded theory of the arranger in *"Ulysses": The Mechanics of Meaning*.

The Consciousness of Joyce is more directly concerned with sources and scrupulously lists in an appendix the contents of Joyce's Trieste library. While Ellmann's critical gifts are effectively displayed in *Ulysses on the Liffey*, his scholarship is a dominant presence in his 1977 study. Commenting on the labors involved in assembling the appendix, Michael Patrick Gillespie remarked: "While often the task must have seemed daunting, scholars familiar with the list have already testified to the merit of Ellmann's work. As researchers develop the information on Joyce's intellectual background, the debt to Ellmann's industry will continue to grow."[11] *The Consciousness of Joyce* also has the usual Ellmann finesse; many passages such as the following display his accustomed pacing, his assurance of the critical act: "Joyce felt more than most writers how interconnected literature is, how to press one button is to press them all. He exhibits none of that anxiety of influence which Harold Bloom has recently attributed to modern writers. Yeats said, 'Talk to me of originality and I will turn upon you with rage.' If Joyce had any anxiety, it was over not incorporating influences enough."[12] The tidy juxtapositions, the elegance of phrasing make for vintage Ellmann. Goethe joins the triumvirate of Homer, Dante, and Shakespeare as being essential to Joyce's enterprise in *Ulysses*. While the German writer is mentioned only in passing in the Joyce biography, he plays a crucial role in *The Consciousness of Joyce*. For example, Ellmann points out that the likely source for Leopold Bloom's taking the name Henry Flower in his epistolary exchanges with Martha Clifford is Faust's taking on the name Heinrich in his relationship with Gretchen.

While the *Ulysses* criticism offered in *James Joyce* is especially notable, Ellmann "reran the reels with a different filter" on two earlier occasions (chapters 15 and 18) with discussions of "The Dead" and *A Portrait of the Artist as a Young Man*. In addition to these set pieces,

there are critical insights sprinkled throughout the narrative—on virtually every page—so many as to overwhelm the casual reader of biography.
The biographer as critic, a role Ellmann is comfortable with, is in no
sense a given. Even though many biographers have also written criticism,
there is no assurance of the coupling of the two. Carlos Baker speaks to
this point in the foreword to his *Ernest Hemingway: A Life Story:*
"Again, although the present work offers a substantial amount of
information about the origin, development, and reception of [Heming-
way's] writings, it is not what is commonly called a 'critical biography,' in which the biographer seeks to explore, analyze, and evaluate
the full range of his subject's literary output simultaneously with the
record of his life."[13] The opposed tendency was expressed by Joseph
Frank in the preface to his *Dostoevsky:* "I sketch in the background
of the events of Dostoevsky's private existence, but I deal at length
only with those aspects of his quotidian experience which seem to
me to have some critical relevance—only with those that help to cast
some light on his books. . . . I do not go from the life to the work, but
rather the other way round."[14] Ellmann's position is somewhere between
Baker's and Frank's, although it tilts in Frank's direction. The difference
between Ellmann and Joseph Frank is that the Joyce biography starts
with the life (actually the prelife, with a chapter entitled "The Family
Before Joyce"), which is allowed free rein in determining the contours
of the enterprise. The life and the work are securely tied together when-
ever possible, but the life story seems to preempt everything, even
(to the despair of a number of reviewers) the details of his creative
process.[15]

If glimpses of Joyce's workshop are offered at oblique angles, one still
comes away from *James Joyce* with a precise sense of how his talent
matured. Ellmann is careful to show how the "epiphanies" Joyce wrote
between 1900 and 1903 offered the beginnings of a career conceived in
the shadows of the French symbolist prose poem. He observes the opening out and gradual thickening of the texture as the works gain in
complexity and assume new experimental possibilities. But Ellmann never
really makes the claim that the historian David Donald made in the
preface of his *Look Homeward: A Life of Thomas Wolfe:* "But chiefly
this book is a study of the creative process, the story of Thomas Wolfe's
evolution as a writer."[16] This is a surprising emphasis for a historian,
but Donald does manage to discredit the widely circulating image of
Wolfe as a "literary naif" and a "Bunyanesque epic singer" in favor of the
image of a more conscious writer aware of the problems of his craft. But
he is not able to offer new readings of Wolfe's fiction, as Ellmann does
with Joyce.

Most literary biographers use the words "life" or "biography" in their subtitles. Witness, for example, Virginia Spencer Carr's *The Lonely Hunter: A Biography of Carson McCullers*, Deirdre Bair's *Samuel Beckett: A Biography*, Joan Givner's *Katherine Anne Porter: A Life*, Matthew Bruccoli's *Some Sort of Epic Grandeur: The Life of F. Scott Fitzgerald*, Joseph Blotner's *Faulkner: A Biography*, Baker's *Ernest Hemingway: A Life Story*, and Donald's *Look Homeward: A Life of Thomas Wolfe*. Ellmann uses neither of these words; in fact, he does not offer a subtitle. None of the above books, not even Donald's, is in any real sense a critical biography. Analysis of the work is usually kept to a minimum; when offered it often tends to be naive—most notably in the case of Bair.[17] The life is, fittingly, of supreme importance in all of these biographies. But so is it in *James Joyce*, despite the fact that there is no subtitle to call attention to it.

A number of the above biographies have been criticized for being mainly inventories of their subjects' "laundry lists." George Steiner, for example, saw in Baker "an interminable record of Hemingway's 'life story' while leaving out all that matters."[18] Even Ellmann's least sympathetic reviewers shy away from that kind of condemnation. Ellmann's biographical voice never seems to permit the accumulation of monotonous detail. It is always hard at work introducing surprising juxtapositions, making incisive comparisons. The first meeting with Yeats, for example, is described as follows:

> Their meeting has a symbolic significance in modern literature, like the meeting of Heine and Goethe. The defected Protestant confronted the defected Catholic, the landless landlord met the shiftless tenant. Yeats, fresh from London, made one in a cluster of writers whom Joyce would never know, while Joyce knew the limbs and bowels of a city of which Yeats knew well only the head. The world of the petty bourgeois, which is the world of *Ulysses* and the world in which Joyce grew up, was for Yeats something to be abjured. Joyce had the same contempt for both the ignorant peasantry and the snobbish aristocracy that Yeats idealized. The two were divided by upbringing and predilection (104).

The details are more figural than literal. Another biographer might have accumulated more conventional information but ended with a far less suggestive vignette.

Ellmann's method seems to thrive on juxtaposition. He often manages his balancing technique in a single sentence: "Before Ibsen's letter Joyce was an Irishman; after it he was a European" (78). When Joyce arrives in Rome at the beginning of chapter 14, another nod is made in the direction of the Norwegian playwright: "Forty-two years before, Ibsen had whiled away a period of exile in Rome thinking about Norway, and Ibsen's example was still one to which Joyce attended. But Ibsen, secure with his small pension, could afford to debate with friends whether it was better to become an office clerk or to swallow the latch key and die of starvation. Joyce, like T. S. Eliot after him, chose to be a clerk" (232). Ellmann provides a number of juxtapositions that involve the brothers. One of the most persuasive occurs at the end of part 3: "It is easy to see that James was a difficult older brother, yet Stanislaus was a difficult younger one. If James was casual and capricious, Stanislaus was punctilious and overbearing. James knew his laxity of behavior to be an appearance he could, in sudden tautness, brush aside; Stanislaus knew his own self-discipline to be largely a revolt against his brother's faults" (496). A Flaubertian tableau is presented when master and disciple are brought together. Although Joyce appears with remarkable frequency in her Beckett biography, Deirdre Bair never approaches the subtlety of the following: "Beckett was addicted to silences, and so was Joyce; they engaged in conversations which consisted often of silences directed towards each other, both suffused with sadness, Beckett mostly for the world, Joyce mostly for himself. Joyce sat in his habitual posture, legs crossed, toe of the upper leg under the instep of the lower; Beckett, also tall and slender, fell into the same gesture" (661).[19] The modern and postmodern perform on stage together.

Ideally, any grammar or poetics of biography should stress the need for the kind of juxtaposed portraits one finds throughout *James Joyce*. As the narrative moves through time, Ellmann seems to know precisely when to introduce a spatial countermovement. Time suddenly stops as elements are placed side by side as in a painting. The insistent piling up of information, which makes for such tedious going in so many literary biographies, is never allowed, for Ellmann applies tight artistic controls. Joyce never goes it alone for very long: Ellmann's "comparative" technique brings him in close proximity with every variety of family member, friend, and fellow writer along the fifty-nine-year biographical way. One can add to the Joyce-Yeats, Joyce-Ibsen, Joyce-Stanislaus, and Joyce-Beckett vignettes quoted above Joyce-Pound, Joyce-Gogarty, Joyce-Svevo, and Joyce-Paul Léon tableaux, among many others.

Horace's famous sideswipe at Homer, "quandoque bonus dormitat Homerus," could appropriately be quoted here; indeed, even the good Richard Ellmann sometimes nodded. Reviewers of both editions of *James Joyce* were quick to point out omissions and lapses. Some felt Ellmann leaned too heavily on Stanislaus's view of matters, resulting in an undeservedly harsh view of Joyce. The attempt to make life and letters converge too neatly unsettled certain critics. These positions are usually responsibly supported, often by people who otherwise admired Ellmann's labors.[20] But it must have been almost impossible not to nod when faced with an undertaking of this size. Ellmann surely earned the right to what Phillip Herring aptly labeled "biographical license" (Herring 115). Ellmann perhaps foresaw the possibility of such license when he suggested that "the form of biography, then, is countenancing experiments comparable to those of the novel and poem."[21] Indeed the pacing and design of *James Joyce* have more than once prompted critics to suggest a kinship with the novel, the literary form that occupied much of Ellmann's attention during his Joyce years.

Ellmann's failures seem insignificant, finally, when measured against the vastness of his enterprise.[22] Joyceans and literary biographers have benefited incalculably from his labors. Herring began the final paragraph of his Ellmann essay with this telling sentence: "Criticizing Ellmann's biography of Joyce, as some of us have done, can hardly dent its greatness, for we are like a few small mice nibbling around a royal wedding cake" (Herring 126). Even his most unforgiving critics must pardon him for writing well.

Richard Ellmann died May 13, 1987, at the age of 69.[23] He had something of a triadic career, which seemed to touch down invariably on Irish soil, as he moved from Yeats to Joyce to Wilde. His last major gesture was to complete his Oscar Wilde biography. He was as good a biographer, critic, and editor as anyone of his generation.[24]

NOTES

1. Irving Howe, "The Wounds of All Generations," *Harper's Magazine*, May 1969, p. 96.

2. Katherine Frank, "Writing Lives: Theory and Practice in Literary Biography," *Genre* 13 (Winter 1980): 500. Subsequent references will be included parenthetically.

3. Ellmann, in a sense, starts the task in *James Joyce* and completes it in such elegant studies as *Ulysses on the Liffey, The Consciousness of Joyce,* a series of prefaces and introductions, and scattered essays. These critical writings serve almost as addenda to the Joyce biography.

4. Richard Ellmann, "Freud and Literary Biography," *American Scholar* 53 (Autumn 1984): 478. See also his "Literary Biography," in *Golden Codgers: Biographical Speculations* (London: Oxford University Press, 1973), 1–16.

5. Erich Auerbach, *Mimesis: The Representation of Reality in Western Literature,* trans. Willard R. Trask (Princeton: Princeton University Press, 1953), 556.

6. See my review of *My Brother's Keeper*, "Out of his Brother's Shadow," *The New Republic,* February 10, 1958, pp. 18–20.

7. A less than laudatory review of the second edition of *James Joyce* by Hugh Kenner carries the title "The Impertinence of Being Definitive," *Times Literary Supplement*, December 17, 1982, pp. 1383–1384. Phillip Herring, in discussing Kenner's review and other matters pertinent to my present labors, speaks of "the advertised definitiveness of *James Joyce*"; see "Richard Ellmann's *James Joyce*" in *The Biographer's Art*, ed. Jeffrey Meyers (London: Macmillan, 1988), 116. Subsequent references to this work are included parenthetically. I am indebted to Herring for allowing me to see this material in manuscript. See also my "Joyce's Life," *The Progressive*, December 1959, pp. 49–50.

8. Richard Ellmann, *James Joyce* (New York: Oxford University Press, 1959), 5. I refer to the first edition of *James Joyce* throughout my essay because of the time period specified for this collection. References are made parenthetically in the text. Reviewers of the 1982 second edition generally agreed that the additions and alterations were not earthshaking. Philip Gaskell, for example, remarked that "this method of producing *JJ* II has not altered the tenor and conclusions of Ellmann's biography in important ways" (*Essays in Criticism* 33 [July 1983]: 253). Denis Donoghue concurred: "Indeed, the revision is pretty light. Ellmann has retained the old structure, and has inserted the new stuff at appropriate points" (*London Review of Books*, September 20–October 3, 1984, p. 15). The one clear advantage of the second edition, as many reviewers have remarked, is Mary Reynolds's scrupulously detailed index. The three sentences quoted in my text, by the way, remain intact in the new edition.

9. Richard D. Altick, *Lives and Letters: A History of Literary Biography in England and America* (New York: Alfred A. Knopf, 1965), 381.

10. Leon Edel, *Writing Lives: Principia Biographica* (New York: Norton, 1984), 185. See also Ira Bruce Nadel, *Biography: Fiction, Fact and Form* (London: Macmillan, 1984), especially 173–74.

11. Michael Patrick Gillespie, *James Joyce's Trieste Library: A Catalogue of Materials at the Harry Ransom Humanities Research Center at the University of Texas at Austin* (Austin, Texas: Harry Ransom Humanities Research Center, the University of Texas, 1986), 12.

12. Richard Ellmann, *The Consciousness of Joyce* (Toronto and New York: Oxford University Press, 1977), 47–48.

13. Carlos Baker, *Ernest Hemingway: A Life Story* (New York: Bantam, 1970), 5.

14. Joseph Frank, *Dostoevsky: The Seeds of Revolt, 1821–1849* (Princeton: Princeton University Press, 1976), xii. Ellmann is fondly acknowledged, by the way, in Frank's preface.

15. Phillip Herring raised this point in his "Richard Ellmann's *James Joyce*" when discussing the second edition: "It does not seem too much to ask that a revised biography of one of the century's greatest writers reveal more about his creative process," especially in light of *The James Joyce Archive*'s appearing in sixty-three volumes several years before 1982 (124).

16. David Herbert Donald, *Look Homeward: A Life of Thomas Wolfe* (Boston and Toronto: Little, Brown, 1987), xvi–xvii.

17. See, for example, Ellmann's review of Bair's *Samuel Beckett: A Biography* in the June 15, 1978, *New York Review of Books*. He found little good to say about it. He shakes his head sadly at "that continuous slight distortion which Miss Bair performs on Beckett in the absence of interpretation. With so amorphous a conception of him, the biography often seems to be a collection of learned gossip."

18. George Steiner, "Across the River and Into the Trees," *The New Yorker*, September 13, 1969, p. 147.

19. See my "Beckett's Life Story," *Contemporary Literature* 20 (Summer 1979): 377–85.

20. Only two of the reviews I have seen appear irresponsibly out of line: Marshall McLuhan's in the Summer 1961 *Renascence* and the unsigned "The Master Builder" in *The Times Literary Supplement* for November 20, 1959. Phrases like "deep misunderstanding of Joyce" and "Ellmann's naive misconceptions are so accessible and startling" are typical of McLuhan's response. *The Times Literary Supplement* reviewer felt that "the grandeur is somehow absent from Mr. Ellmann's record," "his method prevents him from emphasizing anything," and "something . . . appears to have slipped through his fingers."

21. Richard Ellmann, *Golden Codgers*, 15.

22. One oddity that might be pointed out is that in the first edition of *James Joyce*, Ellmann gives as the source of Stephen Dedalus's "Silence, exile, and cunning" Balzac's *Splendeurs et misères des courtisanes* (365). In the appropriate note he offers his authority: "Stuart Gilbert kindly brought this passage to my attention" (786). In the second edition, the source becomes another Balzac novel, *Le Médecin de campagne* (354). The note this time reads as follows: "Stuart Gilbert kindly brought this passage to my attention. See B. Guyon, *La Création littéraire chez Balzac* (Paris, 1951), 66–76" (777). The change from one Balzac novel to another is never explained.

23. See the excellent appreciative piece by Steven Serafin, "Richard Ellmann," in DLB Yearbook 1987, *Dictionary of Literary Biography* (Detroit: Gale, 1988), pp. 226–230.

24. See *Essays for Richard Ellmann: Ommium Gatherum*, ed. Susan Dick, Declan Kiberd, Douglas McMillan, and Joseph Ronsley (Kingston: McGill-Queen's University Press, 1989).

Michael Patrick Gillespie

Kenner on Joyce

> No, assuredly, they are not justified, those gloompourers
> who grouse that letters have never been quite their old
> selves again since that weird weekday in bleak Janiveer
> (yet how palmy date in a waste's oasis!) when to the
> shock of both, Biddy Doran looked at literature (*FW*
> 112.23–27).
>
> Modernism, la la. Yet it once had brave days.[1]

The diversity of James Joyce's writing, the variety of critical approaches that this multiplicity engenders, and the range of insightful responses that numerous readers have articulated make it presumptuous to single out any individual as the preeminent force shaping the study of Joyce's canon. Nonetheless, one might argue that over the last three decades few critics have surpassed Hugh Kenner in the broad influence he has consistently exerted on the general perception of Joyce's works. Even those scholars who reject Kenner's interpretations would agree that the volume of his critical output, his felicity for combining accessibility and sophistication, and the pronounced impact of his views on the thinking of so many other readers make it inevitable that anyone with more than a passing interest in Joyce must also develop an abiding sense of Kenner's canon.

Despite the invariability of the topic and the consistency of Kenner's idiosyncratic style, such a survey stands as anything but predictable or repetitive. Since the publication of *Dublin's Joyce* in 1955, readers have shared Kenner's perspective on Joyce and other stoic comedians (Flaubert and Beckett), become attuned to the full range of Joyce's voices that he discerned, and learned to cast with him a more discerning (if not colder) eye on the "usylessly unreadable Blue Book of Eccles." Few of us have failed to be engaged by these studies, for Kenner's interpretations have always been provocative.[2] At the same time, I do not mean to imply that Kenner's eminence rests merely on cleverness, for throughout his career, intellectual sophistication and critical durability have characterized his work. Over a period roughly corresponding to the length of Joyce's public life, Kenner has consistently produced interpretive responses that go beyond specific illumination to the creation of an ethos for reading that serves as a useful guide to any scholar, whatever his or her particular theoretical predilections. Nonetheless, Kenner's first book-length study of Joyce retains its prominent critical position, for the ideas expressed in *Dublin's Joyce* have so permeated the study of the central figure of modern English literature that for many of us Dublin's Joyce and Kenner's Joyce have become synonymous concepts.

How has this come about? Certainly not through the single-minded pursuit of dogmatic interpretive approaches. Kenner received his critical training at Yale under the tutelage of Cleanth Brooks, and Kenner's close readings repeatedly call to mind the best elements of New Criticism. At the same time, his inclination toward an eclectic historicism repeatedly and determinedly violates the New Critic's presumption of textual integrity. Kenner, in fact, regularly fills his readings with the sort of sociological interpolations and connections initially perceivable only by a mind fascinated with the cultural counterpoint underlying any piece of literature. Kenner's interest in intellectual diversity has placed formulations relating to the consciousness of the artist at the center of his criticism. Nonetheless, allusions to Freud and Jung appear only as historical markers, and serious references to more recent psychoanalytic commentators like Lacan simply do not occur. This by no means reflects a mind dominated by provincial intellectualism and hostile to unconventional methods of perception. Indeed, long before writers like Jacques Derrida called into question traditional linear critical responses, Kenner had been deconstructing Joyce's works. Yet in doing so, he has resolutely avoided the linguistic accouterments adopted by many of the most outspoken proponents of poststructuralism. For that matter, none of the elements making up Kenner's critical personality seems to fit the easy categorization we enjoy applying to leading figures in our field, yet he relentlessly engages our interest and our concern.

Such openness, ingenuity, and accessibility have enabled *Dublin's Joyce*, despite its position as one of the oldest studies of that author, to remain one of the most vibrant and compelling. Many of the views originally presented there by Kenner have become so familiar and are used with such frequency that younger scholars are often unaware of their origin. Other issues first raised in Kenner's study remain the focus of vigorous debate in current Joyce scholarship, yet in few instances do subsequent approaches develop the complexities of these cruxes with greater erudition or sensitivity. Thomas F. Staley, in his detailed survey of major Joyce criticism for *Anglo-Irish Literature,* has commented specifically on the effect produced by the Kenner methodology. He characterizes *Dublin's Joyce* as "a springboard from which several controversies arose. . . . Little that has subsequently been written on Stephen Dedalus fails to take into account some aspect of Kenner's arguments."[3] (Staley underscores his point by emphasizing the signal impact of Kenner's examination of how irony functions in Joyce's writing.) Perhaps most significantly, however, the repeated citation of the book in contemporary scholarship attests to its continuing function as one of the best introductions to the canon still available.

This comes about through an approach reflecting Kenner's admiration for the polymath, making him at once both a delight and a frustration to read. His famous (or notorious) digressions turn each essay into a bravura performance. Deceptively short paragraphs introduce sinuous extrapolations that produce precisely refined readings of specific passages and broad generalization regarding the intellectual process associated with them. His mannerisms madden linear-minded thinkers seeking reductive interpretations of complex ideas, even as they stand as a seductive trap for epigones too eager to emulate his style without the substantive support of his learning.

Perhaps few people who listen to Kenner's public lectures or who read his criticism ever associate this approach to letters with that of Oscar Wilde, but the parallel seems a useful one for explaining, in part at least, Kenner's impact as an intellectual. Like Wilde, Kenner delights in making prose, especially academic prose, a medium for extravagant (but never superfluous) expostulation and in assaulting the complacency of his listeners/readers through paradox. Like any critic, he presents his views with a specific agenda in mind, but unlike most, he does not succumb to the temptation of assuming a didactic rhetorical stance. Rather, Kenner repeatedly affirms the multiplicity inherent in the work of a great author by articulating an overtly idiosyncratic response to Joyce while implicitly inviting us to take up whatever of his views interest us and to develop them in any manner that we choose. He does, of course, present a clear account of the central features of Joyce's writing and of the problems facing anyone seeking to form an intelligent response to any of the works, but at the same time he offers readers the stimulus to develop their own reactions in directions that he himself has not chosen to pursue.

The reader derives this sense of freedom to modify Kenner's views directly from the form of the work. Kenner shapes his study in a style that comes closer to the casual commentary of a bellelettrist indulging the possibilities of intellectual play than to the convoluted and constricted delineations of a pedant seeking to enforce the scholarly certitude of sterile literary criticism.

> Only Dublin had kept its past above the waters; evading the cataclysmic mutation of the Romantic revolt, it had chosen to preserve its form rather than its life. And a man born into that Dublin, exhorted to admire the image of old buildings in the stream, might seek instead to seize the once-living City. Quickened by barroom voices and enraged by the drinkers' opacity, aroused by the civic traditions and exasperated by their street-walking ghosts, loving his city's leisure and hating the lethargy of the living who cut him off from life, such a man—James Joyce, over fifty years ago, at the pivot of an age—would find himself simultaneously citizen and exile.[4]

The grace of Kenner's style, however, can lead the undiscriminating reader to oversimplify the issues he presents. Although his tone exudes an aura of confidence tempting one to elide speculations and facts, the very essence of his method inverts received opinions to develop independent thinking.

This impulse becomes a recurring aspect of Kenner's examination of Joyce's artistic development. It appears most overtly in the chronicling of Joyce's struggle to assuage his own anxiety of influence long before the other Bloom coined the term. Singling out the Citizen from the Cyclops chapter of *Ulysses*, for example, Kenner outlines intellectual idiosyncrasies that might apply to all of Joyce's Dubliners.

> He speaks the language that is given him and entertains the corresponding ideas. No Dubliner acts from his nature, no Dubliner knows what his nature is; he acts on the promptings of *idées recues* and talks in words that have for too long been respoken. Yet the words and actions can partake of a passion it would be difficult to call factitious; human spirits are imprisoned in these husks. Cadence and image crackle with continual racy unexpected-ness, though phrase and action are drearily conventional. (10)

Kenner finds this same inclination shaping Joyce's own process of compo-sition and devotes a great deal of attention to tracing its effect throughout the canon.

As a consequence, Kenner structures much of his study as a direct response to the demands of such a psyche, developed in Joyce's mind and embodied in the characters of his writings. Chapters of *Dublin's Joyce* consistently begin with evocations of historical presence and then pro-ceed in an eclectic, but not aimless, exploration of the forces at work in

Joyce's artistic ambience. To set the scene for full-length examinations of the fiction, Kenner first discusses the impact on Joyce's consciousness of works by writers such as Verlaine, Ben Jonson, Dante, and W. B. Yeats. Through this effort to come to grips with the artistic and intellectual features of Joyce's sensibilities, Kenner struggles with the same influences that Joyce did. Furthermore, he reminds us that we, whether we are conscious of their presence, must struggle with them as well. In Kenner's vision, Joyce measured himself against his artistic predecessors in much the same manner that we now gauge his achievement through analogous associations. In this way, *Dublin's Joyce* stands as a paean to the modernist impulse Kenner twits so playfully in the quotation from *A Starchamber Quiry* that serves as an epigraph for this essay. The implicit paradox works so well because Kenner presents Joyce's canon as an ever-oscillating series of cyclical constrictions and dilations, acutely aware of the influences from which it derives much of its cogency, yet determinedly assertive of its independence.

Instances of seminal criticism abound in each of Kenner's examinations of Joyce's individual works, and despite the subsequent familiarity that these views have achieved, seeing them in context revives a sense of the exhilaration that they imparted to their original readers. An inevitable part of the excitement that one derives from *Dublin's Joyce* lies, then, in the virtuosity of Kenner's critical approach, which never slips into predictable patterns or plodding methodology. His consideration of *Dubliners*, for example, begins with one of the earliest and still most enlightening textual studies of the stories. It moves easily into an archetypal approach, offering what has become the standard outline of the collection's structure—its division into stories of childhood, adolescence, adulthood, and public life. And it ends with a close reading of "The Dead" that remains the basis (often unacknowledged) for countless lectures given by instructors first introducing undergraduates to these stories. Despite all this, however, more than any single conclusion that Kenner presents in the chapter, his format underscores the flexibility open to readers of Joyce, and despite the authority of his own interpretation, it invites extrapolation and diversification.

Less familiar but equally striking evidence of Kenner's critical abilities appears in his examination of Joyce's only extant play, *Exiles*. Many scholars have declined to comment on the drama, for they see it as a problematic, even embarrassing, element in the canon, a work more profitably ignored than explicated. Kenner, on the other hand, has offered a probing analysis that calls attention to its significant place in the evolution of Joyce's artistic consciousness. By developing his concept of Joyce's struggle to attain independence from the creative influences of his youth, Kenner highlights the role of *Exiles* as the final stage of Joyce's transition from emerging artist to mature craftsman. "*Exiles* frees Joyce from Ibsen the undernourished doctrinaire whose 'wayward, boyish' pseudo-rigours of revolt had for some years compromised a portion of his spirit" (69). The play remains imperfect in Kenner's estimation, but its flaws—like the volitional errors of Stephen Dedalus's man of genius—stand out as "the portals of discovery" (*U* 9.229).

Many of Kenner's comments on the play directly illustrate features of his criticism that other students of Joyce have come to see as either the strongest or the weakest aspects of the argument of *Dublin's Joyce*. To maintain a chronology reinforcing the view of *Exiles* as the final transition piece, Kenner relegates *A Portrait of the Artist as a Young Man* to the position of a work associated with Joyce's still-developing artistic sensibilities. His own generally unsympathetic assessment of Stephen (modified in subsequent studies) abets this, and it allows Kenner to emphasize the impact of Ibsen on that novel while pointing out the gradual dimunition of this influence through *Exiles*.

> In the five chapters of *A Portrait of the Artist as a Young Man* Joyce rewrote the five acts of *Brand* in a civic perspective Ibsen knew nothing about. It is from Brand (the name means both "sword" and "fire") that many of the most humourlessly arrogant gestures of Stephen Dedalus are derived. (81)
>
> Exile is [Joyce's] invariable destination as it was for Ibsen. In writing this play Joyce clarified and purged this motive among his many motives for leaving Dublin. In explicating the plight of Richard Rowan, *Exiles* became Joyce's abolition of the last shreds of Stephen. (82)

Other readers have judiciously resisted this view of Stephen. Nonetheless, Kenner's skill at underscoring Joyce's sophisticated treatment of the play's underlying issues enriches any subsequent reading of the drama.

> Richard's way of neither swearing nor expecting eternal fidelity surrounds himself and Bertha with the constant demands of a moral reality too strong for men. We have neither angelic wisdom nor angelic supplies of energy; we cannot live forever on the passionate *qui vivre*; to be neither encouraged nor forbidden at every point is the condition not of human liberty but of human paralysis. Richard rapt himself and Bertha out of a community of paralytics, only to immerse himself and her in a paralysis still more naked; hence the dead stop to which *Exiles* grinds. The guidance of a habitual communal order is not an evasion but a human necessity. (87)

Kenner's Joyce, like Kenner himself, is suspicious of the modernist's inclination to brush aside as irrelevant the weight of social institutions: one might disparage the family, the Church, or the State, but it would never do to ignore their shaping impact on the individual's consciousness. (Prior to writing *Dublin's Joyce*, Kenner had published separate studies of G. K. Chesterton and Wyndham Lewis, each, through his own idiosyncratic expression, representing the antithesis of the modernist view of the world.) At the same time, as a good student of modernism, Kenner cannot escape a fascination for the psyche of the individual artist. Indeed, much more of *Dublin's Joyce* is about Joyce per se than about his works. In writing about Joyce, Kenner set out to master the world in which he existed. Paradoxically, the resulting observations do not represent a regressive form of interpretation; instead, they reflect an approach free of the prescriptive conclusions impelled by too close an adherence to the labels of literary history. "There was a lyric, epic, and dramatic progression not only in writing about Dublin but in experiencing Dublin. Neither himself nor Dublin was his subject, but himself encountering Dublin which was his other self; between lyric and drama the stress shifts from 'self' to 'other'" (98).

In such a passage Kenner's methods apply neither simple historicism nor crude psychoanalysis. Rather, his descriptions of the artistic milieu approach the canon from a perspective aware of its own biases but unencumbered by the imperatives of a specific dogma. Consequently, it raises questions that remain as pertinent to a contemporary poststructural reading as they were to his own interpretation. Even when he most overtly exercises his New Critical tendencies, it would be a mistake to dismiss Kenner's methodology or his findings as anachronistic. Like the best of the recent critical approaches, Kenner's methods remind one of the power inherent in words and of the power inherent in the reader's signification. Nowhere is this more ably demonstrated than in the book's most anthologized chapter, "The *Portrait* in Perspective."

Kenner's reading anatomizes Joyce's first published novel. Simultaneously, by linking *Portrait* to the other works within the canon, Kenner comments on the developing range of Joyce's artistic sensibilities. This critical gesture typifies Kenner's methodology. He places before the reader an articulate rendition of his own complex response to *Portrait*, but he also provides ample opportunities for generating alternative interpretations. The following passage is representative of the way that Kenner offers his views throughout the chapter: "Stephen does not, as the careless reader may suppose, become an artist by rejecting church and country. Stephen does not become an artist at all. Country, church, and mission are an inextricable unity, and in rejecting the two that seem to hamper him, he rejects also the one on which he has set his heart" (121). Although many readers will resist Kenner's conclusion (and perhaps bristle at the term "careless"), thoughtful critics will welcome the opportunity to come to grips with Kenner's observation. Time and again in this chapter, and indeed throughout his book, Kenner's argument does not simply serve to advance his own views about Joyce's writings; rather, it makes us more aware of our own. In doing so, Kenner sets an agenda for scholarly debate still current in studies of Joyce's canon.

In this fashion, *Dublin's Joyce* testifies to Kenner's early demonstration of his formidable critical abilities. One simply cannot read it and remain unimpressed by the sheer volume of information that he adduces from his research. Without benefit of Richard Ellmann's exhaustive biography and with only limited access to select archival material (now readily available to general readers through *The James Joyce Archive*), Kenner draws an amazing amount of convincing evidence from the material at his disposal.

Kenner no doubt derives a portion of his success from an intellectual background that parallels Joyce's own: a Catholicism deeply influenced by Thomistic thought. This enables him—"[s]teeled in the school of old Aquinas"—to articulate significant aspects of the social repertoire informing Joyce's writing that are often overlooked by today's readers.[5] This context remains an essential feature of Kenner's perception of Joyce's writing, yet it by no means relegates his response to a marginal commentary. In fact, this specific sense of the influence that the philosophy of St. Thomas Aquinas must have had on the Catholic education of Joyce allows Kenner to assault Cartesian thinking from a perspective opposite that of deconstructionists but as fully effective and illuminating. "Ultimately, for Joyce, all the 'meanings' are *in Dublin*; ultimately, for the reader, they are all *on the page*. A complex *integritas* has been seized and transferred. Things are not talked about, they happen in the prose" (153, Kenner's emphasis). In consequence, Kenner can reaffirm the basis of Joyce's aesthetic assumptions for a secular world unfamiliar with the scholasticism from which he emerged, and he can simultaneously invite the post–Vatican II mind to elaborate on the implications of this retrospective (re)arrangement.

In addition to sharing with Joyce a common Catholic background, Kenner possesses the same brand of intellectual playfulness, combining boundless curiosity with an irreverence for received ideas. Such an openness demonstrates implicit affinities with contemporary theories of reader response and with current gestures toward a methodology of phenomenological interpretation. In no instance, however, does any approach calcify into dogmatism, for he continually implies that the act of interpretation is much too important to be taken seriously. In summarizing the ethos of *Ulysses*, for example, he comes quite close to articulating the invitation to freeplay (without its deconstructivist connotations) implicit in his own work.

> It is essential to the total effect of *Ulysses* that it should seem to be the artifact of a mind essentially like Bloom's, only less easily deflected; a mind that loses nothing, penetrates nothing, and has a category for everything; the mind that at length epiphanizes itself in the catechism of "Ithaca" (it seems never to have been asked whether it is Joyce *in propria persona* who is asking and answering these droning questions, and if not, what are the implications for the rest of the book). (167)

It is perhaps in *Ulysses*, the repository of Joyce's encyclopedic accumulation of trivia more accessible than *Finnegans Wake*, that the strengths of Kenner's critical approach become most evident. Again like Joyce, Kenner is slow to discount any element of a literary work as insignificant, for he has a finely cultivated sense of possibility and an abiding awareness of the subjectivity (and hence provisionality) of any reader's response. This orientation allows Kenner to rescue putatively banal and mundane elements from obscurity and to recuperate for other readers their significance in Joyce's writing.

Since Stuart Gilbert's pioneering study of *Ulysses*, most critics have acknowledged the novel's Homeric elements as a donnée and then have generally forgotten them. Kenner, however, develops these echoings as more than simple analogues. "The Homeric substructure has been either haggled over in detail, or brushed aside as a nuisance, by readers settling down, cutlery in hand, to a slab of bleeding realism. That the fundamental correspondence is not between incident and incident, but between situation and situation, has never gotten into the critical tradition" (181). For Kenner, Homer stands as a benchmark, "constantly applied in a critical mode," for measuring the narrative strategies of the novel, and the metadiscursive nature of the *Odyssey* becomes both a justification and a goad for Joyce's own efforts. "The moment we stop thinking of Homer's sweaty and quarrelsome Achaeans as unrelaxing heroic posturers, much comes into focus" (193).

All this is not to say that contemporary readers will find themselves completely sympathetic to the view of *Ulysses* presented in *Dublin's Joyce*. The title of chapter twelve, for example—"How to Read *Ulysses*"—suggests that, at this point at least, Kenner has succumbed to a prescriptiveness that belongs to a critical era markedly different from the present one. Yet, as in all of Kenner's writing, despite a tone exuding confidence in the accuracy of his own observations, the approach he outlines leaves ample opportunity for the reader to extemporize. In noting that "Dublin is being presented in a hundred simultaneous perspectives" (198), Kenner in effect acknowledges the inevitability that any given reader will select only a fraction of them to form a text from the novel. In short, in presenting his own view of *Ulysses*, Kenner at the same time legitimizes a range of alternative readings. This stands as a key feature of Kenner's writing throughout *Dublin's Joyce:* he maintains a delicate dialogic balance between the cogency of his own views and the validity of numerous other possible responses.

Some readers might object, with justification, to the apparent narrowness of Kenner's apparently New Critical delineation of the novel's structure—irony juxtaposed with naturalism. One can, with too little trouble, find examples of interpretive digressions in which archness replaces insight and credulity is strained to fit the overriding thesis. Nonetheless, within the limits of his argument, Kenner repeatedly demonstrates his skill as a reader, and through his observations, if not his conclusions, he draws attention to the presence of a wide range of potential interpretations perfectly compatible with poststructural thinking. His sense of the consciousness of Leopold Bloom, for example, deftly outlines the basic elements that still form the starting point for any assessment of that character's nature. "Bloom's discourse . . . coagulates into aphorism. Mottos are conned. Reflection seldom goes a sentence beyond observation" (216). Although his subsequent distinctions between Ciceronian and Senecan philosophers may no longer engage the attentions of other critics, the summation of the Dublin ambience in such metaphors remains a valuable contribution to the scholarship of the book.

Kenner's criticism seems at its best when it moves between precise explications of minute narrative details that most readers elide into their general view of the work and broad generalizations that rarely fail to provoke the reader to respond. It is this dual grasp of arcane knowledge and complex intellectual propositions that accounts for Kenner's broad appeal. When he moves into the middle area of interpretation, articulating his own specific readings of particular episodes, a number of otherwise sympathetic readers will become restive. A clear instance of this occurs in his discussion of the schemata for *Ulysses*, first published in Stuart Gilbert's *James Joyce's "Ulysses,"* as a basis for delineating the basic structure of the book.[6] Kenner's remarks provide a clear outline of the novel's makeup, but the uniform treatment of each aspect of the schemata leads to a rather prescriptive tendency that those not in sympathy with his methodology will find restrictive.

Although he has referred to it selectively throughout his study, Kenner devotes the final section of *Dublin's Joyce* to an examination of *Finnegans Wake.* In many ways, Kenner's approach remains as fresh and engaging today as when he first wrote it, for this analysis effectively combines the strongest features of his interpretive abilities. Rather than offer yet another plot summation (daring as that might seem in light of the novel's convolutions), Kenner teases out the significance of specific elements, giving remarkably fine readings of certain passages and demonstrating with grace and erudition the pleasures inherent in Joyce's final work.

The topics that Kenner chooses to dwell on are nothing if not adventurous. For example, although writing *Dublin's Joyce* in an intellectual climate heavy with discourses punctuated by truncated Freudianisms, Kenner examines the relationship between the author and his father without invoking the impedimenta of psychoanalysis. His views on the son's perception of John Stanislaus Joyce's Dublin enhance one's sense of much of the interplay of paternal imagery without limiting it to the prescriptive interpretations imposed by Freudian criticism.

In an analogous gesture, Kenner applies the same strategy of exploring influence without demanding the primacy of his particular interpretation when he views the impact of the writings of Lewis Carroll on the structure of *Finnegans Wake*.

> All the symbols of the nineteenth century turn up in Dodgson's life with wonderful literalness. Not only did he send his heroine through the looking-glass, but the mirror-girls, innocent and vampire, flit through his biography. Alice Liddell, gentle daughter of the lexicographer, to whom *Wonderland* was dedicated, was supplanted in Dodgson's affections by the emotionally precocious Isa Bowman, who played the part on the stage. Joyce transferred Dodgson's ambivalent relations with Isa to the *Wake* almost unaltered, as HCE's incestuous infatuations with his daughter Iseult. (288)

Throughout this examination, Kenner notes points at which Joyce courted imaginative and emotional convergence. As he does in his discussion of Joyce's father, Kenner introduces significant interpretive possibilities without entangling his argument in predetermined conclusions.

For many scholars of the *Wake* reluctant to undertake a reading of *The New Science*, (*La scienza nuova*), Kenner's greatest contribution remains his discussion of the relation of the writings of Vico to Joyce's final work. "Vico's great insight was that the materials of history, if not its directions, are of human origin. The sphere has two poles; myths, languages, customs, events, may meet in the Logos; but they also meet in the human mind. And the human mind is accessible to investigation, the Logos to speculation only" (329). Kenner builds on the two concepts that he has emphasized throughout his study—the importance to Joyce of philosophical perceptions of the world and the significance of the social ethos from which he emerged—to underscore the conjunctive impact of Vico's influence on the structure of *Finnegans Wake*.[7]

Despite these achievements, the final section of the study becomes, in a *Wake*-like gesture, increasingly fragmented. Although Kenner provides interesting analogues between the composition of the Catholic mass and the framework of *Ulysses*, his commentary on *Finnegans Wake* more often provides discrete insights than overarching interpretations. In the final analysis, that may be the most useful way to deal with the book, but this approach leaves the disconcerting impression that Kenner was gradually losing interest in the topic and stopped abruptly rather than continue searching for the proper voice.

Nonetheless, one should not allow the closing pages of *Dublin's Joyce* to exert undue influence over a response to the entire study. Since its publication Kenner's book has been the starting point for any sophisticated examination of the canon of James Joyce. It places before the reader the considered observations of one of the finest American critics now living, observations that in many cases have become critical commonplaces in Joyce studies. It traces a range of issues central to the comprehension of Joyce and of modernism, and it foregrounds broader questions of epistemology that still concern readers. Although one may feel the temptation to dismiss a study written three decades ago as obsolete or to laud it as a precious object to be revered but no longer consulted, an approach that is more intellectually honest and in the end more rewarding is to take on *Dublin's Joyce* on the same terms under which it was offered over thirty years ago. From this perspective, it remains a vital piece of criticism, as capable of providing insight and of stimulating further response as it was when it first appeared.

NOTES

1. Hugh Kenner, "Notes toward an Anatomy of 'Modernism'," in *A Starchamber Quiry: A James Joyce Centennial Volume, 1882–1982*, ed. E. L. Epstein (New York and London: Methuen, 1982), 3.

2. See, for example, Phillip F. Herring's *Joyce's Uncertainty Principle* (Princeton: Princeton University Press, 1987), 5–6, 37.

3. Thomas F. Staley, "James Joyce," in *Anglo-Irish Literature: A Review of Research*, ed. Richard J. Finneran (New York: Modern Language Association, 1976), 388.

4. Hugh Kenner, *Dublin's Joyce* (1956; reprint, Boston: Beacon Press, 1962), 3. All subsequent quotations are from this edition, and citations appear parenthetically in the body of the essay.

5. James Joyce, "The Holy Office," in *The Essential James Joyce*, ed. Harry Levin (Harmondsworth: Penguin Books Ltd., 1963), 348.

6. Stuart Gilbert, *James Joyce's "Ulysses"* (1930; reprint, New York: Vintage Books, 1955), 30.

7. A recently published study of *Finnegans Wake* provides the first detailed examination of *The New Science* that significantly departs from the views offered in *Dublin's Joyce*. See John Bishop's *Joyce's Book of the Dark*

(Madison: University of Wisconsin Press, 1986). Nonetheless, it is likely that Kenner's approach will continue to exert a profound influence on students of the *Wake*.

Thomas F. Staley

Religious Elements and Thomistic Encounters: Noon on Joyce and Aquinas

From the beginning, students of Joyce have puzzled over what can be called collectively the religious aspects of his art and life: the deeply embedded Jesuit strain, the Scholastic disposition of his thought, the contorted Roman Catholic conscience, the ambivalent spiritual affinity with and simultaneous rebellion against the Roman Catholic church. These elements of Joyce's life and art engage critics not simply because they appear as themes and subjects of his work—which is reason enough to study them—but because Joyce also makes the inseparable connection between aesthetics and religion. Throughout his work, there is a constant discussion of the concept of art, its creation, gestation, and execution— the role of the artist as begetter of the Word. Joyce's art, which is so self-conscious and so absorbed in the process of its own procedures, inevitably draws our attention to those elements that form the basis of his own aesthetic inquiry throughout his works.

But it is not simply on this basis of aesthetic discussion that the religious elements have compelled inquiry. Joyce's work, by reference, discussion, or abuse consistently calls into question the dogma and *magisterium* of the Catholic church. His rebellion, however, is of a special kind. As Umberto Eco has noted, Joyce "abandons the faith but not religious obsession. The presence of an orthodox past reemerges constantly in all his works under the form of a personal mythology and with a blasphemous fury that reveals the affective permanence."[1] Such a disposition, coupled with a fascination for liturgy and rites, quite naturally draws Joyce's readers into the presence of Roman Catholicism throughout his work. Because of these multiple levels and complex strains, critics have approached the religious aspects from widely divergent points of view. The pioneer study of these elements, and what has remained the cornerstone work on the subject, is William T. Noon's *Joyce and Aquinas*, published in 1957.[2] This work marked the beginning of informed critical discussion on a subject of central importance to our understanding of Joyce. Regarding this study two facts are important: Noon was a Jesuit priest, and his study was originally a doctoral dissertation under William K. Wimsatt at Yale. Those familiar with Wimsatt's work can see his clear influence on Noon, not so much in the rigor of textual analysis, although occasionally Noon applies a New Critical approach to a passage in Joyce's texts, but more in Noon's willingness to view Joyce's work as autonomous from his life, especially in separating Stephen Dedalus's ideas and theories from those of Joyce. Given the biographical, apologetic criticism that had been written by many Catholic critics of Joyce, this study became important in the mainstream of Joyce criticism — a work from which other scholars could learn and build. It was referred to as a model of what the knowledgeable and open-minded critic, not narrowed but informed by his religious conviction, could bring to the mainstream of Joyce criticism (though Noon's sympathies lead him to soften on occasion Joyce's harsh vision of Catholicism). Umberto Eco, Maurice Beebe, Jacques Aubert, Robert Boyle, Kevin Sullivan,[3] and other important commentators on the religious and aesthetic aspects of Joyce's work have all acknowledged Noon's seminal contribution. For thirty years the book has been, and remains still, central to the extended critical dialogue on the subject.

There is an additional, related context in which to see *Joyce and Aquinas*. Noon's book confirmed and clarified in an organized and formal way Joyce's use of Scholastic philosophy and other religious elements. The early responses to Joyce's work contained scattered remarks about the religious elements and the spiritual qualities manifest in both theme and subject matter, but it was left to Noon to bring these aspects into systematic focus and analysis.

There is a tendency to assume that after his long and painful publishing difficulties, Joyce, with the exceptions of only the hopeless literary reactionaries, was accorded a central place within the hierarchy of the kingdom of literary modernism. In general, such a scenario is accurate, but a closer look at the initial reception of *A Portrait*, for example, suggests a more diverse pattern of response. This point can be illustrated especially well by measuring the early commentary to the religious aspects of his art. A brief outline provides an important context for Noon's work and this aspect of Joyce criticism generally.

Early American reactions to *A Portrait*, for example, were frequently marked by commentary on the spiritual quality in the novel. Francis

Hackett, in a glowing review in *The New Republic* (March 1917), wrote that "Mr. Joyce is more successful than Samuel Butler in making religious belief seem real." A few months later, Van Wyck Brooks, arguably the most widely read critic of his day, noted in his review of the novel that "you have to go back generations in any other Western country to find a spiritual equivalent to James Joyce . . . he stems from Cardinal Newman as other men stem from Goethe." A year later, the young American poet Hart Crane commented that *A Portrait*, "aside from Dante, is spiritually the most inspiring book I have ever read."[4] Much later, Thomas Merton, the poet and Trappist monk, in his widely read *Seven Story Mountain*, praised the novel for its portrayal of religious crisis. The character of these and other responses was not merely the observation of the religious elements that suffuse *A Portrait* but rather the vivid quality of the deep and complex battle between the shaping artist and one of the most organized of religions.

T. S. Eliot, another American, generally regarded as the century's most influential literary critic in the English language, had written in 1923 that Joyce's method had given "a shape and significance to the immense panorama of futility and anarchy," yet in 1934, in *After Strange Gods*, he wrote that Joyce was "penetrated with Christian feeling."[5] Admittedly, these two statements by Eliot reflect the direction of his own work better than Joyce's, yet the spiritual and religious elements in Joyce's work have engaged a wide range of reaction with very different purposes and opposing points of view. Noon's book had the effect of putting the religious claims in balance, and his investigation of the sources and the analysis of Joyce's use of them has elevated the level of discourse on the subject ever since.

In *Joyce and Aquinas*, subtitled *A Study of the Religious Elements in the Writing of James Joyce*, Noon sets out to locate and describe the Thomism of Joyce, a subject that had frequently been alluded to in Joyce criticism but never systematically studied. Noon contends that Joyce's Thomism is a "highly qualified derivative" of Aquinas's thought, for the most part a matter of thematic correspondence and general categories or affinities of outlook. *Joyce and Aquinas* is an examination of Joyce's theoretical formulations "in the light of the determinable aesthetic and poetic principles of Aquinas" (ix). Noon relates these principles in large part through the order of their development in Joyce's canon: *Stephen Hero* and *Portrait* illustrate the foundation of the aesthetic theories; *Dubliners*, the doctrine of epiphanies; *Ulysses*, the comedy and Trinity themes; and *Finnegans Wake*, the related themes of the poet's role as "creator." Noon's critical schema, even with its obvious overlaps, is not arbitrary, nor does Noon follow it slavishly. His is both a thematic and chronological argument.

Noon's is not a source study that traces, ad infinitum, direct or possible references by Joyce to Aquinas but rather an inquiry into the possible correspondences on "the nature of Aquinian ideas through which Joyce tended to look at other things." The first of these correspondences that Noon treats is in the *Ratio studiorum*, a central document of the Jesuit educational system, which, besides setting out a pedagogy, "assigns a privileged position to the teachings of St. Thomas Aquinas" (2). Noon is careful to note the method by which the Jesuits brought Aquinas into their educational system, because Ignatius Loyola, the founder of the Society of Jesus, believed that everything had a purpose in both its form and its content. Loyola believed, and Joyce certainly proved him right, that the young absorbed by form. Joyce's early education followed the prescription of the *Ratio studiorum* through Clongowes and Belvedere College, but the special charter provisions of University College prohibited the imposition of the traditional Jesuit collegiate curriculum, which required formal courses in Scholastic philosophy. Nevertheless, as Noon makes clear, Joyce had a multitude of opportunities at University College to come under the influence of Aquinas. All aspects of Jesuit education were saturated with Scholastic thought. To be "steeled in the school of Old Aquinas" was not for Joyce to be confronted directly with the *Summa theologica*, but it was to have the Old Dominican everywhere in that world of Jesuit education. Noon was the first to note, however, the absence of direct study of Aquinas in Joyce's academic course. His discussion of this absence against Joyce's claims of Thomistic influence was the first extended critical commentary of this complex influence.

Of Joyce's specific encounters with Aquinas's ideas at University College, we learn more from Ellmann, whose biography was published two years after Noon's study. Ellmann points out that Joyce's Italian teacher, Father Charles Ghezzi, recognized young Joyce's interest in aesthetics and encouraged "him to formulate theories about it."[6] Ellmann amplifies the subject by citing such contemporaries of Joyce as George Clancy, Francis Skeffington, and Thomas Kettle, as well as pointing out the backgrounds of the University College philosophy faculty, but Ellmann does not extend the discussion of Joyce's absorption of Aquinas. In his book, *James Joyce Remembered* (1968), Joyce's classmate Constantine Curran expands somewhat the possibilities of Joyce's personal encounter with Aquinas and locates a particular passage from Rickaby, but he draws on the same textual sources Noon suggests.

As to Aquinas, I must also mention Boedder's *Natural Theology*, the textbook used in the class of religious doctrine open to all students. He had a page or two on Thomistic aesthetics starting out with *pulchra enim dicuntur ea quae visa placent*. Rickaby's *General Metaphysics* was read in the philosophy classes. Joyce could not but have seen it in the hands of his friends who were reading philosophy including, for example, J. F. Byrne (Cranly), who sat at the same table with him in the National Library and at least in the first week of the term would have opened its pages. Rickaby, between pages 148 and 151, holds the marrow of Joyce's aesthetics. It is Rickaby who quotes from St. Thomas well nigh all that Joyce uses touching the good and the beautiful which by its mere contemplation sets the appetite at rest. He discusses its unity, or *integritas*, its harmony of parts, or *consonantia*, and its clear lustre, or *claritas*; commonplaces, it may be said. But for me an intriguing detail is that Rickaby illustrates part of his argument by a sudden unlikely reference to a barn, just as Joyce, in his talk with Lynch, suddenly invokes the basket on the head of a passing butcher's boy.

Noon's study makes it clear that Joyce was not exposed to the formal study of Aquinas, and later studies have confirmed Noon's findings. Joyce never studied Aquinas systematically, even when he read Aquinas and recorded his own aesthetic concepts in Paris, several years later. Noon further contends that Joyce's reading of Aquinas is obviously incomplete and that Joyce misunderstands if not distorts Aquinas at crucial places. Noon writes:

> Joyce's Thomism, whatever we may ultimately decide about it, is never found in isolation in his writings. It is not the crucial Joycean "critical problem"—whatever that may be—and it is not always the same thing when it does make its presence felt in Joyce's different works. Its presence is likely to be most strongly felt, by anyone sensitive to the categories and attitudes of Aquinas, in the general texture or tone of Joyce's writings rather than at those places where the authority of Aquinas is most explicitly invoked. The author of this study considers that Bloom, rather than Stephen, is indisputably the central character of *Ulysses*. But for a study of Joyce's relation to Aquinas, the student finds that Stephen and related artist figures in Joyce's work are more immediately significant than Bloom.
>
> Much in the same way, the conclusions of a study of this sort may easily suggest to the careful student of Aquinas' metaphysics that there has been a misunderstanding, if not a willful distortion, of the Aquinan points of view. (16–17)

Noon's thesis concerning Joyce's version of Aquinas has had important extensions and a few challenges, but the great majority of critics who have followed him have supported his position.[8]

Besides *Stephen Hero* and *A Portrait*, the main early sources of discussion for Joyce's aesthetics are found in his Paris and Pola notebooks, which have been published in *Critical Writings.*[9] The precise sources Joyce used from Aquinas remain baffling. Noon admits his own puzzlement and inability to discover them. Even when Joyce cites a specific reference to Aquinas, as he does in *A Portrait*, the matter cannot be left there. Jacques Aubert, in his excellent work on the sources of Joyce's aesthetic theories, illustrates the difficulty as he pursues his discussion of the "Pola Notebook," where Joyce left fragmentary discussions of Aquinas. He writes:

> First, let us settle the irritating question of the sources. The one which is usually brought up—too often—has the distinction of being precise and obscure at the same time. Precise because it was spelled out in full in *A Portrait:* "The lore which he was believed to pass his days brooding upon so that it had rapt him from the companionships of youth was only a garner of slender sentences from Aristotle's poetics and psychology and a *Synopsis Philosophiae Scholasticae ad Mentem divi Thomae.*" Obscure because, firstly, it had not been possible up to the present to find this text. Noon, having searched in Ireland, began to doubt its existence. Indeed, the work does exist; but—a new perplexity—we don't find there any of the St. Thomas quotations given by Joyce, which, on the other hand, are all in two pages of *The History of Aesthetics.*[10]

In one of his footnotes to this passage Aubert notes that "Noon, in spite of certain ambiguities in his treatment of the subject, learnedly shows everything in Joyce's work which would agree either poorly or not at all with Thomism."[11] Although Aubert has traced the possibility of Joyce's Thomistic sources a bit further than Noon, the matter remains unclear. It is doubtful that Joyce used a single text; fragments of memory served as his source. Aubert's discussion of this and other matters, however, extends Noon's initial speculations and gives added dimension to the Thomistic elements in Joyce's work.

Noon makes it abundantly clear from the beginning of his study that there is no such thing as Thomistic aesthetics and that, indeed, Aquinas himself would have been unfamiliar with the term. In Joyce's extended discussions of aesthetics the concept of "beauty" is central, both in Stephen's discussions in *Stephen Hero* and *A Portrait* and in Joyce's Paris and Pola notebooks. Noon argues that the Thomistic alliance between "art" and "beauty" posed by Joyce is "nowhere stated or taken for granted in the writings of St. Thomas" (19). Nor is there, Noon makes clear, a distinction in Aquinas between a "useful" and a "fine" art. Joyce, according to Noon, is right to use the phrase "applied Aquinas." Joyce, in other words, imbued with the spirit of the Thomistic texts, gave them an interpretation that offered a philosophical justification to the literature he was to write.

There was clearly an affinity between Joyce and Aquinas in their interest in the psychological experience of beauty.

> Like Joyce's putative artist Stephen Dedalus, Aquinas is to a notable extent interested in the psychological experience of beauty, "that which gives delight to the mind." Unlike Stephen, he nowhere seems lost in the Dedalan labyrinth of cognition, "a maze out of which we cannot escape." Moderate realist that he is in his epistemology, he does not, as Joyce's Stephen was later on inclined to do, minimize the force of the extrasubjective factors in the mental experience. The *integritas, consonantia,* and *claritas* (of which Stephen speaks in Aquinas' name) are conceived by Aquinas as qualities of things which the mind comes to know, not as "stages" in the mind's own act of knowing. Furthermore Aquinas does not bear down on these qualities in the same way as Stephen does, though in his effort to keep the objective-subjective scale in a delicate balance he gives in the final *Summa* an increasingly serious attention to the experience of beauty as an act of apprehension: "pulchra enim dicuntur ea quae visa placent." This situation of the experience of beauty as much in the psychological order as in the ontological is in an important sense a clean break with the teaching of Aquinas' master, Albert. Albert was much more inclined to ally beauty with goodness as a reality which satisfies the longings and desires of man's will, of his heart. Aquinas speaks of beauty as satisfying the desire of the mind *to know.* (22)

Because Aquinas situates the experience of beauty as much in the psychological order as in the ontological, there is an important Thomistic alliance between truth and beauty. For Joyce, however, as Noon points out, this alliance is not without strain. Stephen, in his discussions of beauty with Lynch in *A Portrait* ("Is the portrait of Mona Lisa good if I desire to see it?"), carries the discussion far beyond the dimensions of Aquinas's discourse. Aquinas is silent on the question of how far imaginative representations possess ontological goodness or truth. Noon's argument in his second chapter, "The Beauty Maze," makes clear that despite the obvious echos of Aquinas, Joyce has a far more specialized agenda.

In spite of his Scholastic preoccupations, Joyce was endowed with the sensibility of a modernist and was therefore preoccupied with post-Kantian categories, changing patterns of reality that inform Joyce's discussions of such subjects as static art, whereas Stephen's comments in *A Portrait* go beyond his Aristotelian and Thomistic concepts. In *A Portrait*, Stephen views beauty as static, connects beauty with truth, ties by analogy the aesthetic with the religious, and follows the line from Aristotle to Kant through Aquinas. His later preoccupations, in the Proteus episode of *Ulysses*, move even further from Thomistic or Aristotelian categories. The difficulty at this stage of discussion for Noon and all subsequent students of the relationship between Joyce and Aquinas is not so much how far Joyce eventually ends up differing from him (which he does) but rather how Joyce fills in the blanks in the absence of Aquinas's comments on Joyce's particular aesthetic concerns. Aquinas, for example, has little to say about poetry and nothing to say about Stephen's three-form theory, wherein the artist progressively refines himself out of existence in his work. Yet the cast of mind that extrapolates from Aquinas seems so suffused in Aquinas's thought that it is easy to assume Joyce's entire argument is Scholastic, which, as Noon makes clear, it certainly is not.

Having established the intellectual relationship between Joyce and Aquinas and having traced the important religious elements in Joyce's aesthetic theories, including the idea of the epiphany, Noon, by the latter half of his study, moves to interpretations of Joyce's texts. His analysis of "Two Gallants" and especially "The Dead" are read in light of the religious context and the concept of epiphany. Noon's interpretations of these stories do not—certainly not in retrospect, at least—startle with their insight, but they do reveal the complex theological grounding that adheres to their procedures.

The same can be said for Noon's interpretation of *Ulysses*. In spite of his high praise of the book, Noon is frequently at odds with it:

> The Aquinan student of Joyce would be rather myopic himself if he did not see that Joyce's vision of the world is in some respects shortsighted and distorted. There is at times an almost cloacal obsession and antisocial stridency in his images which suggest a kind of pathological protest against the human condition itself. Such a posture is not at all Aquinan or even Christian. One could hardly construct a fair picture either of the Thomist synthesis or of the Irish Christian fact if he had nothing else to work with but the Joycean catharsis. (93)

Noon is obviously uneasy with the larger interpretation of *Ulysses* that characterizes Joyce as a prophet of the void. He struggles with the overwhelming evidence as he sees it and concludes that

> before we characterize Joyce as a metaphysical nihilist, it is for us to ask, and to answer as best we can, of the life symbolized in *Ulysses:* Is this human perfection? Is this rational living? Is this human dignity? Is this the end of the endeavors put forth by the creatures, a little lower than the angels, who are made in the image and the likeness of God? Molly would never think to ask questions like these; Bloom is incapable of asking them; Stephen is too much confused. But we can ask them. Joyce has been asking them obliquely as the novel went along. Joyce is about as far from nihilism

as you can go and still write novels and not "tracts for the times." Nor is he
personally committed to the secularist position which claims you can have
mores without spiritual roots. *Ulysses* as a symbolic construct of the spirit
is at pains to show what happens to mores when these roots in the spirit
have withered away. (103–4)

Noon's conclusion reveals a deep and unsettling struggle with *Ulysses*
that seems to search deeply for a spiritual meaning if only by displace-
ment or implication.

While brilliance of interpretation does not characterize Noon's study,
he is extremely knowledgeable and illuminating when tracing important
philosophical and theological themes. His chapter "Sabellian Subtleties:
The Trinitarian Theme" traces thoroughly and adroitly the important
Trinitarian aspect, "which keeps recurring insistently in *Ulysses* and
Finnegans Wake.

The Trinitarian theme, a central doctrine of the Church, is crucial to
Joyce's artistic theory. In *A Portrait*, Stephen ponders the idea of the Son
as the "image" of the Father:

> The imagery through which the nature and kinship of the Three Persons of
> the Trinity were darkly shadowed forth in the books of devotion which he
> read—the Father contemplating from all eternity as in a mirror His Divine
> Perfections and proceeding out of Father and Son from all eternity—were
> easier of acceptance by his mind by reason of their august incomprehensibil-
> ity than was the simple fact that God had loved his soul from all eternity,
> for ages before he had been born into the world, for ages before the world
> itself had existed.[12]

Noon cites the Jesuit theologian John Courtney Murray, who points out
that " 'all Trinitarian heresies have had one thing in common—an attempt
to explain away the eternal Father-Son relationship as not of the essence
of God' " (109). Noon argues that "Joyce saw too that the principal
Trinitarian heresies may ultimately be reduced to two: Arianism and
Sabellianism" (109). Noon discusses both of these heresies at length. He
concludes that Joyce is not a follower of Arius, who "contended that the
Son was not truly a Son of the Father by nature but a kind of intermediary,
much more than human but a great deal less than divine" (109). The Son,
however *like* God, is not consubstantial with God.

The position of Arius was that the Logos (the Son) was of like
substance (*homoiousios*) with the Father. Although Noon does not mention this, the position of Athanasius, which was opposed to Arius,
became the orthodox position ratified at the Council of Nicaea in A.D.
325. This position held that the Son and the Father were of the same
substance (*homoousios*). Stephen would not accept a theology that removes

the basis of Fatherhood in God. Such a theory would dissolve Stephen's theory that the artist, God, is the Father of his creation. Noon contends that Stephen is in deep sympathy with "Sabellianism, a far subtler, more rationalistic, and quite modernistic heresy," a heresy that Noon argues is the choice "of those who wish to hold a trinity of persons in the Godhead but to do so, at least as Aquinas conceives of the matter, in purely human terms and entirely on the basis of the content of their human experience of personality rather than on the basis of God's revelation about Himself" (110). Sabellius held that the three Persons of the Trinity, the Father, Son, and Holy Spirit, were no more than "modes" or, as Noon writes, "manifestations of God in the outer world" (110). Noon traces Aquinas's concept of the Trinity and notes that Aquinas follows the traditional Patristic axiom: "'*Quo Verbum, eo Imago, et eo ipso Filius'*" (112). Noon sees Stephen as a Sabellian idealist but points out that Joyce's Trinitarian theme also embodies his Shakespeare-Hamlet theme, as well as other intellectual perspectives related to fatherhood and sonship. In his interpretation of Joyce as a Sabellian, Noon seems to argue that Joyce denies that the relations (Father-Son, Father/Son-Spirit) *constitute* the being of God—that God is primordially Trinitarian.

As we explore Stephen's reflections on the Trinity, we must realize that within Thomistic theology, for all its dogmatic ultimacy, the Trinity remains but a (privileged) analogy for *what* God is like. For Aquinas, the fundamental principle always remained *de Deo nescimus quid sit* (we don't know what God is). We have only analogies.

Daniel R. Schwarz, in his recent study *Reading Joyce's "Ulysses,"* takes issue with Noon's argument that Stephen rejects the Arian position and argues that within the narrative framework of *Ulysses* Stephen's movement toward reconciliation follows Arian lines.[13] Noon's argument that Stephen is a Sabellian rationalist leads him to conclude that Stephen "will never be a poet either nor escape out of the labyrinth where a lifeless image and an unquiet imager are one" (125). Schwarz, on the other hand, dismissing Stephen's Sabellianism, draws a more positive conclusion: "Does not Stephen's idea of reconciliation following sundering describe the way that Joyce makes interchangeable the signifier and signified in the novel's extended metaphors? The artist's way of sending himself to redeem the world is to weave the details of his past into unifying patterns and imaginative analogies."[14] Although one might sympathize with Schwarz's reading, it is difficult for this reader to find the hard evidence from the text to support his optimism. Such an extrapolation as Schwarz makes, by the way, would be alien to Noon, the student of Wimsatt.

Noon concludes his study with chapters on Stephen's concept of the artist as creator and on Joyce's use of language within *Finnegans Wake*.

Noon argues that "the principal Aquinan themes which make their presence felt in the writings of Joyce come to a focus sooner or later, unless this study is mistaken, in the question of the meaning of language and the mystery of words" (159). These two important complementary dimensions, one with its comparison of the poet with the God of creation and the other depicting the artist as begetter of the Word, are aspects of Joyce's art that in their movement through his work move far beyond their roots in Thomistic doctrine. In the later chapters of Noon's work, which include discussions of *Ulysses* and *Finnegans Wake*, his application of Thomistic principles in relation to Joyce's larger artistic purposes are less important. This is not to say that Noon's arguments are flawed but rather that they are more fragmentary and remote from the larger questions raised by Joyce's later work.

For over thirty years Noon's study has remained a springboard for scholars who have pursued the religious and Thomistic aspects of Joyce's work, especially as they relate to the aesthetic formulations. Considering the scope and complexity of the subject, *Joyce and Aquinas* is of relatively modest proportions. It makes no pretense to be exhaustive; it is a pioneer study in the best sense of that word, opening up paths and pointing directions for others to follow. There are several studies written near the time his appeared that complement Noon's. J. Mitchell Morse's *The Sympathetic Alien*, Maurice Beebe's *Ivory Towers and Sacred Fonts*, and Kevin Sullivan's *Joyce among the Jesuits* all in different ways deal with the religious complexion of Joyce's art and life.[15] Morse points out Joyce's affinities and debts to Augustine, Dun Scotus, Ockham, and others in a work that is clearly at odds with Noon's Catholic sympathies. Beebe studies Joyce's work from the tradition of the artist as hero in Western literature from Goethe through Proust and finally to Joyce and discusses the religious aspects of Stephen's theories at some length.[16] Sullivan provides important facts on Joyce's education with the Jesuits.

Eco's and Aubert's studies, both important developments of Noon's earlier observations, accept Noon's points on the influence of Aquinas but carry the aesthetic development much further. In *The Aesthetics of the Chaosmos*, Eco sees Joyce as "the node where the Middle Ages and the avant-garde meet."[17] He explores Joyce's medieval sympathies and frame of mind through his affinities with Scholastic thought. For example, on *Ulysses* Eco writes, "Joyce clearly thought of his novel as a *summa* of the Universe."[18] Eco's work is on a much larger scale than Noon's in that he demonstrates how Joyce's penchant for the Scholastic is central throughout his work. Eco is concerned with Joyce's "poetics," which with reference to the Prague school he defines as "the study of the structural mechanism of a given text which possesses a self-focusing quality and a capacity for releasing effects of ambiguity and polysemy." In this context, he sees Joyce's works as being understood "as a continuous discussion of their own artistic procedures."[19] Aubert's work is also informed by later theoretical approaches to aesthetics, and his study represents a development of Joyce's ideas beyond Aristotle and Aquinas.[20]

An example of shorter studies that have further developed Noon's original observations, and in this case counters them, is F. C. McGrath's "Laughing in His Sleeve: The Sources of Stephen's Aesthetics."[21] McGrath acknowledges Noon's account of Joyce's ambiguous sources in Aristotle and Aquinas, but he contends that a more direct source for Stephen's (and Joyce's) aesthetics is in the German idealists, both in their general orientation and in their specific details. This is part of the argument Aubert made earlier. Specifically, McGrath argues that Kant and Hegel are indirect sources for the formulation of Stephen's aesthetic theories. Noon is not unaware of this connection, and McGrath points this out: "After laying the epistemological foundations for his aesthetics, Stephen then builds a specifically literary edifice upon them: his lyric-epic-dramatic progression of the arts. Various attempts have been made to relate these three forms to Aristotle and Aquinas, but William Noon suggests the closest analogue when he cites Hegel's progression of symbolic-classic-romantic from the Introduction to *The Philosophy of Fine Art.*"[22] McGrath concludes his study, however, by arguing the extreme position that Aristotle and Aquinas as sources are "red herrings."

The most recent study, and in many respects the closest to Noon's, is Joseph Buttigieg's *A Portrait of the Artist in Different Perspective.*[23] The author devotes an extensive discussion to the religious context of Joyce's work. He focuses on *A Portrait* but offers a deeply revealing and engrossing study of the religious and aesthetic elements as they relate to Joyce's art. His recognition of both the Ignatian and Thomistic content in *A Portrait* and his subsequent discussion of their place and function is an important reconsideration of these basic aspects that Noon had introduced. Buttigieg goes more deeply than Noon or any other previous critic into the densely theological background that informs *A Portrait* and seems to have shaped Joyce's attitude. He sees Stephen's movement in the novel as "diametrically opposed to the Ignatian program" and to the ideas of Catholic asceticism generally. Buttigieg's discussion of Catholic spirituality and Stephen's rejection of it adds a great deal to our understanding of the ground Joyce was trying to establish in Stephen's imperfect battle to become an artist.

The achievement of Noon's book and its important place in the history of Joyce criticism, like all the books discussed in this volume, are well established, but from the perspective of over thirty years later it is both easier and more difficult to trace with precision its influence and accomplishment. *Joyce and Aquinas* was the first work to question seriously, systematically, and precisely Joyce's fidelity to Aquinas's ideas and the degree to which Joyce used them to shape Stephen's aesthetic concepts as well as his own. The easy assumptions that critics had made regarding Joyce's debt to Aquinas could no longer, after Noon's study, be taken for granted. Noon's careful scrutiny and analysis of Joyce's texts, his investigation of the sources, and his commentary on the religious elements established the foundation for those scholars who followed these lines of inquiry into Joyce's art. No critical study is the last word on an author, but *Joyce and Aquinas* remains a seminal work in a distinguished body of criticism that has illuminated Joyce and his art.

NOTES

1. Umberto Eco, *The Aesthetics of Chaosmos: The Middle Ages of Joyce* (Tulsa, Okla.: The University of Tulsa Monograph Series, no. 18, 1982), 3.

2. William T. Noon, *Joyce and Aquinas* (New Haven: Yale University Press, 1957). Additional citations from Noon appear by page number in parenthesis in the main body of text.

3. Umberto Eco, *Aesthetics;* Maurice Beebe, *Ivory Towers and Sacred Founts: The Artist as Hero in Fiction from Goethe to Joyce* (New York: New York University Press, 1964); Jacques Aubert, *Introduction à l'esthétique de James Joyce* (Paris: Didier, 1973); Robert Boyle, *James Joyce's Pauline Vision: A Catholic Exposition* (Carbondale: Southern Illinois University Press, 1978); Kevin Sullivan, *Joyce among the Jesuits* (New York: Columbia University Press, 1958).

4. Francis Hackett, "Green Sickness," *New Republic* 10, no. 122 (March 3, 1917), 138–39; Van Wyck Brooks, "New Books," *Seven Arts*: 2, no. 7 (May 1917): 122; Hart Crane, "Joyce and Ethics," *Little Review* 5, no. 3 (July 1918): 65; all reprinted in Robert H. Deming's *James Joyce: The Critical Heritage*, 2 vols. (London: Routledge and Kegan Paul, 1970), 1:94–97, 106–7, 123–24.

5. T. S. Eliot, *After Strange Gods* (London: Faber and Faber Ltd., 1934), 48.

6. Richard Ellmann, *James Joyce*, rev. ed. (Oxford: Oxford University Press, 1982), 60.

7. Constantine Curran, *James Joyce Remembered* (London: Oxford University Press, 1968), 36–37.

8. Besides the critical references noted throughout the other endnotes, see Harry Staley, "Joyce's Cathechisms," *James Joyce Quarterly* 6 (1968): 137–53; David E. Jones, "The Essence of Beauty in James Joyce's Aesthetics," *JJQ* 10 (1973): 291–311; and David A. White, *The Grand Continuum: Reflections on Joyce and Metaphysics* (Pittsburgh, Pa.: University of Pittsburgh Press, 1983).

9. James Joyce, *Critical Writings*, ed. Ellsworth Mason and Richard Ellmann (New York: The Viking Press, 1959).

10. Jacques Aubert, *Introduction*, 159. (Citations in text and below are from the French.) Aubert provides the following information on the *Synopsis* in a footnote:

> *Synopsis Philosophiae Scholasticae ad Mentum Divi Thomae, ad utilitatem discipulorum redacta*, Parisiis, Apud A. Roger and F. Chernoviz, editors, via vulgo dicta Grands Augustins, 7, 1892 (2nd ed.). It is an oblong quarto of 71 pages. The title page is followed by a letter from the Archbishop of Cambrai to the Superior, asking him to thank the anonymous author for having written a work so useful for seminarists of the diocese. It is, indeed, true that it is a question here of a school text that aims to train young minds in Thomistic methods, in the exposition and refutation of theses, particularly those of the modern philosophers. (159)

11. Aubert, *Introduction*, 159.

12. James Joyce, *A Portrait of the Artist as a Young Man*, text, criticism, and notes ed. Chester G. Anderson (New York: The Viking Press, 1968), 149.

13. See Daniel Schwarz, *Reading Joyce's "Ulysses"* (New York: St. Martin's Press, 1987), 93–97.

14. Ibid., 96–97.

15. See Beebe, *Ivory Towers*; Sullivan, *Jesuits*; and J. Mitchell Morse, *The Sympathetic Alien: James Joyce and Catholicism* (New York: New York University Press, 1959). See also Bruce Bradley, SJ, *James Joyce's Schooldays* (New York: St. Martin's Press, 1982), which covers knowledgeably and thoroughly Joyce's ten years with the Jesuits. He adds much to Sullivan.

16. Prior to *Ivory Towers and Sacred Founts*, Beebe published the article "Joyce and Aquinas: The Theory of Aesthetics," *Philological Quarterly* 36 (1957): 302–20. In a later review of Noon he notes that "Reverend Noon, a Jesuit Priest, brings to his work not only a broad knowledge of Scholastic philosophy and Joyce, but also a scholarly objectivity and fair-mindedness that go a long way towards settling the question of Joyce's relation to Thomism" (*Modern Fiction Studies* 5, no. 3 [1957]:1).

17. Eco, *Aesthetics*, vii.

18. Ibid., 33.

19. Ibid., 1.

20. Marguerite Harkness's study *The Aesthetics of Dedalus and Bloom* (Lewisburg, Pa.; Bucknell University Press, 1984) sees Joyce's aesthetic influences as coming primarily from nineteenth-century figures. She fails to cite Aubert, Eco, or Noon.

21. F. C. McGrath, "Laughing in His Sleeve: The Sources of Stephen's Aesthetics," *James Joyce Quarterly* 23, no. 3 (1986): 259–75.

22. Ibid., 264–65.

23. Joseph A. Buttigieg, *A Portrait of the Artist in Different Perspective* (Athens, Ohio: Ohio University Press, 1987).

Mary T. Reynolds

Joyce's Shakespeare/Schutte's Joyce

William Schutte's *Joyce and Shakespeare* was published in 1957, shortly before the great change in Joyce criticism that came with the publication of Richard Ellmann's biography and the appearance of a flood of new information from newly released manuscript materials of all kinds.[1] It is a traditional literary study of a kind seldom seen in the 1980s, marked by simplicity and thoroughness, a straightforward investigation. The book (it began as a doctoral dissertation at Yale University) is happily free from modish conceptual formulations and fashionable jargon.

Schutte's subtitle, *A Study in the Meaning of "Ulysses,"* sets the tone of his book. It was the first attempt to explain systematically the function of literary allusion in a major novel and the first large effort toward critical assessment of literariness in Joyce's work. The presence of Shakespeare in *Ulysses* was well known and had been the subject of incidental comment by Stuart Gilbert, Frank Budgen, Harry Levin, and William Tindall. Hugh Kenner described and diagramed Joyce's use of *Hamlet* to augment the basic Homeric structure. Douglas Knight, in a seminal article, said "Hamlet is Stephen's conscious and constant self-referent in Shakespeare, but *Ulysses* makes as much of *King Lear* and *The Tempest* —plays in which the concept of positive and sacrificial loyalty finally triumphs over negative and rapacious treachery." Ellmann, in a 1954 article, said "Hamlet ... is the hero of a revenge-play; however unwittingly and fumblingly, he sheds a great deal of blood. Joyce does not encourage this view of the artist, and so he relates Shakespeare to the suffering father, the victim, rather than to the avenging son. The artist endures evil—he doesn't inflict it." And Richard Kain wrote, "that *Ulysses* is an ambitious technical exercise is well known ... but it is less often recognized that the book is a fulfilment of King Lear's expectation, upon being reunited with Cordelia, that they will 'take upon's the mystery of things / As if we were God's spies.' "[2]

Schutte's argument is presented in nine short chapters with two appendixes. In the introductory opening chapter, the author indicates that he will focus on the ninth episode of *Ulysses*, the Library episode, in which Stephen develops his "Shakespeare theory." Two chapters provide context, one describing Stephen Dedalus prior to the encounter in the National Library, the other describing his three interlocutors, the librarians whose names are combined in the chapter title "Besteglyster." The next four chapters (sixty-eight pages, almost half the book) explore the mind of Stephen Dedalus, and a short chapter (fifteen pages) describes the presence of Shakespeare in the mind of Leopold Bloom. The book concludes with a discussion of the contribution of the Shakespeare allusions to a critical understanding of *Ulysses*.

In an appendix, Schutte sets forth the sources of Stephen's Shakespeare theory: a study by Georg Brandes and a biography by Sidney Lee, both published in 1898, and a series of articles by Frank Harris that was published in book form in 1909. All three sources are mentioned by name in Scylla and Charybdis; all might have been seen by Stephen Dedalus before 1904. Schutte gives a detailed analysis of the statements made by Stephen that might be traced to one or another of these sources. In 1975 William H. Quillian used this appendix as the basis for his discussion of the newly discovered manuscript of Joyce's notes for his lectures on *Hamlet*, given in Trieste in 1912.[3] Quillian called *Joyce and Shakespeare* an indispensable work.

A second appendix lists the quotations from Shakespeare's works as they appear in *Stephen Hero, A Portrait of the Artist as a Young Man*, and *Ulysses*. The quotations are given in four lists: those used by Stephen, those attached to Leopold Bloom, those attached to other characters, and those for which no speaker is specified; they total 215 quotations, of which 202 are found in *Ulysses*. The quotations attributed to Stephen Dedalus, 121 in all, come from a total of twenty-five plays and the *Sonnets*. Bloom's 48 quotations come from eleven plays and Shakespeare's will. It is obvious that the massive presence of Shakespeare in *Ulysses* was carefully constructed by Joyce.

Let us now examine the content of the nine chapters in sequence. To understand the pattern this pioneer study finds in Joyce's use of Shakespeare, it seems advisable to review in some detail Schutte's context for the Shakespeare allusions. In the opening chapter ("Starting Point: the Current Status of Joyce Criticism") Schutte carefully surveys critical attitudes on *Ulysses* and identifies as the central problem in reading the book the question of the novel's resolution. What is the meaning of the eventual meeting between Stephen Dedalus and Leopold Bloom? Schutte's stand is with those critics who take a negative view, concluding that the meeting of the two protagonists has no effect on either of them. "The great irony of the book is . . . that they are unable to take the first step toward the achievement of mutual understanding. The wall between them is impenetrable" (15).

Stephen, in this view, fails to recognize Bloom, the common man, as the predestined subject of his art; "Dedalus has yet to fly. *Ulysses* is the proof that he never will fly." "Salvation was once possible for Stephen, but it could have been achieved only through love. This love Stephen has not. In one sense . . . Bloom . . . is Stephen's predestined subject, the only subject through which the artist can achieve salvation." Bloom seems to be "a contemptible figure" in the eyes of Stephen, and Schutte agrees with this assessment. Bloom "is no more capable of lasting attachments than Stephen. He has no real friend in all the city of Dublin. . . . His brain is a busy brain . . . but because it lacks depth, creative power, nothing ever comes of his schemes or of his friendships. By now he is inured to failure" (14).

Schutte's second chapter ("Stephen before 'Scylla' ") takes a preliminary look at Stephen Dedalus. Examining the nine episodes of *Ulysses* that precede the discussion in the National Library, where Stephen describes his theory of Shakespeare's art, Schutte emphasizes the young man's alienation. "Somewhere between the end of the *Portrait* and the opening of *Ulysses*, Stephen's character has hardened and he has lost much of his capacity for growth" (18). Reviewing Stephen's objectionable qualities, Schutte concludes that he is exactly what Mulligan has called him, "an impossible person."

In this chapter, Schutte draws the portrait of Stephen as Hamlet. Mulligan seems to be "a good friend of Stephen's," but in fact is Stephen's enemy, Rosencranz and Guildenstern to Stephen's Hamlet. According to Schutte's views of the Shakespeare material that goes through Stephen's stream of consciousness in the opening chapters of *Ulysses*, Stephen is also the elder Hamlet to Mulligan's Claudius. The Martello tower, as some early critics had observed, is associated with Elsinore, and Mulligan is the usurper who constantly challenges and undermines Stephen. Both consciously and unconsciously, Stephen's mind is "drenched with Shakespeare." His movements across Dublin involve Shakespeare as he teaches a class in history, walks by himself on the beach, and visits the office of the editor of the *Evening Telegraph*.

The book's third chapter—"Besteglyster"—describes the three librarians whom Stephen meets in the National Library: Thomas Lyster, the director, forty-nine years old in 1904; John Eglinton; and Richard Irvine Best, who later distinguished himself as a Celtic scholar and philologist but who appears in Joyce's chapter as a precious aesthete and admirer of Oscar Wilde. Eglinton, editor of the new magazine *Dana*, later attested the accuracy of Joyce's account, admitting "a twinge of recollection of things actually said." Schutte's attitude in this chapter again seems unsympathetic; he treats Stephen's discussion of Shakespeare as a provocation: "Stephen thinks of the older man less as a partner in a two-way discussion than as an active and dangerous opponent" (47–48). He assumes that Stephen's arrogance and "extravagant forecasts of future accomplishment have made him fair game" and that "the world will seem out of joint because he has not come to terms with it." Stephen's depression on June 16 is unwarranted, "a cloak . . . which he adopted during his quarrel with Mulligan," and Mulligan is right in expecting him to buck up and snap out of it. Stephen "cannot bring himself into harmony with the spirit of the place and time," and if John Eglinton rejects him and his theory, it is only to be expected.

An analysis of Stephen's Shakespeare theory forms the core of the fourth chapter ("A Good Groatsworth of Wit"). Schutte treats it as an attempted scholarly discussion rather than the scaffolding of a theory of aesthetics; he concentrates on the accuracy of Stephen's account of Shakespeare's life and the writing of *Hamlet*. "Stephen's silent admission that he distorted the facts as he knows them serves to cast doubt over all of his facts." From the evidence of factual inaccuracy Schutte concludes that Stephen "has collected a few facts from the biographers and has deduced from them that Shakespeare must have done a certain thing . . . [and has] also taken the dubious step of assuming that Shakespeare's works directly reflect events in his personal life" (54). Schutte dismisses the discussion of Shakespeare on the grounds that "there is no demonstrable historical basis. . . . [Stephen] throws up an intricate series of screens to hide the weakness of his foundations . . . to overwhelm listeners with quantity of material and virtuosity of performance so that they will have no time to weigh the merits of what he says." Schutte concludes that "his work lacks the scholar's fairness and impartiality." A concern with the intentional fallacy was a dominant feature of criticism in the 1950s; "giving a biographical significance to events in the plays and poems" was held to be inadmissible. Reflecting such critical attitudes, which by the 1970s had become less rigid, Schutte's analysis distorts some aspects of Joyce's Library chapter. Shakespeare, Stephen claims, "drew his characters out of his own long pocket" (*U* 1.437; 9.741–742), and when he is asked whether he believes his own theory, Stephen denies it; but as

Richard Ellmann aptly said, this denial means only that the theory is "a parable of the relation of art to life, rather than a biography susceptible of verification."[4]

Schutte's fifth chapter ("The Ordeal of Stephen Dedalus") focuses on the last half of the Library chapter, in which Stephen's efforts are defeated. His treatment is ambiguous; Stephen is an isolated figure, but the reason is not made clear in the chapter except by indirection. Schutte begins by noting that Stephen has decided not to go back to his family; he will break with Mulligan; he will give up his teaching job; he "stands as completely alone as he can make himself — jobless, homeless, friendless. He has deliberately cut himself off from the world about him" (67). The Library chapter is the story of his "misguided but understandable effort to receive recognition from literary Dublin." The reason for his defeat is that "he finds he can only be uncompromisingly himself." He cannot flatter, he cannot compromise with his principles.

In presenting his Shakespeare theory he is "too brilliant." And he jibes at his listeners. "He is properly spanked by Eglinton for his pretensions," but he replies rudely to the editor's comments. He is continually interrupted (indeed, he is not getting a sympathetic hearing), and twice he is "shown his place in the hierarchy of Dublin's intellectual life." The first snub occurs when Eglinton speaks of the planned literary gathering at George Moore's to which Mulligan and Haines have been invited, but Stephen "is carefully not asked" (69); the second, when the well-intentioned librarian speaks of a planned collection of new young poets, to which Stephen "might well have been asked to contribute," but again he has not been included. As Schutte describes the "ordeal," the onus really seems to be on the Establishment figures, who, he makes clear, have written off Stephen Dedalus. They are not judging his work or his ideas, they are judging his rudeness and brashness. Only the "quaker librarian" is really interested. Despite Schutte's negative view of Stephen Dedalus, he gives an excellent analysis of the chapter, impartially contrasting the personal hostility of Eglinton and AE, the two editors, with the more objective interest of Lyster.

Schutte makes an admirable digression to remind us that Stephen was thinking of Shakespeare earlier in the day, as he listened to the description of windy oratory in the newspaper office in the Aeolus chapter. Shakespeare's line "And in the porches of mine ear did pour" suddenly reminds Stephen of Daniel O'Connell, the greatest of Irish orators, whose mass meetings brought an end to the penal laws and began the rise to power of a Catholic middle class. Stephen's silent thought changed the Ghost's words into "Miles of ears of porches." Now, in the library, as he begins his exposition he adapts once more the Ghost's words: "They list. And in the porches of their ears I pour" (*U* 1.299, 421; 7.881, 9.465).

Schutte interprets the passage, which clearly carries another meaning in addition to the obvious one, as an adverse comment by Stephen on his own performance: like O'Connell's speeches, it is doomed to be transient, soon forgotten. But, as a faithful reporter, he quotes Stephen's silent thought: "One day in the national library we had a discussion. Shakes" (212). This comment, at the very end of the chapter, can also be interpreted as a defiant challenge to the Irish Literary Revival, a statement that they will ignore him only to their own loss and that on some future day they will remember this discussion. And in fact, this is exactly what happened to Stephen's author. Joyce's early essay—not on Shakespeare, but, like Stephen's Shakespeare discussion, really an essay about the artist—was rejected by Eglinton as editor of *Dana* in 1904. The essay was then signed and dated by the young Joyce, and the manuscript survives with the particulars of the rejection.

Joyce's truncated "Shakes" seems thus to involve an oblique reference to the patronizing attitudes of the Protestant Anglo-Irish establishment, revealing an unconscious hostility to the emergent Irish middle class, which was a threat to its leadership. Schutte points out in a footnote that the "porches" passage was a late insertion in the text. For a time, after AE's departure, Stephen's discussion goes along well, and, Schutte notes, he seems confident and assured. But then Mulligan arrives; Stephen "understands immediately what will happen" and says "Hast thou found me, O mine enemy?" Mulligan, the mocker, will be welcomed by the editor and the librarian as one of themselves. As Schutte says, "in the next few minutes he will have ample evidence that intellectual Dublin too will slight the Stephens and serve the mocking Mulligans" (74).

Once again, Schutte offers an ambiguous analysis, seemingly uncertain whether Mulligan is a friend to Stephen. As he did with Eglinton and AE, Schutte gives the benefit of the doubt to the Establishment. Mulligan "has made a genuine effort to be a good friend to Stephen"; and again, "the easy-going Mulligan has done his best for Stephen . . . he has tried without condescending to be helpful . . . and no doubt defended Stephen vigorously from the attacks of others" (73–74). But Schutte's description of the chapter also makes it quite clear that Mulligan is destroying Stephen's theory by ridicule, by provoking the audience to laughter. He also describes Mulligan's "honeying malice" in presenting Stephen as dissolute, a companion of prostitutes, a picture not calculated to increase Stephen's popularity with the librarians.

Mulligan's proprietary way with Stephen brings into sharper focus the condescension of the other men in the library and perhaps stands as another section of Joyce's chapter in which the words of the narrative carry a second and a larger meaning. Mulligan is shown as a sponger who takes Stephen's paycheck for drinks at the same time that he jibes at Stephen's poverty, makes him a figure of ridicule, and ultimately makes it impossible for anyone to consider him seriously as an artist. Schutte closes this chapter with one of his memorable insights, a description of the parallel construction Joyce has set up between the concluding lines of Scylla and Charybdis and a similar passage in Aeolus. Lines from *Cymbeline* are used with a delicate resonance to remind Stephen of the druid priests, who guarded ancient, sacred mysteries, as in Stephen's view the artist today serves the modern world.

> Laud we the gods
> And let our crooked smokes climb to their nostrils
> From our blest altars. (*Cymbeline* V.v.476–8)

The words are echoed in Aeolus, and their full repetition as the final words of Scylla recalls a related scene in A *Portrait of the Artist* that occurs on the steps of the National Library, when a younger Stephen has expounded his theories of art; following this, he writes a villanelle that gives the reader "a picture of the poet in the process of creating a poem" (79). The poem presents a priest of art, a picture of "smoke, incense ascending from the altar of the world" (*P* 256).

The repetition of this image in *Ulysses* reminds us, as Schutte points out, that Stephen considers himself "a priest of the eternal imagination" (*P* 260). In A *Portrait*, the scene ends with Stephen at peace, hopeful; in Scylla, he stands again in this peaceful spot on Kildare Street and sees "frail from the housetops two plumes of smoke ascended, pluming." Shakespeare's lines are placed to precede an echo of those lines in *Portrait*: "from wide earth an altar" repeats the controlling image of Stephen's villanelle, "from the altar of the world . . . from the whole earth, from the vapoury oceans" (*U* 215; *P* 256). Schutte was the first critic to bring these significant passages together in a meaningful way.[5]

Schutte's sixth chapter ("The Artist's Role: The God of Creation"), as might be expected, follows the identification of Stephen as a poet with a discussion of his development as an artist. Returning to A *Portrait of the Artist as a Young Man*, Schutte recapitulates briefly the critical reception of Joyce's earlier novel. A major shift in critical views of A *Portrait* came with the posthumous publication of *Stephen Hero*, the unfinished autobiographical prelude to A *Portrait*.

Comparing *Stephen Hero* with A *Portrait*, Schutte describes the published novel as a structure of scenes in which all the elements of society press their claims on Stephen Dedalus, the embryo artist. Art finds no home in this society, the Dublin of 1902; Stephen's developing consciousness of the claims of art will eventually require a rejection of his whole environment. To serve art he will set aside family, nationality, and religion. The institution that makes the strongest claims on his spirit is the Catholic church, but Stephen has experienced a crucial loss of faith and refuses to give lip service. He even concedes the probable existence of the God of the Roman Catholics, and the possibility of his eternal damnation, but he says, "I fear . . . the chemical action which would be set up in my soul by a false homage to a symbol behind which are massed twenty centuries of authority and veneration" (83).

Stephen is invited to join the Jesuit order, and his rejection of this invitation is immediately followed in the *Portrait* by a mystical experience that gives him a sense of destiny. Walking on the beach and thinking of the artist's mission, he has a moment of ecstasy, "an ecstasy of flight" that culminates in the apotheosis of a girl wading in the sea. Schutte calls attention to Joyce's development of the motif that identifies the creative artist; the process of artistic creation "is compared to the process of material creation by God" (84). Thus, his ideal of the artist as creator supplants, if it does not substitute for, the rejected God of the Roman Catholics.

Stephen's first thought of his villanelle is described, therefore, in terms of the Immaculate Conception of the Redeemer. "In the virgin womb of the imagination the word was made flesh. Gabriel the seraph had come to the virgin's chamber." The young man whom we see in *A Portrait* is absolutely dedicated to an ideal of the creative artist, and he leaves Ireland for Paris at the end of the first novel, full of confidence, preparing to forge the uncreated conscience of his race.

As *Ulysses* opens, it is clear that the claims of society are not so easily rejected. In the thirteen months since his departure for Paris, Stephen's mother has died and the family has disintegrated; his father is a spendthrift and drunkard, leaving his sisters dependent on charity for food. Stephen is supporting himself by teaching in a Protestant private school for a few shillings a week, a job without a future and not much of a present. When Stephen meets his sister at a bookstall her wretched poverty fills him with despair. He cannot support the family that his father brought into the world; the effort to do so would drown him along with them. He is haunted by vivid memories of his mother's death and his refusal of her dying request that he be reconciled with the Church.

In this chapter, Schutte begins the development of his principal thesis, that Shakespeare, for Stephen, is the very "type" of the artist and that Stephen will find the secret of the artist's relationship to the world by understanding the relationship of Shakespeare the man to Shakespeare the prolific creator of characters so vividly individualized. Stephen's theory comes out of his search for a key to the close relationship between the life and the art of Shakespeare. This theory requires that the perfect work of art be made of materials that the artist has drawn from the life around him; the artist's own personality, "the distinctive essence which identifies him for the reader as an individual," must be removed, "refined out of existence," absorbed by the characters he creates so that they may exist independently of their author (88).

Shakespeare's plays, Schutte points out, offer the enigma of the man who wrote a series of plays (*Hamlet, Othello, The Merchant of Venice, The Tempest*) that suggest a great deal about their creator yet reveal very little. The Shakespeare of Stephen's aesthetic theory, therefore, is designed in Stephen's own image (89), a solitary figure, isolated and exiled. But as Stephen reflects on the relation of such a mind to the tangible artistic achievement it produced, he brings into the argument "the strongest of family relationships," the union of generations by the consubstantial relationship of father and son, and he offers fatherhood as a view of the artist's role, a "mystical estate, an apostolic succession" (204). Shakespeare the Artist, sundered from his own consubstantial father, became not only the father of his son but "the father of all his race," taking on the role of God the Creator in this mystical communion. Schutte notes that the younger Stephen of *A Portrait* had "already established a rough equation between the role of the artist as creator and that of God as creator" (92). Now he defines the act of artistic creation of individual characters who live because the personality of the artist has vitalized them and then itself been refined out of the work of art. The artist and his material are one, coexistent. "All creation must exist potentially within its creator before it can become actual" (94).

Joyce allows John Eglinton to understand Stephen's point: "The truth is midway. He [Shakespeare] is the ghost and the prince. He is all in all." And Stephen agrees. "The boy of act one is the mature man of act five . . . he acts and is acted on. . . . Lover of an ideal or a perversion, like Jose he kills the real Carmen. His unremitting intellect is the hornmad Iago ceaselessly willing that the moor in him shall suffer." Stephen's isolation in the Dublin of 1904 finds compensation in his identification with Shakespeare; severed from family and friendships, Stephen will discover his spiritual father and will himself become creator.

The last section of Schutte's presentation of Stephen Dedalus takes a significantly different turn. In his seventh chapter ("The Artist's Role: The 'Dio Boia' ") Schutte confronts Stephen's chief inner conflict, his defiance of the "hangman god" (*dio boia*) and the persistent evil in the material world, the destructive instinct that exists to undo and destroy. Buck Mulligan embodies the materialist view of life; Stephen, to the contrary, insists that life must have meaning. Mulligan is a medical student who sees man as a cerebral animal; in Stephen's view, as Schutte aptly summarizes it, "if man is merely a highly developed beast, then the life of the individual . . . has no meaning at all" (96).

Joyce presents this conflict through Stephen's reaction to his mother's death. All day long the terrible memory of her deathbed haunts him. Finally, in the hallucinatory Circe episode, she appears to Stephen as a horrifying apparition, a vivid manifestation of the power of the *dio boia*.

Schutte's discussion of this complex construction was the first full presentation of Buck Mulligan's role in the novel, and it remains the best critical display of the functional importance of Stephen's memories of his mother. The hallucination in which the mother calls for Stephen's repentance is the climax of *Ulysses;* dramatically, it brings to a climax the novel's portrayal of Stephen's developing self-knowledge. Disillusioned, he began in the book's first chapter to think of himself as Icarus rather than Dedalus, a "disillusioned lapwing" in Schutte's words. As the chapters of *Ulysses* unfold, it can be seen that Stephen has lost faith in his destiny, overborne by the hostile world around him; in Circe, when the apparition of his dead mother forces him into action, he finally comes to terms with his central problem, the relation of the creative artist to society. He acknowledges the power of society; he confronts the *dio boia* directly, tacitly admitting that the artist can be both creator and destroyer; he returns a final rebuff to the ghost's insistent plea for repentance and submission to the Church; and he shatters the lamp with his ashplant walkingstick. "The intellectual imagination! With me all or not at all. Non serviam!" (115).

Does this mean that Stephen will continue "to try to live for Art alone" (120)? Joyce, never given to the overt statement, leaves it to the reader to decide about the future of Stephen Dedalus. Stephen's Luciferian denial seems ominous, even final, although in the context of the scene it can also be given a reading limited to a denial of the Roman church's repressive God, who is here represented by his mother's ghost—like the ghost of Hamlet's father, returned from purgatory with a message for her son. Schutte displays the alternatives skillfully and fairly. When Stephen eagerly asks his mother, "Tell me the word, mother, if you know now. The word known to all men" (*U* 2.1269; 15.4228), the ghost replies only by demanding Stephen's repentance, his submission to the Church. Must we read the ghostly apparition's demands as valid? Shall the dead control the living? How else might Stephen have replied? He says, terror stricken, "No, mother. Let me be and let me live." In the terms of the novel as a whole Stephen never denies God; it is the deadening control of the Church that he rejects. When he walked on the beach in the morning he reflected that God made him as he is: "From before the ages He willed me and now may not will me away or ever" (*U* 1.77; 3.47–48). Schutte has repeatedly shown the hostility and lovelessness of Stephen's world, and the horrid image of the mother's ghost in Circe is altogether repressive. Schutte's last word, in these four chapters, is that Joyce holds forth no hope for Stephen. But Joyce is seldom so explicit, and Schutte's analysis allows for another side to the matter.

Schutte disposes of Leopold Bloom in one short chapter of fourteen pages ("Mr Bloom and Shakespeare"). It is a reductive essay. "Bloom's Shakespeare consists largely of literary cliches, some of which he may well use without even knowing that he is quoting" (124). Schutte discusses Bloom's Shakespeare references in the same terms that he used for his treatment of Stephen's knowledge of Shakespeare: he makes an assessment of the quality as well as the quantity of Bloom's knowledge of Shakespeare. It is not surprising that Bloom, as well as Stephen, fails this test. "A man as unliterary in his tastes as Leopold Bloom we should not expect to be on intimate terms with the works of William Shakespeare" (123).

Yet Schutte finds eleven of the plays in Bloom's mind, and he concludes that such a large number of references to the writer whom Bloom calls "our national poet" (*U* 3.1385; 16.782) can hardly be accidental. Indeed not; Mr. Bloom lacks education, but this makes his interest in serious literature only the more striking. We learn from the list of Bloom's books (*U* 3.1561; 17.1365) toward the end of Ithaca that Bloom owns a one-volume edition of the plays and that he searches earnestly in Shakespeare's works for solutions to the problems of life. His efforts are comic but not unworthy. Schutte's point is that Shakespeare's lines have passed into the language; many of the quotations found in Bloom's discourse or in his silent monologue "might easily have been used by a Bloom who had never seen or read Hamlet" (125).

Schutte concludes that the allusions are given to Bloom because "he [Joyce] wants the reader to associate Bloom with Shakespeare . . . since they are commonplaces [they] do not arrest the reader and cause him to wonder why a man like Bloom should be citing Shakespeare. Instead they serve subtly to link the two in the reader's mind . . . to reinforce other devices which Joyce uses to bring Bloom and Shakespeare together" (127). Schutte's argument in this important chapter is that Stephen's Shakespeare theory creates, instead of a biography of the writer, another character who in fact resembles Leopold Bloom. Both are cuckolds; each loses his son; each is ineffectual in his relations with the women in his life; both achieve contentment by returning to the home; and the aims in life of the two have much in common. The parallels between the lives of

Bloom and Shakespeare pass the bounds of coincidence. In Schutte's view, the purpose of Stephen's Shakespeare theory is to define "the conditions and tensions . . . needed to provide the appropriate climate for the production of literary masterworks," and the novel finds in Bloom's life the paradigm of those conditions and tensions.

Schutte subsequently changed his mind; in "Leopold Bloom: A Touch of the Artist," he recants the earlier adverse judgment. To make amends, he recounts in considerable detail the evidence of Bloom's interest in words and in language, showing that Bloom's wit establishes his artistic credentials. "What he says about words is far less important than what he does with them. Like all good writers—and certainly like his creator—he is an incurable tinkerer with language." Examples are given of Bloom's wit, his shrewd perception of relationships, his subtle comments on his world, and his detachment from the prejudiced and preconditioned responses of other Dubliners. Now Schutte concludes that "Bloom is indeed an extraordinary man . . . whose essentially prosaic mode of thought can even rise to the poetic under stress of great emotion."

In his last chapter ("Dublin, Shakespeare, and the Meaning of *Ulysses*"), Schutte returns to the ultimate question, the resolution and meaning of Joyce's novel. He goes back to *Dubliners*, the fifteen short stories that form Joyce's biography of his city. "Since they all concern the period 1890 to 1904, most of them the last few years of it . . . we should expect little change in moral climate as we move from *Dubliners* through the *Portrait* into *Ulysses*. We find none." *Ulysses* completes the work begun in Joyce's first book; it is "an integrated study of the community . . . packed with Dubliners of all descriptions, each one skillfully individualized . . . Each has his story [which] is important only as it takes its place in Joyce's portrait of the whole society" (138–39).

Schutte compellingly summarizes the city's spiritual emptiness and the enervating quality of the moral atmosphere in the Dublin of 1904. "All of the pressures drive man away from man. There are no friends in *Ulysses*; there are only acquaintances" (139). "All kinds of emotion exist in Dublin on June 16, 1904; but love does not" (141). The integrating potential of religion and politics and other forces in society are ineffective, a sorry lot. Dublin is a city in which no creative relationships can exist.

Bloom and Stephen, representing two extremes, meet in the figure of Shakespeare. *Ulysses* brings together the two images of the dramatist— the historical Shakespeare, undisputed master of English literature, and the figure of Stephen's imagination, a "very particular individual" created "out of the obscurity of time and rumor." The function of the Shakespeare material in *Ulysses* turns on the use of this double standard; Joyce "sets up two important contrasts" (142). The standard of the historical

Shakespeare opposes to the great artist those "lesser men who try to walk in his footsteps." The other, subtle contrast is provided between Shakespeare's world and Dublin of 1904; as Schutte sees it, between "the integrated world . . . , in which values exist and in which relationships between man and man are vital and lead through understanding to growth," and the city of Bloom and Stephen, "where values are debased, where men cannot enter into any but the most casual relationships, where the characteristic forces in society act not to integrate but to divide . . . to supply barriers for men to set up against one another."

Schutte's view of Stephen Dedalus, who claims kinship with Shakespeare, ultimately explains Stephen's Shakespeare theory in terms of the world that has formed Stephen. "Stephen inevitably creates a Shakespeare appropriate to [the] conception of the world reflected in the formative influences of his time. Stephen's Shakespeare is isolated from his fellow men, defeated by the forces of his environment, frustrated in his attempts to realize himself" (143). Stephen's Shakespeare is a reflection of a corrupt and debased Dublin; Shakespeare's works mirror the integrated and vital Elizabethan world. "One of the master ironies of *Ulysses* is that this 'Shakespeare reborn' should be Leopold Bloom" (144).

Schutte at this point defines Bloom in the most reductive terms: "only a painfully limited little man who, though he is sometimes shrewd and ever observant, lacks the ability to integrate and so to understand the fragments of experience which life presents to him. It is his inability to come to terms with the world around him that differentiates him most clearly from the Shakespeare of the plays and allies him with the other characters of Joyce's paralyzed community" (144). It is a tribute to the basic objectivity of Schutte's book that his revised judgment of Bloom actually fits his analysis of the Shakespeare material better than does his earlier censure. In Stephen Dedalus's statement that "the boy of act one is the mature man of act five" we hear an echo of Joyce's comment to Frank Budgen: "As the day wears on Bloom should overshadow them all."[6]

Schutte's well-displayed and well-summarized strictures on the Dublin of 1904 point toward a view of *Ulysses* as a condemnation of materialism and sterility in the modern world. The final pages of his book are somewhat weakened by his implicit rejection of Bloom; he interprets the encounters in Hades, Aeolus, Cyclops, and even in Ithaca as "striking evidence of Bloom's futile effort to achieve acceptance by his society." Bloom's failure to "integrate with Dublin society," even more than Stephen's disability, thus becomes a major fault. Stephen's isolation comes from his understanding of "the spiritual squalor of his city" (147) and is deliberately cultivated. Bloom's actions, such as his definition of love as the guide for life and his brave defense of the Jewish nation, are merely exercises in futility; they result only "in a further deterioration of his relations with the men to whom he is talking."

Nevertheless, Schutte's final assessment of the Shakespeare allusions sufficiently admits the evidence for affirmation. Although Bloom and Stephen as individuals "are what they are," with no hope of changing their essential natures, Schutte believes that "for mankind *Ulysses* seems to offer some hope of redemption from the sterility of the present" (148). He reviews the symbolic patterns of the novel and explores briefly the motif of redemption.

Joyce and Shakespeare has been widely read and cited since its publication in 1957. Of forty-two full-length studies of *Ulysses* or of Joyce's works in general, including *Ulysses*, twenty either have made specific references to Schutte's work or have mentioned the book in a bibliography. Twenty-one of the studies in which Schutte is not mentioned contain extensive references to Shakespeare, creating a strong probability that his book had been read. He was especially commended, beginning with Robert Martin Adams's *Surface and Symbol* in 1962, for his discovery of the sources of Joyce's Shakespeare material and his discussion of the Scylla and Charybdis episode.[7] His valuable appendix of Shakespeare quotations was used, with acknowledgment, by Weldon Thornton in his *Allusions in "Ulysses"* (1961), and Schutte subsequently compiled a series of lists of recurrent motifs based on Thornton's book and on his own work.[8] One important effect of Schutte's book, though concealed, was the great increase of critical interest in Joyce's use of allusion and, more generally, in Joyce's complicated wordplay. Eberhard Kreuzer's study, *Sprache und Spiel im "Ulysses" von James Joyce* (1969), shows the influence of Schutte's book, as does Stanley Sultan's *The Argument of "Ulysses"* (1964).[9] Richard Ellmann first noted Schutte's work with the Shakespeare sources in *Ulysses on the Liffey* (1972) and later in his study of Joyce's reading, *The Consciousness of Joyce* (1977); he also praised Schutte's more recent discovery of an essay by George Russell in *Dana*, the magazine that rejected Joyce's early essay, *A Portrait of the Artist.* [10]

Several critics took issue with Schutte, directly or indirectly, on his negative view of Leopold Bloom and on the question of Stephen's chances for redemption—whether he would fulfill the creative potential that is so clearly exhibited in the novel. Edmund Epstein, in an early review, praised the book but felt that Joyce's penchant for ambiguity might have been given greater emphasis. Epstein added two more quotations to Schutte's appendix of allusions, and he gave in full the verses on "lowsie Lucy" that Shakespeare was reputed to have written, which Schutte mentions without quoting.[11]

Arnold Goldman, in *The Joyce Paradox* (1967), continued the discussion begun by Schutte's opening chapter, in which he summarizes the views of critics on the central question of Ulysses—the significance of the meeting of Stephen and Bloom as the final resolution of the novel. Goldman's concise description continues into contemporary criticism:

> The criticism of *Ulysses*, like that of *A Portrait*, subdivides cleanly in respect of Joyce's attitude toward his major characters and toward the direction in which they are assumed to be heading. The direction of the plot, the end to which it apparently moves, is often assumed to be the most telling means of assessing the characters, for by it is constituted a judgment on them by their world and not immediately by their author. Thus we might expect the "end" of Ulysses to have become a moot issue, and William Schutte's review of the various attitudes critics have taken to Stephen and Bloom's meeting alone proves it has.[12]

John Gordon, in *James Joyce's Metamorphoses* (1981), agrees with Schutte that Stephen's Shakespeare theory is "indeed a clue—a guide to the book. The question of consubstantiality, of determining the nature and affinity between first Stephen and Bloom, then Leopold Bloom and Odysseus, is certainly the central problem posed to the reader." Citing Schutte, Gordon suggests that the Hamlet of the Library episode is a nineteenth-century idea that Stephen's theory attacks, and he offers the example of Stephen's comment on the Ghost, "How did he know it?" as "the quite impressive product of a centripetal intelligence working hard to make everything fit."[13]

The permanence of Schutte's *Joyce and Shakespeare* does not depend on the agreement or disagreement of individual critics, such as the examples cited, but rather on the importance of the topic, the largeness of treatment, and the meticulous accuracy of the book's factual approach. Schutte was the first to tackle systematically the issue of Joyce's literariness, his massive use of literary allusions. Lists had previously been made of Shakespeare quotations in Ulysses; Schutte set himself the daunting task of displaying in a critical perspective Joyce's use of Shakespeare, an endeavor that went far beyond the compilation of lists.

Joyce and Shakespeare identified for the first time the modes of Joyce's fictionalization of another author; with great originality, Schutte demonstrates the absorption of Shakespeare and his works into the fabric of another fiction. No one, after reading Schutte's book, could ever again say that the Library chapter of Ulysses is merely decorative, a tour de force, or that Stephen's Shakespeare theory is a diversion not seriously intended.

Because this study focuses on a major author whom Joyce made into a major presence in the novel, it enriches our appreciation of Joyce's methods and means in *Ulysses* and of Joyce's writing in general. Schutte's study is comprehensive and factual, sticking closely to Joyce's text, the product of a sensitive and penetrating intelligence.

NOTES

1. William M. Schutte, *Joyce and Shakespeare: A Study in the Meaning of "Ulysses"* (New Haven, Conn.: Yale University Press, 1957), xiv, 197. Citations in the text appear in parentheses. Citations to *Ulysses* in the text refer to the 1984 edition: *Ulysses: A Critical and Synoptic Edition*, 3 vols., prepared by Hans Walter Gabler with Wolfhard Steppe and Claus Melchior (New York: Garland Publishing Inc., 1954). Citations are abbreviated as *U* followed first by the volume number and page number, then by the episode number and line number. Thus, *U* 1.437; 9.741 signifies volume 1, page 437; episode 9, line 741.

2. Hugh Kenner, *Dublin's Joyce* (London: Chatto & Windus, 1955), 193–95; Douglas Knight, "The Reading of *Ulysses*," *English Literary History* 19, no. 1 (1952): 70; Richard Ellmann, "The Backgrounds of *Ulysses*," *Kenyon Review* 16 (1954): 348; Richard M. Kain, *Fabulous Voyager* (Chicago: University of Chicago Press, 1947), 151–52, 158.

The 1937 *Word Index to "Ulysses"* showed fifty occurrences of Shakespeare's name, two for Dante, two for Goethe, and none for Milton, although all four are clearly present in the novel. Miles L. Hanley, *Word Index to James Joyce's "Ulysses,"* (Madison: University of Wisconsin Press, 1937).

3. William H. Quillan, "Joyce's 1912 *Hamlet* Lectures," *James Joyce Quarterly* 12 (Fall/Winter, 1974–75): 8, 16. The full text of Joyce's handwritten notes is printed as part of this essay, revealing the accuracy of Schutte's work on the sources of Stephen's references to Shakespeare.

4. Richard Ellmann, *James Joyce*, rev. ed. (New York: Oxford University Press, 1982), 364.

5. William M. Schutte, "Leopold Bloom: A Touch of the Artist," *James Joyce Quarterly* 10, no. 1 (1972): 118–31.

6. Frank Budgen, *James Joyce and the Making of "Ulysses"* (New York: Harrison Smith and Robert Haas, 1934), 116.

7. Robert Martin Adams, *Surface and Symbol: The Consistency of James Joyce's "Ulysses"* (New York: Oxford University Press, 1962), 126–28.

8. Weldon Thornton, *Allusions in "Ulysses"* (Chapel Hill: University of North Carolina Press, 1961; reprint, New York: Simon and Schuster, 1973).

9. Eberhard Kreuzer, *Sprache und Spiel im "Ulysses" von James Joyce.* (Bonn: H. Bouvier u. Co. Verlag, 1969); Stanley Sultan, *The Argument of "Ulysses"* (Columbus: Ohio State University Press, 1964). James Atherton's important study of allusions in *Finnegans Wake* unaccountably fails to cite Schutte's work, although a contemporary study of Joyce and Aquinas by Father

William T. Noon, also published in 1957, is mentioned in the bibliography (James Atherton, *The Books at the Wake* [New York: Viking Press, 1960]).

10. Richard Ellmann, *Ulysses on the Liffey* (London: Faber & Faber, 1972), 14; Ellmann, *The Consciousness of Joyce* (New York: Oxford University Press, 1977), 59.

11. Edmund Epstein, "Joyce and Shakespeare," *The James Joyce Review* 1, no. 2 (June 16, 1957): 42–48.

12. Arnold Goldman, *The Joyce Paradox* (Evanston, Ill.: Northwestern University Press, 1966), 74, 85.

13. John Gordon, *James Joyce's Metamorphoses* (New York: Barnes & Noble, 1981), 30–35. See also Brook Thomas, *James Joyce's "Ulysses"* (Baton Rouge: Louisiana State University Press, 1982); 11–13, Lindsey Tucker, *Stephen and Bloom at Life's Feast* (Columbus: Ohio State University Press, 1984), 45–46, 67; Robert Boyle, SJ, *James Joyce's Pauline Vision* (Carbondale: University of Southern Illinois Press, 1978), 71, 117; and John Paul Riquelme, *Teller and Tale in Joyce's Fiction* (Baltimore, Md.: Johns Hopkins Press, 1983), 52–53.

Shari Benstock

In Excess of "And": David Hayman's *Joyce et Mallarmé*

David Hayman's two-volume study, *Joyce et Mallarmé*, was published in 1956 in the *Cahiers des lettres modernes*, in a section of this series entitled "Confrontations."[1] By this time, Hayman was already at the University of Texas, his thesis from the Sorbonne in modern letters (1955) having been revised for publication to incorporate work on Joyce's manuscripts at SUNY–Buffalo and at the British Library in London. By Hayman's own admission, the manuscript materials he had consulted enlarged significantly the scope of his study, forcing him to add hastily before publication (in true Joycean style) some of his discoveries. His continued work on the manuscript and notebook materials of *Finnegans Wake* resulted fourteen years later in *A First Draft Version of "Finnegans Wake"* (1970).[63]

Joyce et Mallarmé bears all the marks of a university thesis, announcing its changes of direction—it had begun under the provisional title "James Joyce and the French Symbolists"—and changes of mind: its eventual "confrontation" between Joyce and Mallarmé was a decision that implied not only Mallarmé's detachment from other symbolists but "the disproportionate influence that he exerted on Joyce" (1:12). The thesis was written in French, and its various publications, first in *La Revue des lettres modernes* (nos. 19, 20, and 21) and finally in book form, were in French—making it an especially singular and overlooked item among American scholarship on Joyce's works. The language of *Joyce et Mallarmé* is straightforward, without pretense or elaborate rhetorical devices, and discloses the time period in which it was written. It celebrates, for instance, what in today's critical climate might be cause for embarrassment and apology—its status as an "influence study." The restrictive practices of this traditional kind of academic scholarship, its need to show when and under what conditions Joyce might have read Mallarmé, to search for quotations, cross-references, and thematic similarities for the Mallarmean influence on Joyce, seem somewhat naive in a more playful and perverse postmodernist environment.

Indeed, David Hayman's role in opening Joyce studies to the postmodern moment—the route that led him from *Joyce et Mallarmé* to *The Mechanics of Meaning* to *In the Wake of the Wake* and beyond—suggests that he has remained over the years more Continental than American in his critical practices, more in the French mode than the English in his theoretical positioning. Thus, *Joyce et Mallarmé* seems retrospectively both a perfectly predictable beginning for this long journey between the American Midwest (where Hayman has taught for more than twenty years) and the Parisian Left Bank. But from a postmodernist perspective, *Joyce et Mallarmé* is also symptomatic of the kind of institutional academic thinking that has forced a reevaluation of critical principles and practices. Joyce's works have become a battleground (or playing field) across which rivals demonstrate the efficacy of their theories of reading and writing. Hayman seems both shortsighted and immensely prophetic in writing that "we recognize that Joyce put everything in his books, but in order to *extract* this message from its *enigmatic envelope* we must have *patience*, a certain sensitivity, and time" (1:13, emphasis added). "Patience" announces a certain form of contemporary criticism that is very much indebted to Joyce's works; Jacques Derrida's continued calls for patient rereadings (particularly of works by Mallarmé and Joyce) are a mark of deconstruction. But the notion that any literary text offers a "message" that must be "extracted" from its "envelope" is a tenet of 1930s New Criticism that feminism, deconstruction, and psychoanalytic critical schools have denounced as a misguided, even dangerous, description of literary critical practice. This view of the scholarly endeavor, however, was certainly dominant both in America and in France in the early 1950s, and the field of literary criticism could hardly be expected to predict the revolutionary effects that "patient reading" might produce.

Thus, a contemporary reading of *Joyce et Mallarmé* is anachronistic in two ways, as though the text were simultaneously out of date and ahead of its time. This is not to fault Hayman's work but rather to suggest that this work is a product of its historical context and also—after the fact— has been subjected to the modernity (what we in America call postmodernism) of both Joyce and Mallarmé. It is here, on a ground he could hardly have suspected to be so slippery, pockmarked, tortuous, and resisting, that Hayman follows a double track: first, to discover the sources of Joyce's "theory of suggestion" and the workings of his "suggestive style"; second, to examine the Mallarmean elements in Joyce's oeuvre, from *Stephen Hero* through *Finnegans Wake*.

Hayman first argues (vol. 1) that Joyce found the "germs of suggestion, words, musical themes, the dualism implied in nature, paradoxes, etc." in Mallarmé's *Crise de vers*, *Un Coup de dés*, and in the collection *Divagations*. Joyce had read all these works—with the exception, perhaps of *Un Coup de dés* —in Trieste, and by the writing of *Finnegans Wake*, he not only possessed a copy of *Un Coup de dés*, but had assimilated its radical linguistic practices. Hayman traces a line of early resistance against the realist novel (the changes that made *Stephen Hero* into *A Portrait of the Artist as a Young Man*) to an increasing interest in the play of language itself, ending in *Finnegans Wake*.

Joyce resisted a straightforward "telling" of his stories, the means of "direct statement," as he explained to Frank Budgen, preferring a method of suggestion, the "analogies, nuances and verbal experiences . . . allusions, musical themes, absence of description, stylistic innovations" (1:186) that Hayman isolates. This stylistics of suggestion included in *Ulysses* the use of Homeric materials, psychological experimentation, the interior monologue, invented words, and even the use (or seeming misuse) of punctuation. These methods, Hayman claims, Joyce found in Mallarmé. The symbolic system is hierarchical, and its elements radiate from words "that form the kernel of the work" (1:187). According to this system, *Ulysses* is more music than prose; every element is a "symbol and is symbolized; it acts on distinct levels, but no level acts alone and no element isolates itself" (1:187). This system constitutes the philosophic base of *Finnegans Wake*, which places itself on paradoxes and dualities that logically result from a style and a method that have their power in words.

Specific instances of how this method—*très Mallarméen* —works in *Ulysses* include the kinds of word games found in the phrase "Molly's legs are out of plumb" (the word "plumb" reverberating multiply, as a kind of *calembour*, but also suggesting a juxtaposition of ideas) and "Perfume of embraces all him assailed" (where, Hayman argues, there is both a juxtaposition of words and an association of ideas). *Ulysses* follows a poetics of suggestion by syntax, repetition, association of ideas, symbols, and a system of symbols and allusions (1:77–80). Hayman illustrates the workings of wordplay with a series of quotations from *Ulysses*, both in English and in French translation, to suggest the visual and aural play of words on the page (1:80–83); he later follows the same exercise through punctuation. Unfortunately, what remains ambiguously unsettled in English is often rendered more straightforward—eliminating some of the "levels" of play—in the French, a condition that is often remarked on today (especially by French critics) but is left unremarked by Hayman. Finally, he lists all the types of wordplay in *Ulysses:* (1) composed words (made up of portions of other words); (2) words formed from an accent on an unaccented syllable; (3) words that, by their position in the sentence, carry a double possibility of interpretation; (4) the "classic *calembour*," or pun, resulting from the juxtaposition of two words that, when joined, reveal a hidden sense; (5) the linkage of two words ("steelhoofs"); and (6) the creation of verbs. These examples are suggestive themselves, and if they seem naive by today's standards, we must remember that it is David Hayman who has patiently educated Joyce's readers in the mechanics of such readings. Excepting Fritz Senn, Hayman has probably done more than any other reader of Joyce's texts to sensitize us to the multidimensional verbality of the Joycean world.

Hayman argues, as others have since him, that the movement of *Ulysses* from daytime to darkness, a move toward the darkened world ahead of *Finnegans Wake*, makes itself felt in a kind of enrichment of suggestive language. One might even say that this text becomes increasingly poetic as it moves away from the daylight rationality. Hayman claims that *Finnegans Wake* is the supreme example of the Mallarmean method in the Joycean oeuvre and that the key text is Mallarmé's *Un Coup de dés*. The "influence" of Mallarmé's text on Joyce's is evident, writes Hayman, in the "striking similarities between these works: their themes, their structure, their technique (this is to say, the manifest principle of suggestion) and their poetry" (1:121–22). Hayman comments that "one finds throughout these two works the same act continually revised from different angles. The themes repeat themselves in a singularly symphonic fashion—each demonstrating a different face of the same problem: the problem of creation, of natural existence" (1:121–22).

One must note in passing, however, that *Un Coup de dés* is a poem, the most radically innovative of the Mallarmean oeuvre, while *Finnegans Wake* retains vestiges of narrative in a sequence of interlocking set pieces that use the elements of narrative even when the story-telling effort is blocked, deflected, or interrupted. Hayman's argument is that in both Joyce and Mallarmé there is a story (*le récit*), often several stories operating simultaneously, that exists and must be discovered behind the "veils" of Mallarmean "evocation." Reading these works "requires an analogous effort to that which created them" (1:123); indeed, the method is one of analogy. At the base of the method, in both Joyce and Mallarmé, is the *word*, words that (in *Finnegans Wake*) "lend themselves to many interpretations" (1:124). Although the basis of the Joycean/Mallarmean method in the *word* has certainly been challenged by postmodernism, which finds one of its richest elements in tracing the undecidable path between the heard and the seen in these texts, observing the ways in which vowel formations regroup themselves outside of words, how consonants drop away from words to float throughout the text (s/p, HCE, and lsp in the *Wake*, for instance), the connections between *Un Coup de dés* and *Finnegans Wake* have been the subject of extensive commentary by French avant-gardists, particularly those associated with the *Tel Quel* group of the early 1970s.[2]

But Hayman is hardly to be faulted for a more conservative approach to the Joyce/Mallarmé connection than might have been provided some fifteen years later in the wake of enormous scholarship on the *Wake*. In the early 1950s, he had only two critical texts on *Finnegans Wake* to guide him—Campbell and Robinson's *Skeleton Key* and *Our Exagmination*. As part of his thesis research, he interviewed Samuel Beckett, Lucie Léon, Stuart Gilbert, Frank Budgen, Maria Jolas, and others who had been associated with Joyce. His thesis, however, was compounded of original research on Joyce's works, and in the field of *Wake* studies he was virtually alone in these years, guided by his sense of the text's directions, his reading practices, and his critical insights. Retrospectively, then, the Hayman commentary on the Mallarmean influence on *Finnegans Wake* is an extraordinary piece of work, a puzzling out of textual methodology in the absence of theoretical models to support his findings and against the reigning dogma of American New Criticism.

Hayman's argument is that Joyce did not destroy language (as some reviewers of the *Wake* had suggested) but worked within the rules of English syntax, semantics, and grammar to render words "more powerful" (1:126). He finds that the four types of wordplay discovered in *Ulysses* (word compositions; words with evocative internal syllables; words that give themselves, according to their sentence position, either to a double application or to a double interpretation; and verbal suggestions) apply to *Finnegans Wake* as well and that all but the first category are found in Mallarmé's works, especially in *Un Coup de dés*. To his original four-part schema, Hayman adds subcategories. Under word compositions he includes words formed from the elements of two or three English words, superimposed or structurally telescoped ("rollorrish rattillary"); words composed with the addition of one or two letters of other words ("spreach," combining "speech" and "preach"); and word creations, from one or several languages, based on sound ("fusefiressense"—"fuse," "fire," and "essence," including the French *essence*, to form a play of "phospherescence"). As examples under category two, where interior syllables of words take on a new dimension, the *Wake* exploits multilingual possibilities (such as "Hoopoe," which combines the name of a bird, *la huppe*, with "hoop" to suggest the cycling of history). It is the third category, however, that proves the most interesting, the most clearly linked to Mallarmé's effort in *Un Coup de dés*. Here the possibilities of meanings rest with the placement of a word in the sentence. In the phrase "till the bark of Saint Grouseus," Hayman finds that bark suggests the bark of a tree, a *barque* (a boat), and the bark of a dog or a human. And the classic *calembour* makes its play across languages: "Loose afore" ("Lucifer"); "foul a delfian" ("Philadelphia").

Hayman adds a final category in which foreign words are used because of their resemblance to English words (or, in the case of Mallarmé's method, to French words). "The wild lac of gotliness," for instance, plays on the French *lac* and the English "lack." In an example from *Un Coup de dés*, "Legs en la disparition," Hayman hears (and sees) the English word "legs" for the French word that suggests legacy and inheritance, where the legatee in the poem is ambiguous—the legatee may be the son, the writer's own oeuvre, or even his own shadow. Headfirst in the way, drowning, the Master is himself in an ambiguous position, legs in air, perhaps. The play on the French *legs* is a favorite of certain contemporary critics, taken from readings of Mallarmé, Plato, Joyce, and others. Derrida plays on this in *Legs de Freud*, and the English translation contains the following comment: "In current French the 'g' is often pronounced, but the original pronunciation was the same as *lais*, from the verb *laisser*, to leave. A legacy is what one leaves, of course; *lais* was both the ancient form of *legs* and the term for a narrative or lyric poem. *Lais* is also the term for the land left bare at low tide. . . . Its principal meaning, however, is the same as the English 'leash.' Thus the paradox implicit in *legs*: it leashes, ties up, *binds* (see *lier*) those to whom it is left, while maintaining resonances of tidal, rhythmic return."[3] Hayman's last category, verbal echoes and onomatopoeic effects, is left without comment from him, but it has proven to be the most fruitful for contemporary readers of the *Wake*, who listen attentively not only to individual words but to the echoing effect of Wakean language, where such effects are part of a superimposition of sounds over other sounds.[4]

Before examining closely the impact of *Un Coup de dés* on *Finnegans Wake*, Hayman analyzes other aspects of the *Wake* narrative in terms of the poetics of suggestion. He argues that syntactic structures remain very much intact in the *Wake* (Joyce's experiments in *Ulysses* with "deregulating" the syntax having proven disappointing to him). That is, the *Wake* achieves its wondrous effects by reliance on the rich vocabulary of English, and here Hayman, along with other early explicators of the *Wake*, such as Clive Hart and Bernard Benstock, suggests that *Finnegans Wake* is a text whose root language is English, from which deformations and deviations are formed. Contemporary reading practices take issue with this claim, of course, arguing that the *Wake* defeats an effort to establish lexical hierarchies.[5] It is punctuation, according to Hayman, that provides Joyce a means of suggesting syntactical ambiguity, an indeterminacy and flexibility of language, implying that a theory of punctuation in the *Wake* might yield interesting evidence of a "root" syntax, if not a primary language as such. This suggestion is one of the most intriguing in Hayman's study, and one that unfortunately has not yet been taken up by *Wake* scholars. Margot Norris has commented recently that she feels an important next stage of *Wake* scholarship might involve a rhetorical study of this text, and an analysis of the place and function of *Wake* punctuation would be essential to such a study.[6] It must be noted, and not for the last time, that the publication of Hayman's initial study in French has denied it a reading public among English-language readers, suggesting—and not for the first time—that Anglo-American dominance in the Joyce industry has resulted in a restrictive monolinguism. Even David Hayman, who has played an instrumental role in bringing the study of Joyce's works—especially *Finnegans Wake* —into an international setting, can state here that "the fact that English is a language very rich in vocabulary explains the structure of *Finnegans Wake*" (1:132). He writes that there are certain Joycean words (in categories comprising common and proper nouns and words suggesting well-known events or quotations) that form a kind of background for the *Wake*, giving passages their "tone" or fixing their "sense." In much the same way, Mallarmé's use of typographical images in *Un Coup de dés* indicates the symbolic importance of the boat, the hat, or the pen by means of suggestion—an action that moves from mere allusions to external elements to the inscription of poetic symbols. Hayman traces these symbols in the *Wake*, finding them in attitudes and qualities associated with the five members of the Wakean family (e.g., Anna Livia with water and river) and in the various plays on the names of family figures, these last often taken from Joyce's notes to "Work in Progress."

In comparing Mallarmé's methods to Joyce's, Hayman notes an almost oppositional positioning: Mallarmé wanted to evoke the world through condensation (*Un Coup de dés* is eleven pages long), tracing its effects in large strokes, "giving the reader the greatest possible imaginative liberty" (1:149); Joyce painted the world through an accretion of small details, his exacting depiction of the world given to us through an attention to worldly problems and antagonisms (Joyce's book, in consequence, is 628 pages long). In order to compare the effects of these two methods, Hayman juxtaposes specific sections of each text to the other, choosing microcosmic cross-sections that can be analyzed according to "the language, style, structure, the nature of characters and actions, in short, all the interactions of the suggestive mechanisms of the work" (1:149–50). The exemplary passage from *Finnegans Wake* is on page 449 ("I could sit on safe side till the bark of Saint Grouseus for hoopoe's hours"); the passage from *Un Coup de dés* is from the third page of the text:

SOIT
     que
        l'Abîme
   blanchi
      étale
         furieux
            sous une inclinaison
              plane désespérément
                  d'aile
                  la sienne
                        par
  avance retombée d'un mal à dresser le vol
              et couvrant les jaillisements
                    coupant au ras les bonds
       très à l'intérieur résume.

Each passage is carefully mined for elements of comparison, and although Hayman's reading is suggestive rather than comprehensive, it yields several insights. He discovers a kind of complicity in these works that has since been described in its minutest details by readers like Philippe Sollers and Jacques Derrida. Hayman writes that "in exploiting to the very depths the possibilities held in words, ideas, and themes, these two works offer us an infinity of effects" (1:171). And it is precisely the term "effects" that has had such reverberations for a contemporary criticism less concerned with source studies and with measuring direct influences of one writer on another than in measuring—with the accuracy of electron microscopes and computerized tuning forks—the effects of certain kinds of literary practices. Among French writers, the key figure is Mallarmé; for English readers in the twentieth century, the most important figure is Joyce (although at the moment of this writing the works of Gertrude Stein appear to offer even more radical possibilities for "effectual" readings).

Hayman admits that Joyce's experiments are far more wide ranging than Mallarmé's (an opinion that might not be endorsed by certain contemporary readers), arguing that the "fine nuances" that so well served Mallarmé were inadequate for Joyce, who needed to find a "more radical system" in his efforts to "deform language" (1:171). What lies behind the assumption of a "deformed" Joycean language is the understanding of language as normative and systematized. Poststructuralist thinking has interrogated this belief in the normative, arguing that language is always "deformed," that is, given to sight and sound effects that open it to multiple meanings and a variety of effects. Joyce did not "deform" language; rather, he followed the routes of non-sense — ways determined by the unconscious — to discover all that "normative" use of language represses and denies.

Joyce's and Mallarmé's works share, however, a system of "suggestion" that can function only by indirection: everything is understood according to "associations, themes or interwoven ideas; no theme or character is isolated in time, for at each moment, it contains the germs of other existences" (1:172). Mallarmé and Joyce also use suggestive elements according to dualism and paradox. The first category works according to couplings: in *Un Coup de dés*, the linking of light/night, man/woman, sky/sea, pen/hat, pen/inkstand, sail/boat; in *Finnegans Wake*, the couplings include Shem/Shaun, Butt/Taff, Cain/Abel, and Sterne/Swift, associations that further represent soul/body, bad/good, wand/rock. Beside these dualisms rest the paradoxes — "contradictory elements that give birth to words" (1:174). For Mallarmé, the effects produced are oppositional: the appearance of a darkness intensified by light effects, a negative presented through a positive, bitterness allied by alchemy to sweetness. Examples from the *Wake* include the "neviewscope" (a telescope used to see nothing) and "goosemother," which suggests both Mother Goose and "go smother," an implicit threat held in the figure of children's stories. Behind innocence lurks the nightmare; behind paradise lurks hell; behind daybreak stands the child of the night — a setting built from the paradoxical. To such intellectual and linguistic effects are added the themes and motifs that Joyce's work shares with Mallarmé's, and Hayman argues that these methods are musical rather than literary. The literary is rendered *through* the musical, which itself is translated from sound to typography to give the texts depth of sound, multiplicity of echoes, and a sonority appropriate to their grand themes. The basic technique in each work is repetition (which has an echo effect) so that the themes, characters, and subjects are juxtaposed, overlapped, and interwoven.

In the second volume of *Joyce et Mallarmé*, Hayman traces specific Mallarmean elements in Joyce's works, noting the reference in *Ulysses* to Mallarmé as the "finest flower of corruption." In the Library chapter, Stephen Dedalus is presented as Hamlet through an allusion to Mallarmé's "Hamlet et Fortinbras" (first published in *La Revue blanche*, 15 July 1896), evoked here through a quotation concerning Hamlet, "il se promène, lisant au livre de lui-même," and Mr. Best's sketch of an advertisement for a production of *Hamlet* in a French provincial town:

HAMLET

ou

LE DISTRAIT

Pièce de Shakespeare

As Hayman comments, this set of allusions to Mallarmé quickly fixes Stephen Dedalus as a Hamlet figure and brings into the context of the Library chapter the influence on Stephen of late-nineteenth-century French decadent writing (2:7–9).

But it is *Finnegans Wake* that provides the richest Mallarmean field, including references to the *Hérodiade*, *L'Après-midi d'un faune*, and *Un Coup de dés*. Hayman counts a minimum of thirty references to Mallarmé's name (2:20) and more than seventy references to *Un Coup de dés*, the most important Mallarmé work in the *Wake* (2:39). Significant references to this experimental work include wordplays on its title, especially when Joyce plays on the phonetic and literal senses of the words. Among these Hayman lists *coup des blés*, *coup de fouet JJ*, *coup de fusil*, and *loup des blés* (2:39). The evidence of Joyce's interest in *Un Coup de dés* rests in the *Wake* notebooks, where Hayman finds Joyce imitating the movement of the wave in Mallarmé's work through the placement of words on the page:

Switch

wave

back   way

ride

and in apparent anagrams

SHEM

HEN

AN

M

R

O

C

K

The Mallarmean links occur not only through this experimentation with word disruptions and displacements across the pages of text but with thematic and symbolic materials. Hayman notes, for instance, the multiple ways in which the crime in the park suggests the role of chance in human endeavor, its effects measured by a kind of "roll of the dice," repeating and reversing patterns of determination and fixity: "Another aspect of the crime: the fact of having acted alone, the fact even of being an individual, implies a role of the dice. Still this 'crime' has a creative side: for psychoanalytic readings, the defecation associates itself at a primitive level with a creative act. This act of HCE has its equivalent in the creation of thought, of babies, of a world, and provokes therefore the anger of the gods that results in the fall" (2:43). Indeed, as Hayman argues, the result of this "roll of the dice," an act of defiance against absolute power, is inevitably the fall of the Master or of HCE, a fall that repeats the movement of the role of the dice, and—according to Joyce's text—"implies nothing definitive" (2:43).

The rolling and overturning effect is repeated variously in the *Wake*, in the route of ALP's letter, in the children's games and the lesson's chapter, in the relationship of Shem the Penman to Shaun the Postman, in the sexual fall of the master and the "crime" in the park, in the disruption and repetition cycles of generation and regeneration. Even the terms of these important incidents in the *Wake* chronicle find their parallels in *Un Coup de dés:* the pen (life wand, penis, symbol of creation), seer, scribe, thunder and storms, Master and Mother (*mère*, sea, and mother), cap, veil/sail (*le voile, la voile*), fortune telling, counting by numbers, and associations of sound across languages—cup, blow, overthrow (*la coupe, le coup*), dice (*dés*) and day (*dés*), etc. At one level, Joyce's use of Mallarmé's text appears through the operation of allusive method: "To fallthere at bare feet hurryaswormarose: Two dies of one rafflement" (*FW* 302, 26–28), which appears in French as: "Pour tomber là à ses pieds nus, vite, pendant qu'il se lève. Deux dés d'un seul coup" (2:52). Hayman comments that the description of ALP's letter and the sexual act that represents one face of HCE's crime are spoken of in terms of Mallarmé's text: the dice that fall to inaugurate a new cycle of history, a fall that completes a previous cycle—a movement that also suggests the generational within families. The tension between the brothers often focuses on the pen and the act of creation through writing, and the implied references from Mallarmé suggest both the power of the pen as sexual power and interpretations of the word "strokes" as both swimming and writing strokes: "Pose the pen, man, way me does. Bould strokes for your life!" (*FW* 303.2–4) translates as "Posez la plume, mon vieux, comme je le fais. Nagez ferme pour avoir la vie sauve" (2:53).

From a contemporary—that is, postmodern—perspective, the most interesting links between the *Wake* and *Un Coup de dés* are those that rest in phonetic representations or in homophonic confusions between French and English. Hayman works with an apparently simple example:

"COME SI . . . LEG IN A TEE" (*FW* 305, righthand margin), translated by Hayman as *"COMME SI . . . JAMBE EN T."* The *"comme si"* finds a direct parallel in *Un Coup de dés*, but the phrase opens itself to all kinds of bilingual reading possibilities: come see (*venez voir*), *comme si* (as if), and *si* as "yes" in both Italian and (in response to a negative question) in French. The second part of the quotation, "leg in a tee," suggests in French a quotation from Mallarmé ("legs en la disparition"), the disappearance of the master-hero, the fall of HCE, whose legs are seen disappearing, the disappearance of the *fils-ombre* in *Un Coup de dés*, and the image of the two legs in the air (\ /) that becomes a visual image across the pages of both *Un Coup de dés* and *Finnegans Wake*. These examples are among several that cross—in sound and sight—the presumed barriers between languages properly separate from each other. In so doing, they suggest not only Joyce's indebtedness to Mallarmé, but also the workings of the *Wake*, a text that continually a/wakes to echoes and images of languages at play.

More generally, the roll of dice suggests the wave/wake motion, the overturning and reversing of solar cycles in both works (2:60–61), sexual couplings and copulation, the violence of war (apparent in the Russian General sequence of the *Wake* and in suggestions of the chance that governs the game of "Russian roulette"), card games, horse races, games of chance involving betting, culpability, sacred numbers ("seven" in both texts), sacred texts (particularly the Bible), erection of false symbols (Babel), and the decomposition of words. The double desire to give oneself up to chance, to the roll of the dice, and to beat chance at its own game governs both texts. Such desire is related to the abyss and the abysmal, as Hayman suggests: "It is the madness of the infinite, the ardent desire to 'become' in the eyes of an infinite universe, to create, to surpass" (2:75). Hayman demonstrates the ways in which the experiment is repeated, Joyce's nods to Mallarmé in the insistence on French spellings of certain key words: *hasard* instead of the English *hazard* and *sang* (which means "blood" in French and which is homonymous to "sang," the past tense of the English "sing"), enforcing a link between blood and violence with poetry and literary creation. The abyssal also suggests a major theme in *Un Coup de dés*, the drowning of the master. Its darkness invokes the shadow-son ("shadow-sun" homophone) of the master, the tensions between father and sons in the *Wake*, and the boys as shadows of each other. The roll of the dice, however, suggests a larger theme for Hayman: "It is the logic of the unconscious-night against the conscious-day. One finds here the fundamental theme of *Un Coup de dés* —that of the cyclical movement that inevitably results in the male-female opposition" (2:86). There is no final "reckoning of accounts" in these two texts, no effort to "even" the odds of a game of chance that each follows through the combinations and improbabilities of nature. Instead, there is a steady overturning of expectation through a repetition of the ordinary, the daily, the cyclical.

As Hayman admits in his conclusion, his major worry had been to "establish the extent of Joyce's knowledge of Mallarmé's works and the 'givens' of his theory of suggestion" (2:99). Such is the project of an academic thesis, a project that in the wake of contemporary criticism— which, in a roll of the dice, has overturned the principles on which "influence studies" premised themselves—is less concerned with tracing the evidence of literary legacies. Although such an effort marks the historical moment of this text—and its author—it also makes important contributions to our current thinking about *Finnegans Wake* and *Un Coup de dés*, of Joyce and Mallarmé as harbingers of an avant-garde that remains for us in the future tense. Of particular interest is the series of appendixes that provides a coda to these two volumes. The mere listing of their contents suggests the kind of painstaking scholarship for which Hayman is well known and the rich imaginative reservoir offered by a juxtaposition—or, in contemporary parlance, a "putting into play"—of the two texts. Appendix A lists Mallarmé quotations from the Trieste notebook; Appendix B lists quotations and paraphrases of Mallarmé in Joyce's works; Appendix C lists appearances of Mallarmé's name in Joyce's works (including the *Wake* notebooks and the *Wake* itself); Appendix D—the longest listing, comprising almost 100 pages of text— lists Mallarmean elements in both the notebooks and *Finnegans Wake*. These listings include references to the *Héroidiade*, *L'Après-midi d'un faune* and *Un Coup de dés*. From this last work, Hayman divides the listings according to Mallarmean figures that appear in the *Wake:* the roll of the dice, elements of the "shadow-son," drowning, waves and undulation, the whirlwind, and madness. The appendixes allow Hayman close attention to the contextual situations of Mallarmean references in the *Wake* and provide source material for further study of the effects of Mallarmé's theory of suggestion on Joyce's works.

NOTES

1. David Hayman, *Joyce et Mallarmé*, 2 vols. (Paris: Cahiers des lettres modernes, 1956). Additional references to this work are made parenthetically in the text. Translations from the French are mine.

2. Derrida has paid particular attention to Mallarmé, publishing *"La Double seance"* in nos. 41 and 42 of *Tel Quel* in 1970, reprinted in *La Dissémination* (Paris: Editions de Seuil, 1972). Barbara Johnson's introduction to her translation,

Dissemination (Chicago: University of Chicago Press, 1981), reprints a letter from Philippe Sollers to Jacques Derrida, a letter written on the margins of both Mallarmé's and Derrida's texts and inserted into the nonspace between the two halves of "The Double Session." According to Johnson, this letter—virtually untranslatable—"transforms [Mallarmé's *Mimique*] by twisting its graphic and phonic signifiers in such a way as to reveal surprising associations and unexpected intersections with the text of 'The Double Session' into which it is inserted" (xix). Mallarmé's writings served as exemplary texts in the work of Sollers and Julia Kristeva through the 1970s. Derrida's interest apparently continues, *Un Coup de dés* echoing throughout his *Ulysses gramophone*, translated by Shari Benstock, in *James Joyce: The Ninth Symposium*, ed. Bernard Benstock (Syracuse: Syracuse University Press, 1988).

3. See the translator's introduction and glossary to Jacques Derrida, *The Post Card*, trans. Alan Bass (Chicago: University of Chicago Press, 1987). Derrida has described this text as a "restag[ing of] the babelisation of the postal system in *Finnegans Wake*" (*Ulysses Gramophone*), and the two sons—Shem the Penman and Shaun the Postman—serve as runners in a postal system to which they have fallen heir: it is their *legacy*.

4. The privileging of sound sense to sight sense in the *Wake* has a long tradition, one explicitly brought to bear as an interpretive model by Philippe Sollers in "Comme si le vieil Homère," *Le Nouvel observateur* (6 February 1982): 73–74. I question his reading/listening principles in "Apostrophes: Framing *Finnegans Wake*," chap. 1 of *Textualizing the Feminine: On the Limits of Genre* (Norman: University of Oklahoma Project for Discourse and Theory, 1991). See also Derrida's "Two Words for Joyce" in *Post-Structuralist Joyce: Essays from the French*, ed. Derek Attridge and Daniel Ferrer (Cambridge: Cambridge University Press, 1984), 145–60.

5. A typical reading strategy for *Finnegans Wake* has long been to "translate" given passages into English, a strategy founded on the assumption that the work is predominantly English, following the syntactic and grammatic structures of English. At a recent workshop at the Zurich James Joyce Foundation (10–15 August 1987), participants were asked—as a first effort to come to terms with a *Wake* passage—to determine what the text would mean in English, a strategy long ago suggested by Clive Hart and continued by Fritz Senn and others. There is room here only to suggest that the foundations of such a practice are questioned by contemporary theory; see Derek Attridge and Daniel Ferrer's introduction to *Post-Structuralist Joyce* (1–13), where the reduction of the *Wake* to an essential English might be one of the "domesticating" reading strategies objected to by poststructuralist criticism. How *Wake* language works, how it eschews hierarchical categories, has yet to be examined carefully by Joyce specialists.

6. These comments were made in response to Richard Lehan's paper at the James Joyce conference, Riverside, California (15 May 1987) and to Shari Benstock in conversation.

Ruth Bauerle

Hodgart and Worthington:
From Silence to *Song**

Scholars who began their Joyce studies after *Song in the Works of James Joyce* was in print find it difficult to imagine functioning without it. Discovered in Northwestern's Deering Library stacks with a glee repressed only by institutional demands for quiet, it was one of the first books that accompanied my inaugural voyage with *Ulysses* in the midsixties, along with Budgen, Gilbert, Ellmann's elegant biography, and Kain's *Fabulous Voyager*.

To explain the significance of such books is as superfluous as to describe why and how ocean voyages are eased by charts or maps. Of course, the lone sailor-reader might set out to enjoy Joyce unaided, hoping to be buoyed by the force and rhythm of his prose rather than washed under and drowned. But like Icarus or Stephen, such a traveler may be burdened by aquaphobia, a fear of losing to the sea's power before the journey ends happily.

Early comment on Joyce scarcely mentioned his use of music. T. S. Eliot, writing on "*Ulysses*, Order, and Myth,"[1] made no mention of music, though he was a delighted habitué of the English music halls whose songs and performers appear throughout *Ulysses*. In the *New Republic*, Clive Bell, discussing the influence of jazz on Joyce's style, suggested that Joyce "does deliberately go to work to break up the traditional sentence. . . . Effectually and with a will he rags the literary instrument. Unluckily, this will has at its service talents which are only moderate."[2]

---

*For assistance in this paper I am indebted to Prof. Zack Bowen, who generously shared his recollections as one of Dr. Mabel Worthington's students.

A general sense of Joyce's musicality was suggested by Ford Madox Ford, who wrote in the *Chicago Tribune Sunday Magazine* that "the pleasure—the very great pleasure—that I get from going through the sentences of Mr. Joyce is that given me simply by the cadence of his prose."[3]

There is no mention of music in Deming's two-volume collection of critical response, *James Joyce: The Critical Heritage*, until pieces written in 1930. Then Frank O'Connor allowed rather grudgingly in the *Irish Statesman* that the melodies of Joyce's brilliant phrases "haunt one's mind long after one has forgotten what they are about."[4] Herbert Read, writing for *The Listener* in August, 1930, saw the possibility of an underlying formal structure "analogous to the structure of a fugue."[5] Read was doubtless prompted by the appearance, that year, of Stuart Gilbert's *James Joyce's "Ulysses,"* with Joyce's own explanation of musical elements in his writing.[6]

When Frank Budgen discussed the rhythms and music of the Dublin odyssey in *James Joyce and the Making of "Ulysses,"*[7] he, like Gilbert, expressed views he had heard directly from Joyce. Mary Colum was also a friend of Joyce, but there is no indication whether she was reflecting his views when in 1937 she averred that his words fell "on the ear as music does" and went on to mention his enormous capacity to summon a mood.[8] Though she sensed similarities between Joyce's prose and music, she did not analyze how far this "master of the evocative method" depended on melodic fragments recalled by textual allusion to aid his recapture of Dublin.

Even the noted Harry Levin generalized, rather than adumbrating particulars, in his pioneering *James Joyce: A Critical Introduction*. Without developing his idea, Levin suggested that music substitutes for direct expression of feeling at the close of "Clay," as Maria sings "I dreamt that I dwelt in marble halls."[9]

Except for the "Sirens" episode, Levin had little more specific to say when he came to *Ulysses*, other than to comment on its musical texture and its modeling after Wagner.[10] He identified "Love's Old Sweet Song" as "the leitmotif of Molly's infidelity,"[11] and he noted verbal themes set to music in *Ulysses*: blasphemy and the mass in the liturgy of May Dedalus's death; cuckoldry in gems from Molly's operatic repertoire; and church and state celebrated in "ribald" songs like the "Ballad of Joking Jesus" and "On Coronation Day." (In fact, "On Coronation Day," at least in any printed versions, is lively and vulgar in the sense of common, but hardly ribald.)

For "Sirens," Levin provided a longer analysis, mentioning by title *"M'appari"* and *"The Croppy Boy."*[12] Two others, "a song from Floradora" and "an air from *La Somnambula*" [*sic*], are less specific references to "Shade of the Palm" and *Tutto è sciolto*. Though Levin commented that "at close range, *Finnegans Wake* seems to realize the aspiration of the other arts toward the condition of music,"[13] he made no note of the thousands of musical allusions Joyce embedded in the *Wake* to realize that aspiration.

Most perceptive was Martin Ross, whose essay "Music and James Joyce" accompanied Hazel Felman's musical setting for "Anna Livia Plurabelle." Though his discussion of Joyce's musicality was quite general, Ross made the point that music is "a black art" that "evokes . . . the strange, dissolving shapes that people our sub-conscious or semi-conscious minds" and that "music can never reproduce the body of life, it can only summon the shadows."[14] Yet he provided no explanation as to how these capacities of music are called into action when the allusions buried in Joyce's prose recall the shadows of memory.

Even into the 1950s, many generalizations appeared without identifying or collecting specific allusions. Vivian Mercier, analyzing Joyce and the Irish parodic tradition in 1956, did identify ten songs, some with multiple allusions.[15] In the same year, Marvin Magalaner and Richard Kain, in their biographical sketch of Joyce near the end of *James Joyce: The Man, the Work, the Reputation*, reflected without citing particulars that "no reader can fail to detect the important role music plays, in fact and in spirit, throughout the works."[16]

Hugh Kenner, also writing in 1956, dealt with few specifics of music in *Dublin's Joyce*. He cited the performance of "*M'appari*" in "Sirens" as marking both Bloom "violated by a voice" as he merges with his absent wife and Bloom fused with Simon Dedalus, transubstantial and consubstantial fathers made one for an instant during this song.[17] When Simon sings, Kenner went on to say, "he sums up his age."[18] Concluding his chapter by quoting the opening line of "Love's Old Sweet Song," Kenner asserted that "on waves of song Dublin was borne toward the hallucination of a lyrical past."[19]

Nevertheless, the need for specific identifications was being felt increasingly. In *Fabulous Voyager* (1947), Richard M. Kain had already identified the task to be done: "To trace the recurrences of these thematic songs would reveal how large a part music plays in the consciousness [of Bloom and Stephen]. . . . Music is one of the most potent of subconscious recalls; it rises unexpectedly to mind and, in turn, leads to appropriate moods."[20]

At that very time, attention was turning to identifying and listing specific allusions. L. A. G. Strong had already enumerated some three dozen musical references two years before Kain's volume; in *The Sacred*

River he listed another 135 items by song title and page location in Joyce's work.[21] Writing concurrently with Strong, Vernon Hall examined closely Joyce's use of *Don Giovanni.*[22] In 1952–53, Joseph Prescott joined the work with articles in the *Modern Language Quarterly* and *Publications of the Modern Language Association,* listing a total of some twenty songs.[23] In those same years Prof. Hodgart, then at Pembroke College, Cambridge, began analyzing musical as well as other allusions in his own "Work in Progress" and "Shakespeare and *Finnegans Wake.*"[24]

Thus, by the time *Ulysses* was thirty years old and *Finnegans Wake* thirteen, scholars had published identifications for about three hundred allusions. It was just about this time, in 1952, that Dr. Worthington, at Temple University in Philadelphia, set out to identify all musical allusions. When she and Hodgart realized, in 1955, that they were engaged on the same research, they agreed to join forces.

In the course of their work, Worthington published several articles incorporating some of her results. These included discussions of Irish folk songs in *Ulysses* (identifying forty-three and giving lyrics);[25] American folk songs in *Finnegans Wake* (forty-nine identifications of folk and early popular music with multiple allusions, omitting lyrics);[26] and nursery rhymes in *Finnegans Wake* (identifying sixty-eight rhymes, again often with multiple allusions).[27]

All of this preliminary inquiry came together at last. The slender size of *Song in the Works of James Joyce* belies both the labor involved and the value of the result. The book includes two essays: "The Sources" (a general survey of the songs discovered, classifying them and totaling the numbers) and "Songs and the Interpretation of *Finnegans Wake*" (incorporating material from Hodgart's two earlier articles). Thereafter come two invaluable lists: the first, with page/line number, identifies each allusion in Joyce's works, taken in an order that appears to focus on the importance of music in each. The poems (as a group) and *Exiles* come first, followed by *Dubliners,* which alluded to seventeen songs among the fifteen stories. *Stephen Hero* precedes *A Portrait of the Artist,* an arrangement illustrating that in rewriting the story, Joyce gave more importance to the music.[28] Whereas *Stephen Hero* has only a dozen melodies listed, *A Portrait* more than doubles that number with twenty-six. (One of these, "Turpin Hero," ought to have been listed also for *Stephen Hero,* whose title derived from that song.)

The gold, as Worthington once described it, came with *Ulysses,* and the real mother lode lay in *Finnegans Wake.* Since no one has ever been able to come up with a universally satisfactory definition of "allusion" to music—an exact quotation, a word, an echo of the language or central image, a rhythm—it has never been possible to obtain an exact count of musical allusions in the larger works. The first essay in *Song in the Works of James Joyce* ("The Sources") estimates the number at over four hundred songs in *Ulysses* and almost a thousand in *Finnegans Wake*.[29] (Many of the songs in *Finnegans Wake* appear also in *Ulysses*.) Also, songs such as *"M'appari"* in *Ulysses* or "Do ye ken John Peel" in *Finnegans Wake* appear repeatedly, so the number of allusions can be estimated as at least 3,500 for all works combined. (Hodgart and Worthington average slightly more than 31 allusions per page in their list, for a total of 3,400. More have since been identified.)

This page-by-page identification of allusions was in itself a stunning achievement. Coming three years after the first edition of Adaline Glasheen's *Census of Finnegans Wake*, *Song in the Works of James Joyce* provided the second scholarly analysis of allusions in the *Wake* and the first to list page/line allusions focused on a single subject for all of Joyce's works. In this respect, the work remains a rare achievement: thirty years later, only a few other studies have followed a single theme, page by page, through the whole Joyce oeuvre.

Later page-by-page companions were perforce indebted to *Song in the Works of James Joyce*. The results of Hodgart and Worthington's research contributed to Clive Hart's *Structure and Motif in "Finnegans Wake"*[30] by "offering a gathering of some of the most important motivistic material." In Hart's words, "that helped me to refine some of my ideas about motiv."[31] It antedated Weldon Thornton's *Allusions in "Ulysses"* (1968) by almost a decade; Gifford and Seidman's *Notes for Joyce: "Dubliners" and "Portrait"* (1967) by eight years; and the same authors' *Notes for Joyce: An Annotation of James Joyce's "Ulysses"* (1974) by fifteen years.

Worthington and Hodgart did not stop with this major advancement in understanding Joyce's work. They also alphabetized the songs they had found, listing after each the relevant page numbers from Joyce. Excluding operas, plays, and operettas, these total 1,181 vocal items, 136 of them nursery rhymes or singing games for children. Also listed are 41 operas like *Il Trovatore*, operettas like *The Gondoliers*, musicals like *No, No, Nanette*, or plays with music like *Arrah-na-Pogue*. (Both these major lists, of course, were achieved before computers made such alphabetizing and cross-indexing relatively easy and fast.)

It is now possible, from the work of these scholars, to confirm allusion to a particular song from the page/line listing. Other occurrences of the same melody or lyrics found in the alphabetical listing provide the basis for a comparative study of Joyce's handling of the song. Because the same list identifies both lyricists and composers, it is also possible, with a little searching, to identify all the Stephen Foster, George

Gershwin, Thomas Moore, or Percy French songs and thus to analyze Joyce's treatment of a given composer.

The alphabetical listing also assigns many songs to categories of nationality and type. Not unexpectedly, classification proved difficult to carry out accurately. Abbreviations for eleven west European and American "nationalities" include, inexplicably, "Elizabethan." There are no entries for east European melodies, however, either because none was found or because so few were identified that a separate grouping was needless.

There are also problems in ordering the songs by type. Is "Has Anybody Here Seen Kelly?" an American popular song or a music-hall ballad? Is "My Wild Irish Rose" American popular or American Irish? Is a cumulative song not also a folk song? Despite such ambiguities, the categories have proved to be helpful guides to the kind of music books in which a given song might be found.

The alphabetical listing serves another role: in it march together nursery rhymes; folk songs from Ireland, the United States, England, Switzerland, and France; popular music from the stage and cinema of at least seven nations; arias—especially tenor arias—from those operas Joyce loved to attend in every city in which he ever lived; hymns; elements of the Catholic mass; national anthems of Ireland, France, England, Norway, the United States, and Germany; nearly all Thomas Moore's *Irish Melodies*; many songs from Bobby Burns; a large number from Stephen Foster; a song of the Wobblies (Industrial Workers of the World) labor movement; songs by Gershwin and Percy French, Gilbert and Sullivan, Balfe and Fitzball and Kipling, Verlaine and Fortunatus, and even by a frontier preacher named Elisha Hoffman. What had earlier been dimly sensed is now confirmed: Joyce's auditory vacuum drew up all sorts of random musical scraps. Each of these was subject to the judgment of Stephen Dedalus on Dublin: they were important because they belonged to Joyce.

The study of these compilations reveals a great deal about Joyce and about his methods. His own poetry, for instance, had seemed more Elizabethan or Jacobean than modern in any possible sense of that word. Yet Hodgart and Worthington found only eleven Elizabethan songs. "I was not wearier where I lay" appears in *A Portrait of the Artist as a Young Man;* "To bed, to bed" (appropriately enough) in *Ulysses.* The other nine are embedded, sometimes repeatedly, in the distinctly un-Elizabethan *Finnegans Wake.*

Sixty-one hymns and religious works, both Christian and Jewish, appear on Hodgart and Worthington's list. These included carols, such as "Silent Night" or "The Holly and the Ivy"; elements of the Catholic mass, such as the *Kyrie Eleison;* medieval hymns, such as *Pange lingua;* American evangelist Ira D. Sankey's "Tell Me the Old, Old Story"; fourteen Negro spirituals; and the Jewish *Kol Nidre*. Hodgart and Worthington also identify sixteen French and twenty-five German vocal pieces, some of them parts of larger operas or included in other groupings such as hymns or carols.

There is also a bibliography of more than two hundred songbooks and a page of discography. There is, however, no key to which books or records include which songs.

The reviews a book receives depend partly on luck. In a sense, Hodgart and Worthington were unlucky in their timing. The *James Joyce Review* had just ceased publication when *Song in the Works of James Joyce* appeared. Neither the *James Joyce Quarterly*, *A Wake Newslitter*, nor *Éire/Ireland* had yet been born, nor, of course, those journals of the last decade, the *James Joyce Broadsheet*, the *Irish Literary Supplement*, *A Wake Circular*, and the *James Joyce Literary Supplement*. Circumstances denied the pair any substantial review by their peers in those early days of Joyce studies.

Though the published reviews were therefore brief, the reviewers were appreciative of the accomplishment. London's influential *Times Literary Supplement*, in a triple review devoting more space to the Hodgart and Worthington volume than to the other two combined,[32] classed *Song* as a "strictly factual" commentary, termed the introduction "illuminating," and called the work an "admirable companion to Mr. James Atherton's recent *The Books at the Wake*." (Atherton's book and *Song in the Works of James Joyce* both appeared in 1960 in England, but *Song* was published a year before Atherton in the United States.) *TLS* concluded "They have done their work well."[33]

Also in London, the *Musical Times* allowed three paragraphs to reviewer Charles Osborne, who seemed dismayed by the two long lists that composed the bulk of the book. Calling the writing of this book "mentally exhausting as well as physically arduous," Osborne cited a *Finnegans Wake* line with double allusion (only two!) and summed up, "Was it worth doing? I prefer to beg the question. There is no doubt that it has been done well."[34]

Clive Hart, who with Fritz Senn was to begin editing *A Wake Newslitter* two years later in 1962, wrote from Lund, Sweden, in the *Modern Language Review*. After commenting on the "vast devotional exercise" of an American composer then trying to set the whole text of *Finnegans Wake* to music, Hart commended the scholarly methods of Hodgart and Worthington. Their "carefully documented results will be of great value" to Joyce specialists," he wrote.[35]

In the United States, Robert Martin Adams included *Song in the*

Works of James Joyce as part of a review essay in the *Hudson Review* on four books.[36] Like Osborne in London, Adams seemed a bit daunted by the lists, calling the book "modest" in bulk, "necessarily short on literary charm," and a "reference-type." Nevertheless, he acknowledged that the authors had "performed a vast and impressive labor in winnowing through the golden acres of music-hall song, nursery rhyme, and operatic libretto; future students of the Joyce canon will find their work indispensable."[37]

Maurice Beebe and Marvin Magalaner also contributed brief notices. Writing in *Modern Fiction Studies*, Beebe mentioned the lists and concluded that this was a valuable reference tool for the study of Joyce.[38] Magalaner evidenced the embarrassment Joyceans often feel about the quality of the music in the allusions. "Because Joyce and his fellow Dubliners were music conscious to an unusual degree—even though they did not always set their musical sights too high," began Magalaner, but he acknowledged the importance of the music and called the book a "useful and seemingly exhaustive list" with "interesting introductory essays."[39]

Robert Kinsman, in *Western Folklore*, used Joyce's extensive allusion to American songs as justification for reviewing such a book in such a journal. Praising the "masterly critical demonstrations" of Hodgart's essay (also praised by Hart in the *Modern Language Review*), Kinsman emphasized Joyce's use of popular culture. He was also the first to respond to the lengthy lists by noting omissions.[40] In the *Virginia Quarterly Review*, an anonymous commentator praised "tremendous comprehension and infinite patience" and rightly judged the work "indispensable" for Joyce scholars.[41] A final American comment in *Nineteenth Century Fiction* gave two sentences to the work. Describing the book as an "attempt" to assess Joyce's musical knowledge and interest, the reviewer concluded provocatively that "the results are startling."[42]

In sum, reviewers admired the industry of the authors, found the sheer bulk of the lists intimidating, yet agreed on the extreme usefulness of the work for all Joyce scholars. The lack of any more extensive analysis may be attributed to the previously mentioned absence of professional journals in an industry just being born; to the overshadowing effect of the mammoth Ellmann biography, which had a wider appeal to an audience even outside the scholarly world; and to the relative shortness of nearly all reviews in those days prior to the scholarly expansion of the 1960s. (One must also note, in passing, the relative speed of the reviews—within a year in almost every instance!)

Surprisingly, no review mentioned what was to seem, within a very few years, the major drawback in Hodgart and Worthington's work. Possibly it was the overwhelming amount of information they had collected;

perhaps it was that xerographic and phototypesetting technology had not yet led us to expect such an inclusion; or perhaps, with so many songs to consider, an unreasonable task seemed a reasonable omission. But *Song in the Works of James Joyce* provided neither words nor music.

Nevertheless, *Song in the Works of James Joyce* became a standard reference, and supplementing it became a regular scholarly activity. A few anachronisms were discovered—songs published after Joyce had already written the "allusive" passage. These few songs had to be cut from the list.[43] Bowen, in his revision of Hodgart and Worthington, dropped several dozen other allusions in the early Joyce because they seemed dubious.[44] Far more often than they reduced the length of the Hodgart and Worthington listings, however, scholars began adding newly identified allusions. Notable among such additions have been Weldon Thornton's more than sixty, plus several operas;[45] forty songs and five nursery rhymes identified by Fritz Senn;[46] and Gifford and Seidman's thirty songs.[47] Bauerle noted more than fifty additional songs (and several hundred additional allusions) in the course of work on the *James Joyce Songbook*. More recently, Leo and Carole Brown Knuth have made an intensive study of Joyce's use of John McCormack's career in *Finnegans Wake*, listing more than eighty melodies sung by McCormack and preserved by Joyce in the *Wake*.[48] Roland McHugh's *Annotations to "Finnegans Wake"*[49] added more than six dozen songs, though many of these were identifications published earlier by others.

These subsequent lists of allusions, even with additions of songs missed in *Song in the Works of James Joyce*, sometimes offered a back-handed tribute to the Hodgart and Worthington accomplishment. Being mortal, the pair made an occasional mistake that persisted among later workers. The ballad "Enniscorthy," for instance, has as its refrain the line "When McCarthy took the flure at Enniscorthy." The attempt at conveying the Irish pronunciation of "floor" was "corrected" by someone to "flute" in the *Song in the Works* listings, and it remains "flute" in the work of Thornton and of Gifford and Seidman.[50]

In the late 1960s and early 1970s, Worthington, with her former student Zack Bowen, then at the State University of New York, Binghamton, set about revising *Song in the Works of James Joyce*. It was planned that Bowen would handle the songs in all Joyce's works through *Ulysses* and that Worthington would deal with all the musical allusions in *Finnegans Wake*. Bowen's completed work appeared as the valuable *Musical Allusions in the Works of James Joyce: Early Poetry through "Ulysses."*[51] This, at last, provided the words for nearly all songs alluded to by Joyce in the works covered and was an immense aid to scholars. Like *Song in the Works of James Joyce*, however, it had an extensive bibliography but did not provide a location list for individual songs. Those who wished to hear the sound of Joyce's music were still frustrated.

Worthington's portion of the revision was never completed, although she had at least three chapters in draft before her final illness and her death in 1977. As she felt less able to work, she asked Kathleen McGrory to complete the revision; McGrory indicates that her work is still progressing.

Hodgart has continued intensive work on Joyce's use of opera, particularly in *Finnegans Wake*. He has in preparation a manuscript with a detailed list of new identifications.

Another effort to supplement the work of Worthington and Hodgart was my *James Joyce Songbook*.[52] In this volume I attempted to collect both words and music for all songs alluded to by Joyce at least five times, or in at least three different works, as well as those songs he was known to have sung. Space prevented including all such songs (219 in all) I located, but as printed, the *Songbook* included 197 songs, accounting for about 1,750 of Joyce's musical allusions; hence, it offered melody and lyrics for more than half his references. Still, there remained another thousand or more songs whose music we did not have readily available, though Bowen, McGrory, and I had all by now built up extensive private collections, as had other scholars, such as James Hurt at the University of Illinois and Vincent Deane and the late Charles Peake—and, of course, Hodgart—in England. Deane has been publishing songs, as space permitted, in the *Finnegans Wake Circular*.[53]

More than listing songs, Hodgart and Worthington made possible other kinds of scholarly work. Their volume lies behind Cheryl Herr's recent work on Joyce and popular culture[54] and James V. Card's paper on Molly Bloom as professional singer.[55] And *Song in the Works of James Joyce* stimulated other projects, too. Bowen and others at the State University of New York made five Folkways records (of "Lestrygonians," "Calypso," "Lotus Eaters," "Hades," and "Sirens").[56] These productions antedated Bowen's volume on Joyce's early musical allusions by a decade. Each had appropriate musical background to convey the genuine Dublin atmosphere. They were most significant, however, in solving a problem that had troubled scholars at least since Budgen noted it in 1934:

> Notes lie like words on paper *nebeneinander* and like words they float in the air—or seem to float in the air—*nacheinander*. Poet and musician only part company when the musician writes his notes *übereinander* and sends them forth on the airs in clusters and swarms. . . . Joyce can give some of the effect of four voices singing together, but not the fact. The reader speaks the words and the sounds fall from his lips one after the other, for all parts must be sung with his voice, and he has only one.[57]

With sound recording, Bowen achieved Joyce's "simultanist manner,"[58] giving us the music and the text at the same instant, as Joyce intended us to hear them.

It became a practice, after the James Joyce Symposia began in 1967, to include at least one musical program in each year's events. Musicians such as Kevin McDermott; Irene Wymann and Michael Schar; and Donna Janusko and Dorothe Isler have delighted their audiences with melodies from Joyce's work. Recordings also developed from the Hodgart and Worthington identifications. The James Joyce Cassette Series was announced in 1975, with Worthington as general editor and an editorial board including Kathleen McGrory, Joseph Phillips, James Murphy, and Thomas Horan.[59] Fifteen cassettes of Joyce songs were planned, but only four or five tapes were produced before Dr. Worthington's final illness. The New Hutchinson Family Singers (led by James and Phyllis Tilton Hurt and including Dennis Michael Davis, Julianne Macarus, and Thomas Schleis) recorded twenty-five songs spanning the whole of the Joyce oeuvre.[60] Kevin McDermott recorded his program on long-playing disc. And at the Leeds University *Finnegans Wake* Conference in 1987, Charles Peake and a group of musicians gave a warmly received program of music appearing in Joyce, now available on tape.[61]

There were also new musical compositions that derived, after several generations, from *Song in the Works of James Joyce*. Margaret Rogers's *A Babble of Earwigs: A "Finnegans Wake" Chorale* (premiered at the Joyce in Milwaukee Conference, University of Wisconsin–Milwaukee, June, 1987) incorporated melodic themes from *The James Joyce Songbook*, which, of course, derived from Hodgart and Worthington's work.

If early reviewers were dumbfounded by the extent of the lists, recent scholarship has been more perceptive of the contribution made by the Hodgart and Worthington book. Its authors appear in the acknowledgments of volume after volume of Joyce criticism through the decades. Worthington, who was a student of William York Tindall at Columbia, must have been especially pleased by his inclusion of her work in the bibliography for *A Reader's Guide to "Finnegans Wake."*[62] At the 1969 James Joyce Symposium in Dublin, Zack Bowen opened his paper, "Libretto for Bloomusalem in Song: The Music of Joyce's *Ulysses*," by referring to "the pioneering work done by Hodgart and Worthington."[63] More recently, in the *Companion to Joyce Studies*, Barbara diBernard, writing on "Technique in *Finnegans Wake*," asserted that "*Song in the Works of James Joyce* has not been surpassed for an examination of the use of song in *Finnegans Wake*."[64]

The debt owed these pioneering Joyce scholars is also personal in many instances. Mabel Worthington was enthusiastic about *The James*

Joyce Songbook when I proposed it, and so long as health allowed her, helpful to my slow progress. She lent copies of music, pointed me to sources, suggested leads, and read preliminary drafts. Had there been no *Song in the Works of James Joyce*, I would never have attempted the *Songbook*. Had there not been personal encouragement from Worthington, I might never have finished it.

Bowen had similar substantial aid in preparing his *Musical Allusions*, for Worthington had been his teacher, as Tindall had been hers. In a recent letter he said

> I had the privilege of being Mabel Worthington's student when I was an M.A. candidate at Temple University from September, 1958 to January, 1960. During my first semester I enrolled in her Joyce seminar and was never the same after. At the time she was in the process of reading galley proofs from *Song in the Works of James Joyce*, and then, as ever, thinking constantly of music.
>
> She told me that during her time as a graduate student at Columbia she had worked in a singing Irish bar, and had heard a lot of music associated with Joyce there. . . . Her particular interests were in folksongs and nursery rhymes, and she had the Opies' books just about memorized. . . .
>
> She was an avid collector of records and folklore books especially, and she loved to spend evenings in the company of singers. She established a Joyce society in Philadelphia which held meetings at an Irish bar where the music associated with Joyce was frequently sung by the patrons as well as itinerant performers. . . .
>
> She left her students a legacy of intense interest in Joyce and music. . . .
>
> We worked together for the academic year 1971–72 on a grant from SUNY Binghamton, Mabel on the *Wake* and I on the earlier works, and it was Mabel who wrote to Wayne D. Shirley and Joseph Hickerson at the Library of Congress Music Division, who eventually discovered in an uncatalogued old carton in the basement the music to "Seaside Girls," a song I had sought for years at the Dublin National Library, the British Museum, the Library of Congress, the New York Public Library and every other substantial music collection in the United States. It was a happy day when a xeroxed copy came from those unheralded Joycean musicians in Washington.
>
> The substantial sub-industry of Joyce music really got its start from the pioneering investigations of Hodgart and Worthington. The rest of us, in copying, researching and explicating the songs to which they led us, were like engineers making practical application of the original inspiration of inventors. Now no one detracts from the enormous importance of music and musical references in Joyce's work. The credit is due primarily to Matthew Hodgart and Mabel Worthington.[65]

Even those scholars who have never had the opportunity to meet or work with Hodgart or Worthington owe a special debt to them. It is some centuries since we were told that the person who makes our songs is more important than the one who makes our laws. If Joyce did not make, he at least chose our songs for us. They echo in our heads as we read his work, in our letters as we write one another. I have never known a Joyce meeting that did not have, in addition to formal musical programs, a spontaneous outburst of singing—at dinner, in the streets, in pubs, wherever we gathered. It may not be beautiful, but for all of us, it is music. Faulknerians do not warble of Yoknapatawpha, nor Emersonians of Concord. No other scholarly group, to my knowledge, has this heritage that has helped bond Joyceans in fellowship. It is part of what makes our gatherings so much fun. And fun is a serious matter.

Until the songs were identified, they couldn't be found; until they were found, they couldn't be sung. Until they were sung, they couldn't be heard. Till they were heard, Joyce was unheard. We had to sing these songs before they—and Joyce himself—could sing in us.

A last detail perhaps sums up the place won among Joyce scholars by *Song in the Works of James Joyce*. Now, almost universally, it is referred to simply as "Hodgart and Worthington." Their names have become their title. A well-earned title it is.

NOTES

1. T. S. Eliot, *"Ulysses,* Order, and Myth," *Dial*, Nov. 1923, pp. 480–83, reprinted in *James Joyce: Two Decades of Criticism*, ed. Seon Givens (New York: Vanguard, 1963), 198–202.

2. Clive Bell, "Plus de Jazz," *New Republic* 28 (21 September 1921): 92–96, in *James Joyce: The Critical Heritage*, 2 vols., ed. Robert Deming (New York: Barnes and Noble, 1970), 1:183.

3. Ford Madox Ford, "Literary Causeries: vii: So She Went into the Garden," *Chicago Tribune Sunday Magazine* (6 April 1924), in Deming, *Heritage*, 1:306.

4. Frank O'Connor, "Joyce—The Third Period," *Irish Statesman* (12 April 1930): 114–16, in Deming, *Heritage*, 1:517.

5. Herbert Read, "The High Priest of Modern Literature," *The Listener* (20 August 1930): 206, in Deming, *Heritage*, 1:521.

6. Stuart Gilbert, *James Joyce's "Ulysses"* (London: Faber and Faber, 1930; N.Y.: Knopf, 1931; reprint, New York: Random House Vintage Books, 1955), 240–57 on "Sirens."

7. Frank Budgen, *James Joyce and the Making of "Ulysses"* (London: Grayson, 1934; Bloomington: Indiana University Press, 1960), 132–39.

8. Mary Colum, *From These Roots*, in Deming, *Heritage*, 2:652.

9. Harry Levin, *James Joyce: A Critical Introduction* (Norfolk, Conn.: New Directions, 1941), 33–34.

10. Ibid., 79, 89.

11. Ibid., 85.

12. Ibid., 98–105.

13. Ibid., 184.

14. Martin Ross, "Music and James Joyce" (Chicago: Argus Bookshop, 1936; reprint, Folcroft, Pa.: Folcroft Library Editions, 1973), 5, 6. Includes Hazel Felman's music to accompany "Anna Livia Plurabelle."

15. Vivian H. S. Mercier, "James Joyce and an Irish Tradition," in *Society and Self in the Novel* (English Institute Essays 1955), ed. Mark Schorer (New York: Columbia University Press, 1956), 78–116.

16. Marvin Magalaner and Richard M. Kain, *Joyce: The Man, the Work, the Reputation* (New York: New York University Press, 1956), 312.

17. Hugh Kenner, *Dublin's Joyce* (Bloomington: Indiana University Press, 1956), 25.

18. Ibid., 26.

19. Ibid.

20. Richard M. Kain, *Fabulous Voyager: James Joyce's "Ulysses"* (Chicago: University of Chicago Press, 1947; reprint, New York: Viking, 1959), 144.

21. L. A. G. Strong, "James Joyce and Vocal Music," *Essays and Studies by Members of the English Association* 31 (1945): 95–106; Strong, *The Sacred River: An Approach to James Joyce* (New York: Pellegrini and Cudahy, 1951).

22. Vernon Hall, "Joyce's Use of Da Ponte and Mozart's *Don Giovanni*," *PMLA* 66 (1951): 78–84.

23. Joseph Prescott, "Local Allusions in Joyce's *Ulysses*," *PMLA* 68 (1953): 1223–28; Prescott, "Notes on Joyce's *Ulysses*," *MLQ* 13 (1952): 149–62; Prescott, "A Song in Joyce's *Ulysses*," *Notes and Queries* 197 (5 Jan. 1952): 15–16. Re. "Love and War," Deming 1st ed., item 868.

24. Matthew J. C. Hodgart, "Shakespeare and *Finnegans Wake*," *Cambridge Journal* 6 (1953): 735–52; Hodgart, "Work in Progress," *Cambridge Journal* 6 (1952): 28–31.

25. Mabel Worthington, "Irish Folk Songs in Joyce's *Ulysses*," *PMLA* 71 (1956): 321–39.

26. Mabel Worthington, "American Folk Songs in Joyce's *Finnegans Wake*," *American Literature* 28 (1956): 197–210.

27. Mabel Worthington, "Nursery Rhymes in *Finnegans Wake*," *Journal of American Folklore* 70 (1957): 37–48.

28. Matthew J. C. Hodgart, and Mabel Worthington, *Song in the Works of James Joyce* (New York: Columbia University Press, 1959), 59–61.

29. Hodgart and Worthington, *Song*, 6, 12. More than twenty years later, I placed the estimates at 350 in *Ulysses* and more than a thousand in *Finnegans Wake*. (Ruth Bauerle, *The James Joyce Songbook* [New York: Garland, 1982], xvii.)

30. Clive Hart, *Structure and Motif in "Finnegans Wake"* (Evanston, Ill.: Northwestern University Press, 1962).

31. Letter from Clive Hart to Ruth Bauerle, 20 Oct. 1987.

32. "Echoes From Dublin," *Times Literary Supplement* no. 3040 (Friday, 3 June 1960): 354. Reviewed with: Tindall, *A Reader's Guide to James Joyce,* and Magalaner, *Time of Apprenticeship: The Fiction of Young James Joyce. Song* received a generous four paragraphs to Tindall's two and Magalaner's one.

33. Ibid.

34. Charles Osborne, *Musical Times* [London] 101 (May, 1959): 302.

35. Clive Hart, *Modern Language Review* 56 (Oct. 1961): 4, 602–3.

36. Robert Martin Adams, "In Joyce's Wake," *The Hudson Review* 12 (Winter 1960): 627–32. Other books considered were Ellmann's *James Joyce* (three and a half pages); Mason's and Ellmann's *The Critical Writings of James Joyce,* (one page); and Sylvia Beach's *Shakespeare and Company.* Just under a page went to *Song in the Works of James Joyce.*

37. Ibid., 631.

38. Maurice Beebe, "Song in the Works of James Joyce," *Modern Fiction Studies* 5 (1960): 367.

39. Marvin Magalaner, "Song in the Works of James Joyce," *Books Abroad* 35 (Spring 1961): 186.

40. Robert S. Kinsman, *Western Folklore.* 19 (July 1960): 218–19.

41. *Virginia Quarterly Review* 36 (Winter, 1960): xx.

42. "Notes and Reviews," *Nineteenth Century Fiction* 14 (March 1960): 374.

43. See, for instance, Alan M. Cohn, "Some Anachronisms in and an Addition to Hodgart and Worthington," *A Wake Newslitter,* n.s., 4 (July 1962): 3.

44. Zack Bowen, *Musical Allusions in the Works of James Joyce: Early Poetry through "Ulysses"* (Albany: State University of New York Press, 1974).

45. Weldon Thornton, *Allusions in "Ulysses"* (Chapel Hill: University of North Carolina Press, 1968).

46. Fritz Senn, "A Throatful of Additions to *Song in the Works of James Joyce,"* *Joycenotes* 1 (June 1969): 7–17.

47. Don Gifford and Robert J. Seidman, *Notes for Joyce: An Annotation of Joyce's "Ulysses"* (New York: Dutton, 1974); their revised edition, titled *"Ulysses" Annotated* (Berkeley: University of California Press, 1989), adds another sixteen songs (two of them anachronisms and six of them already in Bowen's work) and drops two. Don Gifford and Robert J. Seidman, *Notes for Joyce: "Dubliners" and "A Portrait of the Artist as a Young Man"* (New York: Dutton, 1967; 2nd rev. ed. titled *Joyce Annotated* [Berkeley: University of California Press, 1982]).

48. Carole Brown [Knuth], "Will the Real Signor Foli Please Stand Up and Sing 'Mother Machree'?" *A Wake Newslitter* 17 (Dec. 1980): 99–100; Carole Brown Knuth and Leo Knuth, "More Wakean Memories of McCormack: A Centenary Tribute," Colchester, Essex: A Wake Newslitter Occasional Paper no. 4, Sept. 1984; Knuth and Knuth, *The Tenor and the Vehicle: A Study of the John McCormack/James Joyce Connection* (Colchester, Essex: A Wake Newslitter Press, 1982).

49. Roland McHugh, *Annotations to "Finnegans Wake"* (Baltimore: Johns

Hopkins University Press, 1980); McHugh, "Two More Songs." *Joycenotes* 1 (June 1969): 17.

50. Hodgart and Worthington, *Song*, 64, 159, 209. Cf. Thornton, *Allusions*, 87, 553; Gifford and Seidman, *Notes for Joyce: An Annotation of Joyce's "Ulysses,"* 76, 551; Gifford and Seidman, *"Ulysses" Annotated*, index. Ellmann's *James Joyce* (New York: Oxford University Press, 1959; rev. ed., 1982) gives the title as "The Man Who Played the Flute at Inniscorthy" (p. 53; it remains thus in the rev. ed., p. 52). Since Ellmann's book was published almost simultaneously with that of Hodgart and Worthington, it is uncertain where "flute" originated. The ballad was correctly identified after being located at the New York Public Library's Lincoln Center Library for Music and the Performing Arts by Victory Pomeranz; see *James Joyce Quarterly* 11 (Fall 1973): 52–54. Bowen uses the correct title in his 1974 work.

51. Bowen, *Allusions*.

52. Bauerle, *Songbook*.

53. Vincent Deane, ed., *A Finnegans Wake Circular*. Anna Villa, Ranelagh, Dublin 6, Ireland.

54. Cheryl Herr, *Joyce's Anatomy of Culture* (Urbana: University of Illinois Press, 1986).

55. James V. Card, "Molly Bloom, Soprano," *James Joyce Quarterly* 27 (Spring 1990): 595–602.

56. Zack Bowen, director, "Calypso" (Folkways FL 9835, 1963); "Hades" (Folkways FL 9914, 1964); "Lestrygonians" (Folkways FL 9562, 1961); "Lotus Eaters" (Folkways FL 9836, 1964); "Sirens" (Folkways FL 9563, 1966).

57. Budgen, *Making of "Ulysses,"* 133.

58. Ibid., 139.

59. Mabel Worthington, general ed, *James Joyce Cassette Series: Songs and Commentary*. Brookfield, Conn. (P.O. Box 97, 06804): Joyce Cassettes, 1975 and after.

60. New Hutchinson Family Singers, "The Joyce of Music" (Urbana: University of Illinois Press, 1983). Includes 32-page booklet with words to the songs and audio cassette.

61. Charles Peake and Company, *Song in "Finnegans Wake,"* *James Joyce Broadsheet*, c/o Pieter Bekker, 4 Moorland Road, Leeds LS6 1AL.

62. William York Tindall, *A Reader's Guide to "Finnegans Wake"* (New York: Farrar, Straus and Giroux, 1969).

63. Zack Bowen, "Libretto for Bloomusalem in Song: The Music of Joyce's *Ulysses,"* in *New Light on Joyce*, ed. Fritz Senn (Bloomington: Indiana University Press, 1972).

64. Barbara diBernard, "Technique in *Finnegans Wake,"* in *A Companion to Joyce Studies*, ed. Zack Bowen and James F. Carens. (Westport, Conn.: Greenwood Press, 1984).

65. Letter from Zack Bowen to Ruth Bauerle, 14 October 1987.

Alan M. Cohn

Some Other Landmarks of Joyce Literature

The following is a selective, chronologically ordered list of pre-1960 works on Joyce, offered as a supplement to those treated in the preceding essays. I have expanded the scope of this list beyond the area of criticism to include such items as editions, bibliographies, and so on, in recognition of the important contributions they have made to Joyce studies. The responsibility for any idiosyncracies of admission or omission are mine.

Larbaud, Valery. "James Joyce." *Nouvelle revue française* 1 (Apr. 1922): 385–409.
Larbaud introduces *Ulysses* to the French; English translation published in 1922 in *Criterion*.

Pound, Ezra. "James Joyce et Pécuchet." *Mercure de France* 1 (June 1922): 307–20.
Important early exploration of the form and content of *Ulysses*.

Eliot, T. S. "*Ulysses*, Order, and Myth." *Dial* Nov. 1923, pp. 480–83.
The seminal and oft-reprinted review.

Wilson, Edmund. "James Joyce." In *Axel's Castle*. New York: Scribner's, 1931.
First important critical essay anticipating the direction of twentieth-century literature.

U.S. District Court. New York (Southern District). United States of America, libelant, v. one book called *Ulysses*, Random House, Inc., claimant. *Opinion*. A. 110–59. [New York: 1933.]
Judge John M. Woolsey's decision allowing the publication of *Ulysses*.

Broch, Hermann. *James Joyce und die Gegenwart.* . . . Vienna: Herbert Reichner, 1936.
  Argues that *Ulysses* is a work of great artistic and ethical magnitude.

Hanley, Miles L. *Word Index to James Joyce's "Ulysses."* Madison, Wis.: n.p., 1937.
  Forerunner of the many concordances to Joyce's works.

Gorman, Herbert. *James Joyce.* New York: Farrar & Rinehart, 1939.
  The first full-scale biography, written with Joyce's cooperation but also under his ultimate control.

Gillet, Louis. *Stèle pour James Joyce.* Marseille: Sagittaire, 1941.
  A collection of early articles by a French critic and friend of Joyce, [later (1958) translated into English by Georges Markow-Totevy].

Spencer, Theodore, ed. *Stephen Hero.* New York: New Directions, 1944.
  The first scholarly edition of a work by Joyce.

Levin, Harry, ed. *The Portable James Joyce.* New York: Viking Press, 1947.
  This collection has served as an introduction to Joyce's work for a multitude of students and other readers.

Given, Seon, ed. *James Joyce: Two Decades of Criticism.* New York: Vanguard Press, 1948.
  Gathers nineteen important essays, mostly reprinted.

Parker, Alan. *James Joyce: A Bibliography of His Writings, Critical Material, and Miscellanea.* Boston: F.W. Faxon, 1948.
  The pioneer bibliography.

Jolas, Maria, ed. *A James Joyce Yearbook.* Paris: Transition Press, 1949.
  Consists mainly of English translations of Continental works on Joyce.

Byrne, J. F. *Silent Years: An Autobiography, with Memoirs of James Joyce and Our Ireland.* New York: Farrar, Straus and Young, 1953.
  Background material from the model for Cranly of *A Portrait of the Artist.*

Slocum, John J., and Herbert Cahoon. *A Bibliography of James Joyce, 1882–1941.* New Haven: Yale University Press, 1953.
  Still the standard primary bibliography.

Magalaner, Marvin, and Richard M. Kain. *Joyce: The Man, the Work, the Reputation.* New York: New York University Press, 1956.
  A critical examination of the massive literature on Joyce.

Epstein, Edmund L., ed. *James Joyce Review.* Vol. 1–vol. 3, no. 1/2 (1957–1959).
The first of the journals devoted to the man and his works.

Gilbert, Stuart, ed. *Letters.* New York: Viking Press, 1957.
Reedited by Richard Ellmann in 1966, with two additional volumes conjoined.

Colum, Mary, and Padraic Colum. *Our Friend James Joyce.* Garden City, N.Y.:
Doubleday, 1958.
Reminiscences of both the Dublin and Paris years.

Joyce, Stanislaus. *My Brother's Keeper: James Joyce's Early Years,* edited by
Richard Ellmann. New York: Viking Press, 1958.
Posthumously published account of Joyce's first twenty-two years as seen
by his brother and confidante.

Sullivan, Kevin. *Joyce among the Jesuits.* New York: Columbia University Press,
1958.
A close examination of Joyce's education.

Beach, Sylvia. *Shakespeare and Company.* New York: Harcourt, Brace, 1959.
Reminiscences from the publisher of *Ulysses.*

Mason, Ellsworth, and Richard Ellmann, eds. *Critical Writings.* New York:
Viking Press, 1959.
Mainly Joyce's early and uncollected essays and reviews.

Magalaner, Marvin. *Time of Apprenticeship: The Fiction of Young James Joyce.*
London and New York: Abelard-Schuman, 1959.
Extensive study of Joyce's early development, concentrating on *Dubliners.*

Morse, J. Mitchell. *The Sympathetic Alien: James Joyce and Catholicism.* New
York: New York University Press, 1959.
A controversial examination of Joyce's use of Catholic teachings.

Contributors

Ruth Bauerle, retired from the English faculty of Ohio Wesleyan University, remains fully committed to research and writing. Her publications include *The James Joyce Songbook* and *A Word List to James Joyce's "Exiles"*; essays on *Exiles* and "The Dead"; and notes, articles, and reviews in many professional journals.

Michael H. Begnal is professor of English and comparative literature at Pennsylvania State University, where he also serves as director of graduate studies in English. He has published widely on James Joyce and modern literature. His most recent work is *Dreamscheme: Narrative and Voice in Finnegans Wake*.

Bernard Benstock, professor of English at the University of Miami and editor of the *James Joyce Literary Supplement*, has written, coauthored, edited, or coedited thirteen books on Joyce, including the recent *James Joyce: The Augmented Ninth* and *Essays on Joyce's "Ulysses."* Separate volumes on the narrative con/texts of *Ulysses*, *Dubliners*, and *Finnegans Wake* are forthcoming.

Shari Benstock, professor of English and director of women's studies at the University of Miami, is coauthor (with Bernard Benstock) of *Who's He When He's At Home: A James Joyce Directory*, author of *Women of the Left Bank: Paris 1900–1940* and *Textualizing the Feminine: On the Limits of Genre*, and editor of *Feminist Issues in Literary Scholarship* and *The Private Self: Theory and Practice of Women's Autobiographical Writings*.

Alan Cohn, bibliographer of the works of James Joyce, was the humanities librarian at Southern Illinois University from 1955 until his death in 1989. Editor of *Work in Progress: Joyce Centenary*

Essays, he published articles and checklists in *PMLA,* the *Journal of Modern Literature, Modern Philology,* the *Revue des lettres modernes, Papers of the Bibliographical Society of America, Notes and Queries,* and the *James Joyce Quarterly.*

Janet Egleson Dunleavy is professor of English and comparative literature at the University of Wisconsin–Milwaukee. In addition to having published various studies of nineteenth- and twentieth-century Irish writers and related aspects of Irish culture, she is coauthor (with G. W. Dunleavy) of *The O'Conor Papers* and *Douglas Hyde: A Maker of Modern Ireland* and coeditor (with M. J. Friedman and M. P. Gillespie) of *Joycean Occasions.*

Melvin J. Friedman, professor of comparative literature and English at the University of Wisconsin–Milwaukee, serves on the editorial boards of numerous scholarly journals and on the selection committee for the Ritz Paris Hemingway award. Coeditor of *Pound/The Little Review: The Letters of Ezra Pound to Margaret Anderson,* he has written extensively on Beckett, Styron, Ionesco, Flannery O'Connor, and other twentieth-century authors.

Michael Patrick Gillespie, associate professor of English at Marquette University, has published on a wide range of writers of the modernist period, including Joyce. His most recent book is *Reading the Book of Himself: Narrative Strategies in the Works of James Joyce.*

Clive Hart, professor of literature at the University of Essex, is cofounder (with Fritz Senn) of *A Wake Newslitter,* coeditor (with David Hayman) of *James Joyce's "Ulysses": Critical Essays,* coauthor (with Philip Gaskell) of *"Ulysses": A Review of Three Texts—Proposals for Alterations to the Texts of 1922, 1961, and 1984,* and author of *A Topographical Guide to James Joyce's Ulysses, Structure and Motif in "Finnegans Wake,"* and other books on Joyce. He writes also on other aspects of modern literature and on the early history of flight.

Suzette A. Henke is professor of English and comparative literature at the State University of New York at Binghamton. She is author of *Joyce's Moraculous Sindbook: A Study of "Ulysses"* (1978) and co-editor of *Women in Joyce* (1982). Her publications in the field of modern literature include essays on Virginia Woolf, Anaïs Nin, Dorothy Richardson, Doris Lessing, Linda Brent, Samuel Beckett, W. B. Yeats, and E. M. Forster. Her recent book, *James Joyce and the Politics of Desire,* was published by Routledge, Chapman and Hall in 1990. She is presently working on a study of "women's life writing" in the twentieth century.

Morton P. Levitt, professor of English at Temple University and editor of the *Journal of Modern Literature,* is the author of *Bloomsday: An Interpretation of James Joyce's "Ulysses,"* with engravings by Saul Field; *The Cretan Glance: The World and Art of Nikos Kazantzakis;*

and *Modernist Survivors: The Contemporary Novel in England, the United States, France, and Latin America*, as well as many articles on contemporary fiction.

Patrick A. McCarthy is professor of English and director of graduate studies in English at the University of Miami. Author of *The Riddles of "Finnegans Wake," Olaf Stapledon*, and *"Ulysses": Portals of Discovery*, he is the editor of *Critical Essays on Samuel Beckett* and *The Legacy of Olaf Stapledon: Critical Essays and an Unpublished Manuscript*. His work in progress is a study of Malcolm Lowry.

Richard F. Peterson, professor and chair of the department of English at Southern Illinois University, is the author of *James Joyce: A New Look, Mary Lavin*, and *William Butler Yeats;* coeditor (with Alan Cohn and Edmund Epstein) of *Work in Progress: Joyce Centenary Essays;* and a frequent contributor on Joyce and other modern Anglo-Irish writers to the *Journal of Modern Literature, Modern Fiction Studies, Journal of Irish Literature, James Joyce Quarterly, Yeats Annual*, and *Sean O'Casey Review.*

Mary Reynolds, recently retired, taught for many years in the Yale University College Seminar program. Her publications in the field of Joyce Studies include *Joyce and Dante: The Shaping Imagination*, essays, and reviews. She serves on the board of both *Joyce Studies* and the *James Joyce Quarterly.*

Bonnie Kime Scott is professor of English at the University of Delaware. Her essays on Irish literature, women writers, and feminist theory have appeared in numerous journals and collections. She is author of *Joyce and Feminism, James Joyce*, and *New Alliances in Joyce Studies.*

Fritz Senn, director of the Research Centre of the Zürich James Joyce Foundation and a principal organizer since 1967 of the biannual international Joyce Symposia, often serves as visiting professor of English and comparative literature in the United States. Cofounder and coeditor with Clive Hart of *A Wake Newslitter*, he has published many articles and notes on Joyce and his work, including those collected in *Nichts gegen Joyce: Joyce versus Nothing* and *Joyce's Dislocutions: Essays on Reading as Translation.*

Thomas F. Staley is director of the Harry Ransom Humanities Center, Chancellor's Council Centennial Professor in the Book Arts, and professor of English at the University of Texas at Austin, where he also edits a new journal, *Joyce Studies*. A founder and general editor for twenty-six years of the *James Joyce Quarterly*, he is author or editor of eight books on Joyce. He writes also on British women novelists, including Jean Rhys and Dorothy Richardson, and has frequently contributed essays on modern literature to journals in the United States and abroad.

Index